R. Gupta's®

HARYANA

GENERAL KNOWLEDGE

A Concise Description of
History, Geography, Economy, Polity, Flora & Fauna, Culture etc.

by
RPH Editorial Baord

2025
EDITION

RAMESH PUBLISHING HOUSE, NEW DELHI

Published by
O.P. Gupta *for* Ramesh Publishing House

Admin. Office
12-H, New Daryaganj Road, Opp. Officers' Mess,
New Delhi-110002 ✆ 23261567, 23275224, 23275124

E-mail: info@rameshpublishinghouse.com
For Online Shopping: www.rameshpublishinghouse.com

Showroom
- Balaji Market, Nai Sarak, Delhi-6 ✆ 23253720, 23282525
- 4457, Nai Sarak, Delhi-6, ✆ 23918938

Book Code: R-505

ISBN: 978-93-5012-635-6

Price: ₹ 120

Printed at: Deepak Offset, Delhi

CONTENTS

CHAPTER 1

HARYANA : A FACTFILE

Date of Formation: 01-11-1966

THE LAND

Location	:	North-western India
Latitude	:	27° 39' (north)
Longitude	:	30° 55' (east)
Area	:	44,212 square kilometres
Terrain	:	(A) Shivalik Hills (B) Ghaggar Yamuna Plain (C) Semi-desert Sandy Plain (D) Aravalli Hills
Average Rainfall	:	45 cm.
Soil	:	*Loamy*, Alluvial, Sandy, Rocky, *Marl*
Average Temperature	:	39-45°C (Summers)
Average Temperature	:	10-21°C (Winters)

THE DEMOGRAPHY

Population	:	25,351,462 (2011)
Males	:	13,494,734 (2011)
Females	:	11,856,728 (2011)
Overall Literacy Rate	:	75.6 % (2011)
Male Literacy Rate	:	84.1 % (2011)
Female Literacy Rate	:	65.9 % (2011)
Population Density	:	573 persons per square kilometre
Sex Ratio	:	Male: Female: 1000-879

Populace : Hindus
Muslims
Sikhs
Christians
Others

Language Spoken : Hindi, Punjabi

ADMINISTRATIVE STRUCTURE

Capital : Chandigarh
Jurisdiction : Punjab and Haryana High Court at Chandigarh
Districts (Jan. 2024) : 22
Divisions (Jan. 2024) : 6—Ambala, Hissar, Rohtak, Gurugram, Karnal and Faridabad
Sub-divisions (Jan. 2024) : 80
Tehsils (Jan. 2024) : 94
Sub-tehsils (Jan. 2024) : 49
Blocks (Jan. 2024) : 143
Villages : 6,841
Cities : 154
Strength of Legislature : 90
Seats in Lok Sabha : 10
Seats in Rajya Sabha : 5

DISTRICTWISE DATA

District	*Date of Formation*	*Area (sq. km)*	*Population 2011*	*District HQ*
1	*2*	*3*	*4*	*5*
Ambala	1 Nov., 1966	1,574	11,28,350	Ambala
Kurukshetra	23 Jan., 1973	1,530	9,64,655	Kurukshetra
Karnal	1 Nov., 1966	2,520	15,05,324	Karnal
Jind	1 Nov., 1966	2,702	13,34,152	Jind
Sonepat	22 Dec., 1972	2,122	14,50,001	Sonepat
Panipat	1 Jan., 1992	1,268	12,05,437	Panipat
Rohtak	1 Nov., 1966	1,745	10,61,204	Rohtak
Faridabad	2 Aug., 1979	741	1,809,733	Faridabad

1	2	3	4	5
Gurugram	1 Nov., 1966	1,258	15,14,432	Gurugram
Mahendragarh	1 Nov., 1966	1,899	9,22,088	Narnaul
Bhiwani	22 Dec., 1972	4,778*	16,34,445*	Bhiwani
Hissar	1 Nov., 1966	3,983	17,43,931	Hissar
Sirsa	26 Aug., 1975	4,277	12,95,189	Sirsa
Rewari	1 Nov., 1989	1,594	900,332	Rewari
Kaithal	1 Nov., 1989	2,317	10,74,304	Kaithal
Yamunanagar	1 Nov., 1989	1,768	12,14,205	Yamunanagar
Panchkula	15 Aug., 1995	898	5,61,293	Panchkula
Fatehabad	15 July, 1997	2,538	9,42,011	Fatehabad
Jhajjar	15 July, 1997	1,834	9,58,405	Jhajjar
Nuh (Mewat)	4 April, 2005	1,507	1,089,263	Nuh
Palwal	13 August, 2008	1,359	1,042,708	Palwal
Charkhi Dadri	1 Dec., 2016	—	—	Charkhi Dadri

* Data of Charkhi Dadri district are included in it.

CHIEF CENTRES OF TOURIST INTEREST

(A) Kasna Lake Resort (Uchana)
(B) Morni Hill Tourist Complex (Morni)
(C) Jyotisar, (Kurukshetra District)
(D) Brahma Sarover (Kurukshetra)
(E) Black Partridge Tourist Complex (Abubshehr)
(F) Yadvindra Gardens (Pinjore)
(G) Badkhal Lake (Surajkund)
(H) Rajhans (Surajkund)
(I) Skylark Tourist Complex (Panipat)
(J) Magpie Tourist Complex (Faridabad)
(K) Sohna
(L) Sultanpur Bird Sanctuary (Sultanpur)
(M) Parakeet (Pipli)

MAJOR EDUCATIONAL CENTRES

Universities

(A) Kurukshetra University, Kurukshetra
(B) M.D. University, Rohtak
(C) Chaudhary Charan Singh Agricultural University, Hissar

(D) Guru Jambeshwar University, Hissar
(E) Chaudhary Devi Lal University, Sirsa

RESEARCH INSTITUTES

1. National Dairy Research Institute, Karnal

EDUCATION (ENROLMENT)

Arts and Science Colleges	91.04%
Teacher Training Colleges	1.11%
Medical Colleges	1.66%
Agricultural Colleges	1.00%
Engineering Colleges	3.20%
Veterinary Colleges	0.33%
Physical Educational Colleges	0.59%
Oriental Study Colleges	1.47%

RIVERS

1. Yamuna
2. Ghaggar
3. Saraswati (Now extinct)
4. Dohan
5. Tangri
6. Krishnawati
7. Sahibi
8. Markanda

CANALS

1. Western and Eastern Yamuna Canal
2. Gurgaon Canal
3. Bhakra Canal
4. Jawahar Lal Canal
5. Bhiwani Canal

LAKES

1. Damdama
2. Khalilpur
3. Sultanpur
4. Kotla
5. Badkhal

GOVERNORS OF HARYANA

1.	Shri Dharamvir	1.11.1966–31-3.1967
2.	Shri B.N. Chakravarty	15.9.1967–26.3.1976
3.	Shri R.S. Narula	27.3.1976–14.8.1976
4.	Shri Jai Sukhlal Hathi	18.8.1976–23.9.1977
5.	Shri Harcharan Singh Brar	24.9.1977–8.12.1979
6.	Shri S.S. Sandhawalia	10.12.1979–28.2.1980
7.	Shri G.D. Tapase	28.2.1980–13.6.1984
8.	Shri S.M.H. Burney	14.6.1984–21.2.1988
9.	Shri H.A. Barari	22.2.1988–6.2.1990
10.	Shri Dhanik Lal Mandal	7.2.1990–13.6.1995
11.	Shri Mahavir Prasad	14.6.1995–13.6.2000
12.	Shri Babu Parmanand	14.6.2000–2.7.2004
13.	Shri A.R. Kidwai	7.7.2004–July 2009
14.	Shri Jagannath Paharia	July 2009–July 2014
15.	Shri Kaptan Singh Solanki	27.07.2014–25.8.2018
16.	Shri Satyadev Narayan Arya	25.8.2018 – 06.07-2021
17.	Shri Bandaru Dattatraya	07.07.2021 – ....

CHIEF MINISTERS OF HARYANA

1.	Sh. B.D. Sharma	1.11.1966–23.3.1967
2.	Sh. Virender Singh	24.3.1967–20.11.1967
3.	Sh. Bansi Lal	31.5.1968–30.11.1975
4.	Sh. B.D. Gupta	1.12.1975–30.4.1977
5.	Ch. Devi Lal	21.6.1977–28.6.1979
6.	Sh. Bhajan Lal	29.6.1979–4.6.1986
7.	Sh. Bansi Lal	5.6.1986–19.6.1987
8.	Ch. Devi Lal	20.6.1987–1.12.1989
9.	Sh. O.P. Chautala	2.12.1989–22.5.1990

10.	Sh. B.D. Gupta	23.5.1990–11.7.1990
11.	Sh. O.P. Chautala	12.7.1990–17.7.1990
12.	Sh. Hukam Singh	17.7.1990–22.3.1991
13.	Sh. O.P. Chautala	23.3.1991–6.4.1991
14.	Sh. Bhajan Lal	23.6.1991–10.5.1996
15.	Sh. Bansi Lal	11.5.1996–June, 1999
16.	Sh. O.P. Chautala	24.7.1999–Feb., 2000
17.	Sh. O.P. Chautala	2.3.2000–March, 2005
18.	Sh. Bhupender Singh Hooda	5.3.2005–25.10.2014
19.	Sh. Manohar Lal Khattar	26.10.2014-11.03.2024
20.	Sh. Nayab Singh Saini	12.03.2024 — ....

FAMOUS PERSONALITIES

Lala Duli Chand	(1873-1965)
Sir Shaadi Lal	(1874-1941)
Sir Chhotu Ram	(1881-1945)
Dr. Gopichand Bhargava	(1886-1966)
Pt. Neki Ram	(1887-1956)
Chaudhary Devi Lal	(1914-2001)
Pt. Bhagwat Dayal Sharma	(1918-1993)
Kapil Dev Nikhanj	(1959-)
Rao Tula Ram	(1825-1863)
Altaf Hussain Haali	(1837-1914)
O.P. Chautala	(1934-)

TRANSPORT

(Upto 31-10-2023)

Total road length	:	31,422 km
National Highway	:	3,391 km
State Highway	:	1,659 km
Major District Roads	:	1,375 km
Other District Roads	:	24,997 km
Bus fleet	:	3,369 buses
No. of large bus depots	:	24
No. of sub-depots	:	13
Total length of railway lines	:	3,737.91 km

STATE CABINET*

Nayab Singh Saini

CABINET MINISTERS

Name	Ministry
Nayab Singh Saini	Chief Minister, Home, Finance, Institutional Finance & Credit Control, Planning, Excise and Taxation, Town & Country Planning and Urban Estates, Information, Public Relations, Language and Culture, Administration of Justice, General Administration, Housing For All, Criminal Investigation (C.I.D), Personnel & Training, Law and Legislative, Any other department not allotted to any other Minister.
Anil Vij	Energy, Transport, Labour
Krishan Lal Panwar	Development and Panchayat, Mines and Geology
Rao Narbir Singh	Industries and Commerce, Environment, Forest and Wild Life, Foreign Cooperation, Sainik and Ardh Sainik Welfare
Mahipal Dhanda	School Education, Higher Education, Parliamentary Affairs, Archives
Vipul Goel	Revenue and Disaster Management, Urban Local Bodies, Civil Aviation
Arvind Kumar Sharma	Co-operation, Jails, Elections, Heritage and Tourism
Shyam Singh Rana	Agriculture and Farmers Welfare, Animal Husbandry & Dairying, Fisheries
Ranbir Gangwa	Public Health Engineering, Public Works (Building & Roads)
Krishan Kumar	Social Justice, Empowerment, SCs and BCs Welfare and Antyodaya (SEWA), Hospitality, Architecture
Shruti Choudhry	Women and Child Development, Irrigation and Water Resources
Arti Singh Rao	Health, Medical Education and Research, AYUSH

MINISTERS OF STATE (Independent Charges)

Name	Ministry
Rajesh Nagar	Food, Civil Supplies and Consumer Affairs, Printing and Stationery
Gaurav Gautam	Youth Empowerment and Entrepreneurship, Sports, Law and Legislative

* As on October 28, 2024

Rural and Urban Population of Haryana - Districtwise, Population of age-group (0-6) and population of literates (2011)

S. N.	State / Dists	Total Rural/ Urban	*Total Population 2011*			*Population of age group (0-6)*			*Literates*		
			Persons	*Male*	*Female*	*Persons*	*Male*	*Female*	*Persons*	*Male*	*Female*
1	2	3	4	5	6	7	8	9	10	11	12
	Haryana	Total	25351462	13494734	11856728	3380721	1843109	1537612	16598988	9794067	6804921
		Rural	16509359	8774006	7735353	2285112	1245090	1040022	10158442	6140099	4018343
		Urban	8842103	4720728	4121375	1095609	598019	497590	6440546	3653968	2786578
1.	Panchkula	Total	561293	299679	261614	66302	35583	30719	405318	229862	175456
		Rural	248063	133153	114910	32010	17107	14903	163427	95926	67501
		Urban	313230	166526	146704	34292	18476	15816	241891	133936	107955
2.	Ambala	Total	1128350	598703	529647	127689	70541	57148	818025	461288	356737
		Rural	627576	331703	295873	74425	41467	32958	426642	244282	182360
		Urban	500774	267000	233774	53264	29074	24190	391383	217006	174377
3.	Yamuna-nagar	Total	1214205	646718	567487	146789	80393	66396	832457	474793	357664
		Rural	741376	393957	347419	93904	51380	42524	477813	276833	200980
		Urban	472829	252761	220068	52885	29013	23872	354644	197960	156684

1	2	3	*4*	*5*	*6*	*7*	*8*	*9*	*10*	*11*	*12*
4.	Kurukshetra	Total	964655	510976	453679	116957	64320	52637	646893	370828	276065
		Rural	685430	361020	324410	86773	47734	39039	437671	253287	184384
		Urban	279225	149956	129269	30184	16586	13598	209222	117541	91681
5.	Kaithal	Total	1074304	571003	503301	139393	76258	63135	646529	385782	260747
		Rural	838293	445931	392362	110499	60425	50074	485223	293066	192157
		Urban	236011	125072	110939	28894	15833	13061	161306	92716	68590
6.	Karnal	Total	1505324	797712	707612	196610	107797	88813	978013	564516	413497
		Rural	1050514	557110	493404	142691	78011	64680	647883	380886	266997
		Urban	454810	240602	214208	53919	29786	24133	330130	183630	146500
7.	Panipat	Total	1205437	646857	558580	169662	92380	77282	786599	464136	322463
		Rural	650352	349642	300710	94584	51786	42798	402944	243714	159230
		Urban	555085	297215	257870	75078	40594	34484	383655	220422	163233
8.	Sonepat	Total	1450001	781299	668702	188262	104693	83569	998316	589881	408435
		Rural	996637	538750	457887	132007	73328	58679	665141	400112	265029
		Urban	453364	242549	210815	56255	31365	24890	333175	189769	143406
9.	Jind	Total	1334152	713006	621146	168554	91710	76844	832758	502049	330709
		Rural	1028569	550519	478050	131390	71437	59953	617715	377967	239748
		Urban	305583	162487	143096	37164	20273	16891	215043	124082	90961

1	2	3	4	5	6	7	8	9	10	11	12
10.	Fatehabad	Total	942011	495360	446651	121024	65279	55745	557578	327471	230107
		Rural	762423	400814	361609	99259	53426	45833	434531	258814	175717
		Urban	179588	94546	85042	21765	11853	9912	123047	68657	54390
11.	Sirsa	Total	1295189	682582	612607	157667	84684	72983	782897	456968	325929
		Rural	975941	514177	461764	120421	64422	55999	559635	331990	227645
		Urban	319248	168405	150843	37246	20262	16984	223262	124978	98284
12.	Hissar	Total	1743931	931562	812369	215167	116229	98938	1114311	670200	444111
		Rural	1190443	634139	556304	150650	81222	69428	714796	439026	275770
		Urban	553488	297423	256065	64517	35007	29510	399515	231174	168341
13.	Bhiwani	Total	1634445	866672	767773	212011	115756	96255	1069871	643158	426713
		Rural	1313123	696212	616911	172608	94039	78569	840162	511763	328399
		Urban	321322	170460	150862	39403	21717	17686	229709	131395	98314
14.	Rohtak	Total	1061204	568479	492725	129330	71041	58289	747582	436025	311557
		Rural	615040	332034	283006	77793	42691	35102	412667	248850	163817
		Urban	446164	236445	209719	51537	28350	23187	334915	187175	147740
15.	Jhajjar	Total	958405	514667	443738	120051	67380	52671	676091	399480	276611
		Rural	715066	384219	330847	89704	50465	39239	496455	296833	199622
		Urban	243339	130448	112891	30347	16915	13432	179636	102647	76989

1	2	3	4	5	6	7	8	9	10	11	12
16.	Mahendra-garh	Total	922088	486665	435423	111181	62638	48543	630255	380440	249815
		Rural	789233	416358	372875	95381	53778	41603	533442	324741	208701
		Urban	132855	70307	62548	15800	8860	6940	96813	55699	41114
17.	Rewari	Total	900332	474335	425997	113893	63743	50150	636947	375453	261494
		Rural	666902	349710	317192	84052	47154	36898	464452	276558	187894
		Urban	233430	124625	108805	29841	16589	13252	172495	98895	73600
18.	Gurgaon	Total	1514432	816690	697742	202602	110705	91897	1111116	638666	472450
		Rural	472179	251462	220717	67473	37469	30004	324087	192288	131799
		Urban	1042253	565228	477025	135129	73236	61893	787029	446378	340651
19.	Mewat	Total	1089263	571162	518101	248128	130168	117960	454897	308435	146462
		Rural	965157	506086	459071	225069	117967	107102	384749	266086	118663
		Urban	124106	65076	59030	23059	12201	10858	70148	42349	27799
20.	Faridabad	Total	1809733	966110	843623	251955	136679	115276	1272739	734940	537799
		Rural	370878	198103	172775	60653	33077	27576	227022	139717	87305
		Urban	1438855	768007	670848	191302	103602	87700	1045717	595223	450494
21.	Palwal	Total	1042708	554497	488211	177494	95132	82362	599796	379696	220100
		Rural	806164	428907	377257	143766	76705	67061	441985	287360	154625
		Urban	236544	125590	110954	33728	18427	15301	157811	92336	65475

Haryana : Districtwise Population and Growth Rate in a Decade–2011

S.N.	*State Districts*	*Census 2011*				
		Persons	*Male*	*Female*	*1991-2001*	*2001-2011*
	Haryana	2,53,51,462	1,34,94,734	1,18,56,728	28.43	19.90
1.	Panchkula	5,61,293	2,99,679	2,61,614	50.91	19.83
2.	Ambala	1128350	598703	529647	25.78	11.23
3.	Yamunanagar	1214205	646718	567487	29.19	16.57
4.	Kurukshetra	964655	510976	453679	23.32	16.86
5.	Kaithal	1074304	571003	503301	21.02	13.55
6.	Karnal	1505324	797712	707612	23.06	18.14
7.	Panipat	1205437	646857	558580	38.58	24.60
8.	Sonepat	1450001	781299	668702	22.39	13.35
9.	Jind	1334152	713006	621146	21.36	12.13
10.	Fatehabad	942011	495360	446651	24.76	16.85
11.	Sirsa	1295189	682582	612607	23.59	15.99
12.	Hissar	1743931	931562	812369	27.11	13.45
13.	Bhiwani	1634445	866672	767773	22.49	14.70
14.	Rohtak	1061204	568479	492725	21.00	12.88
15.	Jhajjar	958405	514667	443738	23.06	8.90
16.	Mahendragarh	922088	486665	435423	19.16	13.48
17.	Rewari	900332	474335	425997	25.34	17.64
18.	Gurgaon	1514432	816690	697742	44.15	73.14
19.	Mewat	1089263	571162	518101	45.67	38.65
20.	Faridabad	1809733	966110	843623	58.88	32.54
21.	Palwal	1042708	554497	488211	34.21	25.76

CHAPTER 2

The Epic

INTRODUCTION

The Bhagwad Gita is the most widely read and revered religious text of the world. The State of Haryana is proud of the fact that this legendary epic was orated by Lord Krishna at Jyotisar (Kurukṣhetra), which is located here. Further, it was also compiled by Veda Vyasa on the bank of river Saraswati, which was once a perennial river of this State. Hence, the greatest philosophy of life is associated with Haryana because Lord Krishna had given the Supreme Sermon to Arjuna on this land.

This poem is long poem, which, in fact, describes the gist of life, *karma* and duties of an individual. Lord Krishna narrates to Arjuna how he should do his duty and become a part of the Ultimate Soul. This poem forms the sixteenth chapters (adhyayas) of the Mahabharata, written by Veda Vyasa. It is in the form of Sanskrit hymns (*Shlokas*). Let us study, in brief, what *The Bhagwad Gita* tells every human form of the world.

THE BHAGWAD GITA

The Gita had little religious impact until Shankaracharya's commentary appeared. From this time onward, it had an important influence on Hinduism. Krishna, presented in the poem as Vishnu in the flesh, is the spiritual teacher who recited the Gita. Most of *The Bhagwad Gita* consists of a dialogue between Krishna and Arjuna o the battlefield on Kurukshetra. That is where the armies of the ro cousins, the Pandavas and the Kauravas, face each other for the de battle to end their feud. *The Bhagwad Gita* debates the right and wrong of conflict. It also discusses a person's duty to himself, or herself, his or her fellow human and God. It explores God's relationship with humans. It shows how people can begin to understand God and thus, free themselves from the burden of *Karma* (deeds done in previous lives and in this present life).

Krishna and Arjuna are not the only speakers in *The Bhagwad Gita.* King Dhritarashtra, the father of the Kauravas, asks the charioteer, Sanjay, to describe the course of the battle for him. The remainder of *The Bhagwad Gita* deals with the report of Sanjay, who describes what he sees in a trance. Prince Arjuna watches his cousins and brothers preparing for the battle and is greatly troubled. He asks Krishna, who acts as his charioteer, how he can justifiably take part in the battle because it must be wrong to slay his kinsfolk for the sake of power. He would rather die than kill his relatives. Due to this dilemma, he throws down his weapons and gives up the fight.

Krishna thinks Arjuna is merely showing signs of weakness. But when He realizes that the prince is genuinely anxious about where his duty lies. He speaks as God Vishnu. He explains the nature of the *atman* (soul). The *atman* can never be killed nor can it kill. When the body dies, it simply passes into another body and continues to live. Death must come to all who live and rebirth must come to all who die. Why mourn for what cannot be avoided? It is Arjuna's duty to fight in a war for the right cause. He is soldier and his responsibility is to fight. Real sin lies not in the killing of his enemies but in failing in his *dharma* (duty).

Krishna instructs Arjuna about three ways to have union with God. The first is *Karma Yoga* (the Way of Action). Every person should do his or her duty according to caste, without hope of personal benefit or ambition, but with faith in God. Those who go through the motions of performing rituals without care or interest, or do their work only for profit, will never be released from the cycle of birth, death and rebirth. Only if a person acts with his or her mind fixed on *Brahman* (God), will he or she become free. Moreover he will also remain at peace and unified with the Almighty. Anyone in that state feels no disturbing desires. Where there is no desire, there is no disappointment and there are also competitive ambitions. In work, one's sole ambition should be to serve as an example to others so that they too may do their duty.

The second way is *Jnana Yoga* (the Way of Knowledge). Through this method also, the contemplative person can seek union with God. Such a person has great self-control and spend much of his or her time in meditation. Through God's grace, he or she will come to realize that *Brahman* and *Atman* are one. Arjuna asks, which one of these two paths is the best. Krishna replies that the result will be the same, whichever path is followed. The end means absorption is *Brahman*. The entire universe exists because of *Brahman* but only few are only mature enough to perceive His power. Most people are absorbed with their own petty and temporary concerns, which are only *maya* (illusion); and *maya* can not last but must pass away in time.

The third way is *Bhakti Yoga* (the Way of Devotion). This is one of the most important contributions made by *The Bhagwad Gita* to the development of modern Hinduism. Krishna becomes the Ishvara (personal God), who may be worshipped as a spirit or as an image by his followers. He will accept any offering, however humble, as long as it is made with love. Every worshipper, who approaches with a loving heart, is welcomed. Union with God and release from the sufferings of birth, death and rebirth shall be bestowed on all those who are devoted to Krishna.

Krishna then reveals Himself to Arjuna as Lord Vishnu, Arjuna is overwhelmed and bursts into a great hymn of praise. He is fearful and ashamed because he had addressed Krishna as his friend. But Krishna is merciful and returns to the human form to comfort Arjuna . He explains to Arjuna that His Majesty is too great for human beings to behold. Krishna continues to teach Arjuna about the nature of man. He defines the qualities that bring people nearer to Brahman and those that tend to lead them astray. The individual nature of people decides what and how they worship. Some people look to God, others to worldly things. When people make an offering to God, it must be made in faith, otherwise it is unreal and cannot bring good results.

The Bhagwad Gita provides a summary of the Hindu religious thought and practice; much of it is based on the Upanishadas. These are part of the *Vedas*, the oldest sacred books of Hinduism. It gives a methodology for developing belief as well as for forging a personal relationship between the deity and his/her worshipper. It offers a new approach to the full perception of, and absorption in, *Brahman.*

The Mahabharata

This is one of the two great epics that were written in India nearly 3000-4000 years ago. *The Bhagwad Gita* is a part of *The Mahabharata.* The latter was written by the sage Veda Vyasa after the Mahabharata war. It has 18 Chapters (Adhyayas). It describes the ascent of the Kauravas, the entire story of the Kauravas and Pandavas, the war and finally, the Supreme Sermon of Lord Krishna to Arjuna. This sermon is in the form of *The Bhagwad Gita.* The epic concludes with the ultimate migration of the Pandavas into heaven; Yudhishthira went to the same in his mortal form while other Pandavas and Draupadi died while they were on their last journey (on a mountain).

The entire epic has been written in Sanskrit, the language of the Aryan race during the historic times. It is the longest poem of the world.

For more details, please read the chapter on history in this book.

CHAPTER 3

HISTORY

The Region that gave Birth to History

"There is a region called Haryana which is like a heaven on earth"- Quoted from the inscription found in Sarwan district near Delhi in Vikrami Samwat 1385.

Haryana was formed as a new State of India on Tuesday, 1 November 1966. Replete with myths, legends and Vedic references, Haryana's 5,000—year old history is steeped in glory. It was here, 3,000 long years ago, that Lord Krishna had preached *Bhagwad Gita* to Arjuna at the set of the great battle of Mahabharata. He had stated, "your right is to do your duty and not to bother about the fruits (outcomes) thereof. Since then, this profound philosophy of the supremacy of duty has become the foundation of Indian culture and thought. It was on this soil that saint Veda Vyasa had written Mahabharata. Before the Mahabharata war, a battle of ten kings took place in the Kurukshetra region in the Saraswati valley. But it was the Mahabharata War fought approximately in 900 BC, which gave worldwide fame to the region. The Mahabharata names Haryana as *Bahudhanyaka*—the land of plentiful grains and *Bahudhana*—the land of immense riches. The word Haryana occurs in the Sanskrit inscription dated 1328 AD, which is kept in Delhi Museum. This inscription refers to this region as "the very heaven on earth". It was here that the Aryans had kindled their first sacrificial fires. Their culture took birth, bloomed and matured in this very region.

Excavations of archaeological sites at many places in Haryana, such as Naurangabad, Mittathal and Tigrana in Bhiwani, Kunal in Fatehabad, Agroha and Siswal near Hissar, Rakhi Garhi and Balu in Jind, Rukhi near Rohtak and Banawali and Bari near Sirsa have unearthed evidences of pre-Harappan and Harappan culture in India. Sizeable findings of pottery, sculpture and jewellery at sites located in Kurukshetra, Pehowa, Tilpat, Panipat, Sonepat, etc. have established the credibility of the Mahabharata war. These are the places, which have been mentioned in the Mahabharata as Prithudaka (Pehowa), Tilprastha (Tilput) Panprastha (Panipat) and Sonprastha (Sonepat).

The legendary tales state that Manu had deemed this area the creation of gods (*devatas*). Hence it was also called Brahmavrata. The excavations at various sites of the State have revealed that the Indus Valley Civilisation and the Mohenjodaro culture had flourished here. Ancient Scriptures also call Brahmavrata as Brahmarishi Pradesha or the "Uttarvedi of Brahma". This State is also believed to be the place of creation of the universe. It is also believed that Manu was the entrant of this region. Artefacts obtained from Harappan, Pre-Harappan, Post-Harappan sites confirm the existence of many cultures in this region during the pre-historic eras. Such artefacts have been collected at Banawali, Seeswal, Karnal, Mirzapur, Daulatpur and Bhagwanpura.

The ancient king, Sudasa, who was from the Bharata clan, started his victory campaign from this region. He organised the Aryan forces, which expanded their areas of influence to far east and south in due course of time. The name of India was christened Bharata because of the sagas of victory and valour of these Aryan ancestors of the yore.

Pre-Mahabharata Times

Much before the war of Mahabharata, the Kurus (of Aryan descent) had started the era of agriculture in this region. According to the Puranas, the 48 kosas of the land of mother Adiroopa were made cultivable by the Kurus. The region came to be known as Kurukshetra, because it was owned by these Kuru rulers. Later, a great part of the land between, the Ganges and the Saraswati came to be known as Kuru Pradesha (Kuru Land)

The Mahabharata Era

As would be explained in this book at a later stage, the war of Mahabharata was fought in 900 B.C. At that time, the Aryan civilisation was at its peak. Lord Krishna gave the legendary sermon to Arjuna at jyotisar (near Kurukshetra). His sermons are better known as *The Bhagwad Gita.*

The Post-Mahabharata Era

The Aryakulas of the region fought many wars against the invaders. This era proved to be a dark chapter in the history of India. The area was divided into Janapadas; a cluster of villages was deemed a Janapada. The combination of some Janapada was called Gana. The Gana was a political unit and the Ganasabha was arranged/organised by the representatives of Janapadas. Several Ganas used to make a Sangha; it was also called Gana Sangha. One Gana Sangha ruled the land starting from Shatadru (Sutlej) up to Ganga (the Ganges). The Gana system was respected even by the erstwhile monarchs and emperors. This system had become deeply embedded in the social system of the populace. The Supreme panchayat of Haryana region was respected by Harshavardhana. It continued to reign supreme till the end of the Mughal empire.

The region has been theatre of many a war because of its status of "the gateway of north India". As years rolled by, successive streams of Huns, Turks and Afghans invaded India and decisive battles were fought on this land. After the downfall of Gupta Empire during the middle of sixth century AD, north India was again split into several independent kingdoms. The Huns established their supremacy over the Punjab. It was this period that one of the greatest King of ancient India, Harshavardhana had initiated his rule. He became the king of Thanesar (Kurukshetra) in 606 AD and later, became the ruler of most of northern India.

At the end of the fourteenth century, Tomars led an army through this area to Delhi. Later, the Mughals under Babar, defeated the Lodhis in the First Battle of Panipat in the year 1526. Another decisive battle was fought in Panipat in 1556, establishing the reign of the Mughals for centuries to come. Taking advantage of Humayun's death, Hemu has marched to Agra and Delhi and occupied it without difficulty. In response, Bairam Khan (Akbar's guardian) marched towards Delhi. Both the armies clashed in the Second Battle of Panipat. Hemu was in a winning position when a stray arrow struck him in the eye. He fell unconscious, causing panic among his troops. The tide of the battle turned and the Mughals won the battle. Towards the middle of the eighteenth century, the Marathas had established their supremacy over Haryana. The entry of Ahmed Shah Abdali into India, culminated in the Third Battle of Panipat in 1761. Marathas' defeat in this battle marked the end of their ascendancy and the decline of the Mughal Empire, leading to the advent of the British rule.

In 1857, the people of Haryana joined the Indian leaders in the revolt against the British government. By the end of June, 1857, most of the present Haryana region was liberated from the British. But the British managed to put down the rebellion in November, 1857 by bringing in additional forces from outside this area.

The history of India is replete with tales of heroism of the highest order and in this context, the historic significance of the battles of Panipat and Kurukshetra in Haryana cannot be ignored by any means. The new State, which emerged as a separate political entity of the Indian union on November, 1966, is considered to be the cradle of rich Indian cultural heritage. In terms of development, Haryana, indeed, has come a long way during past years.

THE MAHABHARATA WAR

It was fought in 900 BC. Mahabharata is the longest poem in the world, made up of 220,000 lines divided into 18 sections. It was written in Sanskrit, the ancient sacred language of India. It tells the story of a great battle that occurred about 3000 years ago. It was on the banks of river Saraswati the saint Veda Vyasa wrote Mahabharata in 900 BC. Lord Krishna preached *The Bhagwad Gita* the gospel of duty, to Arjuna at the onset of great battle. Since then, this profound philosophy of the supremacy of duty has become the foundation of Indian culture and psyche. The Mahabharata knows Haryana as *Bahudhanyaka*—the land of plentiful grains, and *Bahudhana*-the land of immense riches.

Dhritarashtra and Pandu were born to Bhishma's brothers. Dhritarashtra was born blind and though he was the elder one, he had to forfeit his claim to the throne due to this physical defect. Pandu became the king. Dhritarashtra married Gandhari, whereas Pandu, the younger, had two wives—Kunti and Madri. Gandhari was so devoted to her husband that she bandaged her eyes, not to enjoy anything that she could not share with her royal husband and remained voluntarily blind for life. She became the mother of the Kauravas, 100 in total whereas Kunti got three sons from Pandu and Madri got two.

One day while hunting, Pandu accidentally killed the wife of a sage, who got enraged and cursed Pandu that if ever he had intercourse with a woman, he would die instantly. Pandu renounced his crown to become a religious hermit and went to the jungle with his two wives, Kunti and Madri. But in day, Pandu could not resist himself and had intercourse with Madri and died. Madri immolated herself and walked into her husband's funeral fire leaving behind her two sons Nakul and Sahadev in the custody of Kunti, who already had three sons Yudhishthira, Bheema and Arjuna. After the Pandu's death, Dhritarashtra became the king and the five sons of Pandu, known as the Pandavas grew up under the guardianship of Kunti. The five Pandava princes were educated along with Kaurava boys under the supervision of Bhishma and the patronage of Dhritarashtra. Drona, though a Brahmin, was a very skilful and efficient teacher, who taught them the art of archery and the various techniques of warfare.

Yudhishthira the eldest of the Pandavas, was so righteous that he gained the name Dharmaputra. Bheema was a giant in terms of physical strength. Arjuna was handsome and the most skilful archer of his times. Dharmaputra was the beloved of the people and being the eldest among the 105 princes, was naturally, and by his right, the heir to the throne. Duryodhana, the eldest of the Kauravas, however was jealous of the Pandavas and tried every method and machination to destroy them. When Yudhishthira was proclaimed king, Duryodhana could not sit quiet and watch. Dhritarashtra loved all the 105 princes alike and there was no partiality in his mind between his own sons and nephews, the Pandavas. The great blind royal father, came under the bad influence of Duryodhana and though directly not an evil-doer, was in sympathy with his son's disappointments and sorrows.

Duryodhana plans to kill the Pandavas like giving poison to Bheema, burning down the lac-house etc., failed miserably. Bheema was strong enough to digest the poison. The Pandavas were warned in time by their uncle Vidura and so in the darkness of the night, the five brothers, along with their mother, escaped into the jungle from the burning lac-house. After their miraculous escape from the lac-house, they did not return to the palace. They roamed about in the guise of Brahmins with their mother. Everyone, including the Kauravas, believed them to be dead.

During that time, they heard of the *Swayamvara* of Draupadi. The qualification to marry her lay in the extraordinary skill of archery in hitting a moving target. Arjuna easily won. Everybody congratulated the winner and discovered that it was Arjuna. Thus the Pandavas were in the limelight once again. Then, Arjuna took his bride to their hut and called to his mother to come outside and see what he had brought. Instead of doing so, she answered back, "My dear children, whatever it be, you share it among yourselves". Therefore, Draupadi became the common wife of all the five Pandavas. Krishna, who was also present at the marriage ceremony, became a great friend of the Pandavas from then onwards. On Bhishma's advice, the kingdom was divided into two parts. Naturally, the better part of the half was taken away by the Kauravas. Still, the Pandavas built a wonderful city in their own part and called it Indraprastha. Duryodhana was jealous of the increasing prosperity of the Pandavas and could contain himself no longer. He openly challenged Dharamputra for a game of dice, Shakuni, deceit in a human form, was the maternal uncle of the Kaurava. He played for them. Inevitably Dharamputra lost everything-his kingdom, his brothers and also his wife.

Not satisfied with this gain, Duryodhana tried to insult Draupadi in the royal court. Due to Krishna's power, nothing disastrous happened. Dhritarashtra, fearing that this might bring unforeseen calamities, begged Draupadi to take whatever she wanted. She asked for the freedom of her husbands. It was granted. Dhritarashtra due to his excessive love for the eldest son, was blind to what was right or wrong. So again, Duryodhana invited Dharmaputra for another game of dice and the bet was that the losers would live in the forest for 13 year without any claim to the kingdom, the last year however to be spent incognito. But if in the thirteenth year, they were detected, then again a round of 13 years of exile would be in force; and this would go on forever.

Dharmaputra lost again. During the stay of twelve years in the forests, the Pandavas visited many holy places. They had many interesting adventures during the course of this time. One of them led to Hanuman's friendship and grace. Arjuna is called Kapidhvaja as he kept on his flag the emblem of Hanuman. Krishna visited them now and then. Arjuna, at the advice of Vyasa, practised penance, propitiated Shiva and got from Him the mighty weapon, the Pasupatastra. He propitiated the other gods, too, like, Indra, Agni, Varuna and others and got very powerful weapons from all of them. Thus twelve years were not wasted but spent in securing the divine, weapons, which were to be used at the opportune moments of time.

In the thirteen year, hiding all their weapons in the hollow trunk of a tree in a burial ground, all the Pandavas along with Draupadi, went to the palace of the king of the Viratas and stayed there as servants. Duryodhana was making frantic efforts to discover them. When he heard about the strange murder of Kichaka the brother-in-law of the king, he concluded that the Pandavas must be in the Virata country. So, the Kauravas attacked the Viratas, with the apparent purpose of carrying away its cattle wealth. Of course, the Pandavas took part in the battle, but when they were recognized as Pandavas the time limit of thirteen years had already passed.

Dharamputra was fond of peace, and was in favour of eschewing violence. So, he sent Krishna as a messenger to Hastinapur to claim his kingdom back from Duryodhana. But Duryodhana had become used to treating Indraprastha as his own. He not only refused to give their kingdom back, but also refused to give even five houses for the five brothers to live! Thus, a war was fought at Kurukshetra. Hundred Kauravas, Bhishma, Drona, Asvatthama etc., were on one side and the Pandavas, Krishna, Drupada, etc., were on the other. Krishna did not actually fight. He was the charioteer of Arjuna and hence, he is called Parthasarathy. Krishna was very impartial. He gave his army to the Kauravas and himself offered to serve the Pandavas. The Kaurava and the Pandava armies planned for the war. The Kauravas planned their attacks under the supervision of Bhishma and under Bheema's directions, the Pandava army marched ahead. This is the point at which, Arjuna had second thoughts about fighting in the battle. Krishna gave Arjuna good advise that brought back his war-spirit. This advice came to be known as *The Bhagwad Gita*.

Lord Krishna gave the Supreme Advice to Arjuna at Jyotisar, which is very close to Kurukshetra. All the Kaurava princes died in this battle and Yudhishthira became the king. He continued to reign until he felt that he had completed his life's work. Then, he renounced the throne and set out for heaven with the other Pandavas and Draupadi. With them, also went to a dog, which represented Dharma the God of duty and moral law. After more adventures, the Pandavas were finally united in heaven.

This story, which forms the main theme of the Mahabharata, makes up only about a quarter of the poem. The Mahabharata contains many other popular stories, including the tales of Nala and Damayanti, Savitri and Satyawan, Dushyant and Shakuntala etc. The battle of Kurukshetra offers an opportunity to discuss military strategy. But the underlying theme of the Mahabharata relates to moral duty and right conduct. The long and complex dispute that divides the royal family of Bharata affords an opportunity to explain the duties and conduct expected of a king. It also shows the ideals of behaviour for subjects, soldiers, religious hermits and people suffering due to misfortune.

Sage Ved Vyasa is traditionally regarded as the author of the Mahabharata but he is more likely to be its compiler. The epic seems to be a collection of writings by several authors who lived at various times. The oldest parts are probably about, 3,000 year old while others can be traced to as late as 500 A.D.

The God Vishnu became a very personal deity for his worshippers through his appearance as Krishna, the adviser and friend of Arjuna in the Mahabharata. About 1,300 greatly varying manuscripts of the Mahabharata exist today. All of them show the poem in its latter form because the earliest of them goes back only to the 1400s.

The Treatise on Karma

The most famous addition to the Mahabharata is *The Bhagwad Gita*. It finds its place in the sixth book and is now the most widely recognized of Hinduism's sacred texts. *The Bhagwad Gita* tells how Arjuna, the third of the Pandavas princes, has misgivings about whether he should be fighting his cousins, the Kaurvas. Krishna, speaking with the authority a deciding of God Vishnu, persuades him that his action is just, and then Arjuna's military skill becomes a deciding factor in the ensuing Pandava victory. The teaching of *The Bhagwad Gita* are fundamental to Hinduism.

THE VARDHANA DYNASTY—Harshavardhana (606-647 AD): After the downfall of the Gupta Empire in the middle of the sixth century AD, north India was again split into several independent kingdoms. The Huns established their supremacy over the Punjab and certain other parts of central India. The northern and western regions of India into the hands of a dozen or more feudatories. Gradually, one of them, Prabhakar Vardhana, the ruler of Thanesar, who belonged to the Pushabhukti family, extended his control over all other feudatories.

Prabhakar Vardhana was the first king of the Vardhana dynasty with his Capital at Thanesar, which is now a small town in the vicinity of Kurukshetra. It is located at a distance of nearly 150 km. from Delhi. After his death in 606 A.D, his eldest son, Rajya Vardhana ascended the throne. He was killed in a battle, which he won against Devagupta. The latter had killed Grahavarman, the husband of his sister Rajyashri and usurped the throne of Kannauj.

Harsha ascended the throne at the age of 16. Though quite a young man, he proved himself to be a great conqueror and an able administrator. After his accession, Harsha first rescued his sister just as she was going to commit sati. At the request of his sister, he united the two kingdoms of Thanesar (Kurukshetra) and Kannauj and transferred his Capital from Thanesar to Kannauj. Harsha waged many wars. He defeated Sasank of Bengal. He also brought the five Indies—eastern Punjab (The present-day Haryana), Kannauj, Bengal, Bihar and Orissa—under his control. He conquered Dhruvasena of Gujarat. He also conquered Ganjam, a part of the modern Orissa state.

His empire included territories of distant feudal kings too. Harsha governed his empire on the same lines as those of the Guptas. The kings whom he conquered paid him revenues and sent soldiers whenever he was fighting wars. They accepted his sovereignty but remained rulers over their own kingdoms. Harsha's ambitions of extending his power to the Deccan and southern India were stopped by Pulakesin II, the Chalukya king of Vatapi in northern Mysore.

His reign is comparatively well-documented, thanks to his court poet Bana Bhata and Hieun Tsang. Bana composed an account of

Harsha's rise to power in *Harshacharita.* Hieun Tsang was a Chinese Buddhist pilgrim who came to India during this time to collect Buddhist literature and visit places connected with Buddhism. He wrote a full description of his journey in his book *SI-YU-KI. Harsha* died in the year 647 AD. He ruled over India for 41 years. He was the last empire builder of ancient India. Harsha supported the development of philosophy and literature and wrote three well-known plays-Nagananda, Ratnavali and Priyadarshika.

After Harsha's death, apparently without any heir, his empire died with him. The kingdom disintegrated rapidly into small states. The succeeding period is very obscure and badly documented but it marks the culmination of process, which had begun with the invasion of the Hunas in the last years of the Gupta's empire. Meanwhile, the kingdoms of the Deccan and the south became powerful.

The Mughals

First Battle of Panipat (1526 AD): The First Battle of Panipat gave a death blow to the Lodhi empire and marked the end of the Delhi Sultanate's rule in India. It led to the establishment of the Mughal Empire in India. Mongol prince, Zahir-ud-Din Muhammed, known as Babar, had promised to help Daulat Khan Lodhi, the Governor of Lahore, to fight the Sultan of Delhi, Ibrahim Lodhi in 1523 and undertook many raids into the Punjab. Babar, after occupying the whole of the Punjab by 1525 AD, marched towards Delhi. In November, 1525 he set out to meet the Sultan of Delhi. Passage across the Indus took place on 15th December. Babar had about 12,000 soldiers. They crossed Sutlej at Ropar and reached Ambala without meeting any resistance. On April 1st, Babar reached Panipat. It was barren wasteland, dry and naked with few thorny bushes. Rumours came that Sultan was coming with an army of 10,000 soldiers and 1,000 war elephants. The Afghan Sultan of Delhi, Ibrahim Lodhi advanced from Delhi to meet invader. Babar had a strong artillery, which was effectively pressed into service.

The battle started at six o'clock in the morning. Sultan Ibrahim Lodhi advanced rapidly. At about 400 yards, Babar's cannons opened fire. Noise and smoke from the artillery terrified the Afghans and their attacks lost momentum. Babar sent his flanking columns to envelop the Sultan's army. Here, the Afghans met for the first time the real weapon of Mongols—Turko-Mongol Bow. Its superiority lay in the fact that it was the weapon of the nobles and the finest warriors. Such a bow in the hands of a Mongol warrior could shoot three times as rapidly as a musket and kill, at a distance of at 200 yards.

Attacked from three side, the Afghans jammed into one another. Elephants heard the noise of cannons at close ranges ran and out of control. Ibrahim Lodhi and about 6,000 of his troops were involved in actual fighting. Most of his army, stretching behind up to mile, never saw action. Battle ended in about three hours with the death of Ibrahim Lodhi who was at the forefront.

And at the place where fighting had been the fiercest, among the heap of Mongol bodies, lay the vain but courageous Sultan, Ibrahim Lodhi. His head was cut off and taken to Babar. Ibrahim Lodhi's tomb is still present at Panipat. When the Afghans fled, they left 20,000 dead and wounded behind Lodhi's. Losses to Babar's army were heavy; 4000 of his troops were killed or wounded. Had Sultan Ibrahim survived another hour of fighting, he would have won as Babar had no reserves and his troops were rapidly tiring under the Indian mid-day sun. Babar observes in his autobiography, "The mighty army of Delhi was laid in the dust in the course of half a day". In the words of Rushbrook Williams, "If there was one single material factor, which more than any other conduced to his ultimate triumph in Hindustan, it was his powerful artillery". The elephants trampled their own soldiers after being frightened away by the explosion of gunpowder. Two weeks later, the victorious Babar entered Agra where he was presented with the famous diamond Koh-i-noor. Babar celebrated his victory in a lavish manner and occupied Delhi and Agra.

The Apex of the Mughal Era

On 24th January, 1556 AD., the Mughal ruler, Humayun, slipped while climbing down the steps of his library and fell to embrace his death. His son, Akbar, was only thirteen year old when he ascended the throne. At the time of Akbar's accession to the throne, the Mughal rule was confined of Kabul, Kandhahar and parts of the Punjab and Delhi. Akbar was then campaigning in the Punjab with his chief minister Bairam Khan. On February 14, 1556, in a garden at Kalanaur, Akbar was enthroned as emperor. Hemu (Hemchandra) was a military chief of the Afghans King, Muhammad Adil Shah, who had established himself at Chunar and was seeking to expel the Mughals from India. Taking advantage of Humayun's death, Hemu marched to Agra and Delhi in October and occupied it without difficulty and became the ruler under the title Raja Vikramaditya.

To counter this, Bairam Khan (Akbar's guardian) marched towards Delhi. On November 5, both the armies met at Panipat. Hemu with a large army, including 1,500 war elephants, had initial success. There was a pitched battle and Hemu was on a winning spree when a stray arrow struck him in the eye. He fell unconscious. As has been proved in many other battles, the loss of the leader caused panic among the troops and turned the tide of the battle. The Mughals won the battle. Shah Quli Khan captured the Hawai elephant with its occupant and took it directly to Akbar. Hemu was brought unconscious before Bairam Khan and Akbar. Bairam pleaded Akbar to perform the holy duty of slaying the infidel and earn the Islamic holy title of Ghazi. Akbar severed the head of unconscious Hemu with his sabre.

Some historians claim that Akbar did not kill Hemu himself but just touched the infidel's head with his sword and his associates finished the gory holy work. After the battle, Hemu's head was sent to Kabul as a sign of victory to the ladies of Humayun's harem and Hemu's torso was sent to Delhi for exposure on a gibbet. Iskandar Khan chased the Hemu's fleeing army and captured 1,500 elephants and a large contingent. Hemu's wife escaped from Delhi with the treasure and Pir Mohammed Khan's troops chased her caravan without success. There was a great slaughter of those who were captured and in keeping with the custom of his ancestors. Akbar had a victory pillar built with their heads. This battle, known as Second Battle of Panipat, was an epoch-making event in the history of India as it resulted in re-establishment of Mughal empire in India.

Battle of Karnal 1739 AD (Feb. 24, 1739)

This was fought between the forces of Nadir Shah, an Iranian adventurer and Muhammed Shah, the Mughal emperor of India, at Karnal, 125 km north of Delhi. The Mughals suffered a decisive defeat.

Nadir Shah led about 55,000 troops, and Muhammed about 15,000. But both sides, especially Indians, had large numbers of non-combatants. Nadir Shah had become the ruler of Persia by deposing the King in 1732.

The End of the Mughal Era

Nadir began his invasion in 1738 A.D. by pursuing fugitives from Kandhahar to Mughal-held-Kabul (both now in Afghanistan). The alleged violation of promises by Muhammed Shah and the ill-treatment of his envoys by Delhi Court served as the alleged cause for his invasion. Divided counsels prevented a Mughal stand until Nadir reached Karnal. Jealousy and rashness led to the Indian defeat and emperor was besieged in his entrenched camp. Nadir marched to Delhi and massacred its inhabitants on March 11. He left on May 5, with large sum of booties, including the famous Peacock Throne of Shah Jahan and the Koh-i-noor diamond. The Mughal Empire never recovered from this blow to its prestige.

The Fall of the Marathas

The Third Battle of Panipat (1761) : Towards the middle of the eighteenth century, Marathas, under the leadership of the Peshwas, had established their supremacy over Haryana and most of north India. The intrusion of the Afghan, Ahmed Shah Abdali into India, culminated in the Third Battle of Panipat on January 14, 1761. Ahmad Shah defeated the Marathas and this marked the end of the Maratha ascendancy. The defeat of the Marathas led to rapid decline of the Mughal empire after Aurangzeb's death, leading ultimately to the advent of the British rule.

The main reason for the failure of Marathas was the absence of allies. Though their infantry was based on European style contingent, they failed to woo allies in north India. Their earlier behaviour and their political ambitions, which led them to loot and plunder, had antagonized all the powers. They had interfered in the internal affairs of the Rajputana states and levied heavy taxes and huge fines on them. They had also made huge territorial and monetary claims upon Awadh. Their raids in the Sikh territory had incensed the Sikh chiefs. Similarly, the Jat chiefs, on whom, also they had imposed heavy fines, did not trust them. They had therefore, to fight their enemies alone, except for the weak support of Imad-ul-Mulk. Moreover, the senior Maratha chiefs constantly bickered with one another. Each one of them had ambitions of carving out their independent states and had no interest in fighting against a common enemy.

Ahmad Shah (1722-73), the first amir of Afghanistan, was the hereditary chief of the Abdali tribe of Afghans, whom he later renamed as the Durrani. He led a contingent of his tribesman in the service of Nadir Shah, the king of Persia, who won control over most of Afghanistan and part of India. When Nadir Shah died, Ahmed Shah founded an independent Afghans kingdom. He invaded the Indian Punjab six times between 1748 and 1752 and seized and looted Delhi. Although he was a powerful military leader, yet Ahmed never succeeded in ruling India on a permanent basis. He subsequently withdrew into Afghanistan.

The Advent of the British

(1803 to 1857) : The year 1803 is an important year in the history of Haryana. In this year, the area of what is now present-day-Haryana and Delhi came under the control of the East India Company of Britain. At that time, Delhi was being ruled by old and week Mughal ruler, Shah Alam. But the real power lay in the hands of the Maratha leader Daulat Rao Sindhiya, who acted as his Regent. On 6th September, 1803, the battle between General Lake's British forces and the Marathas took place near village Partapganj, 6 miles south of Delhi. Many people from Haryana fought along with the Marathas against the British. Among them were: the Jats, led by Hari Singh, the king of Ballabhgarh; the Ahirs, led by Rao Tej Singh of Rewari; and 5,000 Sikhs. The Marathas fought bravely but lost due to the cowardice of French officers who were assisting them. When the British entered Delhi on 14 September, 1803, the Mughal ruler, Shah Alam, surrendered. On 30 September, 1803, the Maratha leader, Daulat Rao Sindhiya, also decided to make peace with the British by signing a treaty with the East India Company. Under this treaty, the areas of Haryana and Delhi came under the control of the British.

British Rule Over Haryana

In 1805, the British divided this area into two parts due to administrative and political reasons. A smaller part called the Assigned Territories, was kept directly under the control of the Company. The larger part was divided and handed over to various local rulers who were faithful and loyal to the British. The Assigned Territory consisted of the areas under Panipat, Sonepat, Samalkha, Ganaur, Palam, Palwal, Nuh, Nagina, Hathin, Ferozpur Jhirkha, Sohna and Rewari. This area was administered by East India Company's officer, called the Resident and he reported directly to the Governor General. The other larger part was divided into various princely states and handed over to loyal local king and nawabs. But these arrangements didn't go too well with the people of Haryana who are by nature independent minded and don't like outsiders meddling in their affairs. Therefore, they, especially the Jats of Rohtak and Ahirs and Meos of Gurgaon, rose again in revolt against the rulers. But by 1809, British had established full control over the territory of Haryana.

The year 1833 was another important landmark in Haryana's history. In this year, the Bengal Presidency under the East India Company, was divided into two provinces of Bengal and North Western Province. Most areas of Haryana and Delhi together became one of the six divisions of north western Province, called the Delhi division. The Delhi division was further sub-divided into seven princely states and five districts. The princely states were Bahadurgarh, Ballabhgarh, Dujana, Farukhnagar, Jhajjar, Loharu and Pataudi. The five districts were Delhi, Gurgaon, Rohtak, Panipat and Hissar. These districts were divided into Tehsils and Tehsils were bifurcated into Zails. The officer heading the Delhi division was called a Commissioner instead of the Resident. At this time, some areas of the present-day Haryana were outside the Delhi division and were considered to be a part of the "upper region". These were the districts of Ambala and Thanesar and the princely states of Buria, Chhachhrauli and Jind. But the people of "upper region" and Delhi division, though administratively in different provinces, were closely bound by socio-cultural ties. This administrative system continued till the Revolt of 1857.

The Mutiny of 1857

The Revolt of 1857 was sparked by the introduction of the Enfield rifle in the Indian Army. The cartridges of this new rifle were greased with an ingredient containing cow's fat and hog's lard. This news spread like wild fire among the sepoys of the army. Both Hindus and the Muslims were shocked and outraged at the use of cow's fat and hog's lard, respectively. They soon formed panchayats in all corps and decided to socially boycott any sepoy who used these cartridges. This feeling continued to grow until mutiny started and spread throughout northern India and Bengal. The first military station in northern India, where the mutiny started, was Ambala; the day was 10 May, 1857. Except for the princely states of Jind, Kalsia, Buria and some small Jagirs in Ambala and Thanesar, the entire Haryana region was severely affected by the revolt. An important aspect of the uprising in Haryana was complete communal co-operation and amity. By the beginning of June, 1857, almost whole of Haryana had become independent of the British rule. It took almost six months for the British to take back the control of Haryana. The superior firearms, artillery and the help of some loyal rulers of princely states proved to be handy for the British. The rebels were ruthlessly crushed by them. While doing so, they burned down hundreds of villages and indulged in wanton killings. After the 1857 Revolt, the British removed Haryana from the north western province and merged it with Punjab in February, 1858. The region of Haryana was divided into two divisions that of Delhi and Hissar. The Delhi division consisted of the districts of Delhi, Gurgaon and Panipat while the Hissar division consisted of the districts of Hissar, Sirsa and Rohtak. These districts were further divided into tehsils, tehsils into zails and zails into villages. The Punjab government, in 1871, ordered the setting up of district committees or Zila Samitis. The Punjab District Board Act (1883) gave more powers to these Zila Samitis.

The Arya Samaj

The formation of Arya Samaj on 10 April, 1875 played a very important role in the history of Haryana region. The founder of Arya Samaj, Swami Dayanand Saraswati (1824-1883) was a great Sanskrit scholar. Swami Dayanand came to Haryana in 1880. He stayed in Rewari for some time to preach against superstitions and illiteracy. He also established a branch of Arya Samaj in Rewari. Later, another branch was established in Rohtak. Later, Lala Lajpat Rai played an important part in popularizing Arya Samaj in Haryana's villages. Arya Samaj played a great role in removing backwardness in the farming community of Haryana, especially among the Jats.

The Congress

The formation of the Congress party in 1885 speeded up political activities in the Haryana region (1885 to 1947). After the formation of the Congress in 1885, the political activities in Haryana accelerated. In 1905, the British partitioned Bengal and this directly challenged the Congress programme. The Congress responded by the Swadeshi Andolan. Murlidhar from Ambala and Lala Lajpat Rai in Hissar actively participated in this agitation. In October, 1907, in Ambala, a state-level conference was organised by the Congress. A large number of people from every corner of the Punjab and Haryana participated in this conference. Under the leadership of Lala Lajpat Rai, the conference decided to form branches in every district. Till this time, the Congress's Swadeshi Andolan did not have much force outside the urban middle class of the region. As a result of the Ambala conference's decision, district-level branches were formed in all the districts of Haryana and the Punjab

On 9th May 1907, the British exiled Lala Lajpat Rai to Burma. This caused a severe setback to the activities of the Congress party. Due to increasing criticism, the British were forced to bring Lalaji back on 14 November, 1907. But the bitter fight between the *garam dal* (Extremists) *and naram dal* (Moderates) factions of the Congress resulted in its activities coming to a standstill. Due to this and various other reasons, the agitation for independence ran out of steam and it remained so till the end of the First World War.

The First Great War

After the commencement of the First World War, the Congress held a conference in Madras where it passed a resolution to support the British in its war effort. Four annual conferences were held by the Congress during the period of the war and in each one of them, similar resolutions were passed for helping the British. As a result, Congress workers from Haryana also started helping the British in their war efforts. The main reason was that the leadership was in the hands of the middle class urban people and they thought that by doing this, they would be able to get some personal benefit.

During the war, a very large number of Haryanavi youth got themselves enlisted in the army. In Rohtak district alone, more that 20,000 young men were recruited in the army by the British. Businessmen and other rich people donated large amounts of money to help the government. While the *naram dal* faction of the Congress was helping the British during the war, the *garam dal* faction led by Bal Gangadhar Tilak. Ms. Annie Besant started the Home Rule League agitation. In Haryana, Pandit Neki Ram Sharma was at the forefront of this agitation. After the Calcutta Conference in 1917, Tilakji asked Pandit Neki Ram Sharma to lead the Home Rule agitation in the Haryana region.

Pandit Neki Ram Sharma concentrated his activities particularly in the Rohtak region. Perturbed by this, the government threatened him with imprisonment and also tried to buy him out with offers of land and money but to be no avail. Disturbed by the failure of the Home Rule agitation he decided to invite Tilakji to Haryana but the government reached by banning Tilakji from coming to Punjab and arrested Pandit Neki Ram Sharma.

Annexation of Haryana to Punjab

The region of the present-day Haryana was made a part of Punjab in 1858 by the British. Due to the active role of the people of Haryana in the Revolt of 1857, this region was punished and no significant development work took place. The people of Haryana region were treated as second-class citizens. Moreover, there were many differences between the people of these two regions like language, clothing and other habits. The demand for a separate state got a boost with the demand of Master Tara Singh for a Punjabi Suba in 1948. Moreover, there were problems due to the language conflict between the Hindi-speaking and the Punjabi-speaking people. Note that during the medieval age and also during the British rule, Punjab was called the

Panjab. But after independence, it came to be known as Punjab. Hence, from now onwards, we shall mention it as Punjab. In order to solve this problem the then Punjab Chief Minister, Bhimsen Sachchar, introduced the Sachchar formula on 1 October, 1949. According to this formula, the State was sub-divided into two parts : 1. Punjabi Area 2. Hindi Area. The Hindi area included the districts of Rohtak, Hissar, Gurgaon, Kangra, Karnal and the Tehsils of Jagadhari and Naraingarh. It was decided that the official language of the Punjabi area would be Punjabi (Gurumukhi script) and the official language of the Hindi area would be Hindi (Devnagari script). The then State PEPSU also decided to follow the same formula. But the Sachchar formula could not succeed and it became especially unpopular in the Hindi area.

On 25 December 1953, the Indian Government set up a Commission under the Chairmanship of Syed Faizal Ali for suggesting the reorganization of States according to language and culture. The proponents of Panjabi Suba and Haryana both appeared before the Commission with their respective demands. But the Commission did not approve of the division or reorganization of Punjab. This decision of the Commission caused great despondency in the region.

Punjab government tried to find a solution to this difficult problem by suggesting the division of the state into Panjabi-speaking and Hindi-speaking areas. According, in April, 1956, the Indian Government declared Punjab to be a dual-language state divided it into Panjabi Area and Hindi Area. Both Hindi and Panjabi were declared its Official languages . The Hindi Area included the districts of Hissar, Rohtak, Karnal, Gurgaon, Mahendragarh, Shimla, Kangra and the tehsil of Ambala, Jagadhari, Naraingarh, Jind and Narwana. But in 1957, due to certain actions of Pratap Singh Kairon, the then Chief Minister of Punjab, this solutions too failed.

The Demand for Statehood

The failure of this solution accelerated the demand for separate states in both the regions. In 1960, Master Tara Singh launched a *morcha* for his demand of Punjab Suba. He was promptly arrested on the orders of Punjab CM, P.S. Kairon. On the arrest of Master Tara Singh, Sant Fateh Singh took over the leadership of the agitation. Because Sant

Fateh Singh was a secular person and well connected with the masses, he became more popular. He went on a fast unto death to force the Government to accept their demand for the Punjabi Suba. More than 57,000 people went to jail in this *satyagraha*. Both the Union Government and Punjab Government were shaken by this agitation. The wily Punjab Chief Minister, Kairon, then played his trump card and released Master Tara Singh from jail. Master Tara Singh was greatly disturbed by the increasing popularity of Sant Fateh Singh. He took the leadership of the agitation back from Sant Fateh Singh and persuaded him to break his fast. Then, he himself, decided to go on a fast unto death, but broke the fast after 48 days. This caused Master Tara Singh to lose his popularity and Sant Fateh Singh became the leader of Panjabi people, especially of the Sikhs. Meanwhile discontent kept simmering among the people of Haryana region for a separate state.

In 1965, Sant Fateh Singh again decided to go on a fast on 10 August, 1965 to press for the demand of the Panjabi Suba. He further threatened self-immolation if the demand was not accepted with in 25 days. The Hindus of the Panjabi Area opposed the demand for the division of the State, fearing that they would be in a minority in the new State. The local Press, which was also controlled by the Hindus, too joined them and openly opposed the division. The People of Haryana region, except for RSS and Jan Sangh followers, supported the demand for the division of Punjab into Hindi-speaking and Panjabi-speaking states.

Reorganisation of Punjab

Finally, bowing to the growing pressure from the people of both the regions, the Indian Government announced the setting up of a parliamentary committee for reorganization of Punjab on 23 September, 1965. This committee was headed by Sardar Hukam Singh. Meanwhile, in October, all the legislatures belonging to the Haryana region got together and discussed the issue of the new state. On 17 October, 1965, in a meeting in Rohtak, three important resolutions were passed. They were: (A) A new Hindi-speaking State should be formed, which shall include, in addition to the Hindi-speaking areas of Punjab, some areas of Delhi, Rajasthan and Uttar Pradesh. (B) If the States of Rajasthan and Uttar Pradesh do not agree, then the new State should be formed consisting of Hindi speaking areas of Punjab. (C) The people of Haryana region would not tolerate any division of the Hindi-speaking areas and whole of this area should constitute the State of Haryana.

The Hukam Singh Committee agreed to division and reorganization of Punjab and recommended that a Boundary Commission may be set up to facilitate this division. On 23 April, 1966, acting on the recommendation of the Hukam Singh Committee, the Indian Government set up the Shah Commission under the Chairmanship of Justice J.C. Shah, to divide and set up the boundaries of Punjab and Haryana. Haryana was carved our of the Indian State of Punjab on 1 November, 1966. This State was formed on the recommendation of the Sardar Hukam Singh Parliamentary Committee. The formation of this committee was announced in the Parliament on 23 September, 1965. On 23 April, 1966, acting on the recommendations of the Hukam Singh Committee, the Indian Government set up the Shah Commission under the Chairmanship of Justice J.C. Shah, to divide and set up the boundaries of Punjab and Haryana.

The Commission gave its report on 31 May, 1966. According to this report, the districts of Hissar, Mahendragarh, Gurgaon, Rohtak and Karnal were to be a part of the new State of Haryana. Further the Tehsils of Jind (district Sangrur), Narwana (district Sangrur) Naraingarh, Ambala and Jagadhari were also included. The Commission recommended that Tehsil Kharar (including Chandigarh) should be part of Haryana. After receiving the report of Shah Commission, the Indian Government passed Punjab reorganization Bill, (1966) on 18 September, 1966. According to this Bill, the boundary of Haryana was demarcated as follows:

The districts of Hissar, Rohtak, Gurgaon, Karnal and Mahendragarh; the Jind and Narwana tehsils of Sangrur district; the Ambala, Jagadhari and Naraingarh tehsils of Ambala district; the Pinjore circle of Kharar tehsil (district Ambala); and the part of Mani Majra circle of Kharar tehsil, it was also decided that the two States of Haryana and Punjab would have a common High Court, called the Punjab and Haryana

High Court. The other parts of the Bill dealt with issues like division of the Parliamentary seats in the Lok Sabha and Rajya Sabha.

A State is born

Finally on 1 November, 1966 the State of Haryana emerged on the Indian peninsula, after a lot of turmoil, political negotiations and movements on a mass scale.

CHAPTER 4

GEOGRAPHY

INTRODUCTION

The State of Haryana is located in the north-western part of India. The river Yamuna flows on the eastern boundary of the State. The Shivalik mountain range flanks the State on its north, the State of Himachal Pradesh is also on its northern side. On the western side, it is flanked by the State of Punjab. At the southern side, the State is flanked by the Aravalli Hills and the desert of Rajasthan. On the eastern side, Uttar Pradesh is the neighbouring State, which touches it only for a limited length. As soon as one crosses the Yamuna river on the eastern side, one enters Uttar Pradesh.

The total area of the State of Haryana is 44,212 square kilometres. Its total population is 2,53,51,462 as per Census (2011). Areawise, Haryana is a moderately large State; all other States of the country are larger (in terms of area) except Kerala, Goa, Mizoram, Nagaland, Sikkim, Tripura, Meghalaya and Manipur. The population of Haryana is more than those of Goa, Arunachal Pradesh, Mizoram, Manipur, Nagaland, Sikkim, Himachal Pradesh, Uttarakhand, Tripura and Meghalaya.

TERRAIN

Haryana is at a height of 700-900 feet above the Mean Sea Level (MSL). Its terrain can be divided into four parts. The brief description of its towns, cities and terrain is as follows:

Haryana has a total of 154 cities and towns. It has 6,841 villages. For administrative purposes, the whole State has been further sub-divided into six division—Ambala, Rohtak, Gurugram, Hissar, Karnal and Faridabad. Till January 2024 there are 22 districts, 80 sub-divisions, 94 tehsils, 49 sub-tehsils and 143 blocks.

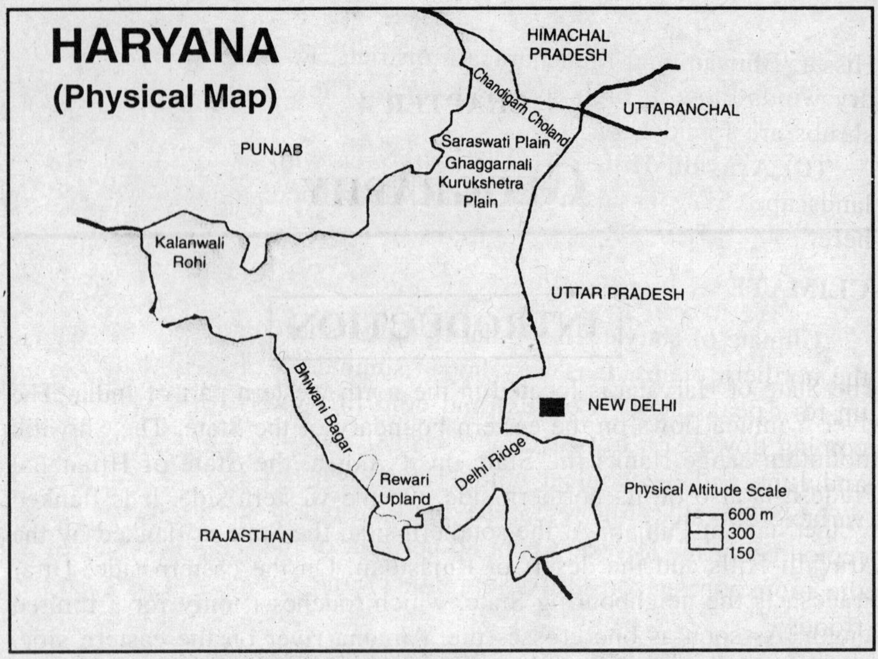

Haryana is situated in the north between 27°37' to 30°35' Latitude and between 74°28' to 77°36' Longitude. Haryana has Uttar Pradesh on eastern border, Punjab on its western border, Himachal Pradesh and Shivalik Hills on its northern border and Delhi, Rajasthan and Aravalli Hills on its southern border. The altitude of Haryana varies between 700 feet to 900 feet above the Mean Sea Level. Haryana has four main types of terrain, as follows :

(A) Shivalik Hills : Their altitude varies between 900 to 2,300 metres. These hills are a source of rivers like Saraswati, Ghaggar, Tangri and Markanda. It is a cold region, which receives rainfall in plenty.

(B) Ghaggar Yamuna Plain : It is divided into two parts—the higher one is called Bangar while the lower one is called Khadar. This alluvium plain is made up of sand, clay, silt and hard calcareous balls like gravels. Winters are very cold whereas summers are very hot. Rainfall occurs in plenty. Trees of Sheesham, Peepal, Banyan, Mango, Neem and Jamun are found here.

(C) Semi-desert Sandy Plain : This area borders the State of Rajasthan and includes the districts of Sirsa and parts of Fatehabad,

Hissar, Bhiwani and Mahendragarh districts. Rainfall is scarce and hot dry winds blow at high speeds. Keekar, Thor, Kair and other thorny shrubs are found here.

(D) Aravalli Hills : This is a dry area with uneven and irregular landscape. Slate is taken out of this area. There is minimum rainfall here.

CLIMATE

Climate of Haryana is similar to those other States of India lying in the northern plains. It is very hot in summer (with temperature going up to a peak of 50° Celsius) and cold in winters (with temperature coming down to a lowest of 1° Celsius). The hottest months are May and June and the coldest being December and January. Rainfall is variable Shivalik Hills region having the highest and the Aravalli Hills region being the lowest. About 80 per cent of the rainfall occurs during the monsoon season (July-September) and sometimes causes local floods.

RIVERS

There are (or were) eight major rivers in Haryana—Yamuna, Ghaggar, Saraswati, Dohan, Tangri, Krishnawati, Sahibi and Markanda.

Yamuna: Yamuna river forms the eastern boundary of Haryana with Uttar Pradesh. It enters Haryana near the Kalesar forest in Yamunanagar district. It flows due south along the districts of Yamunanagar, Karnal, Panipat, Sonepat and leaves Haryana near Hasanpur in district Faridabad. At Tajewala barrage in district Yamunanagar, the water of the river Yamuna are diverted to the western Yamuna canal for irrigation. There is a nice tourist spot at Hathni Kund near this barrage. The world famous Taj Mahal is situated on the banks of this river in Agra, Uttar Pradesh. It is also called Yamna, Jamna and Jamuna in local dialects. This revered river originates from the Champasar Glacier at an altitude of 4,421 m in the State of Uttarakhand. Some say that the source of the river is the Saptarishi Kund, glacial lake. There is a sacred shrine of Yamunotri or Yamnotri, near this source at an altitude of 3,235 m. There is a temple dedicated to Goddess Yamuna, which remains closed from November to May. At Hanumanchatti or Hanuman Ganga merges with Yamuna river.

Yamunotri finds a special mention in the Hindu mythology. According to a legend, this secluded hilly spot was the home of an ancient sage, Asit Muni.

From Uttarakhand, the river flows into the State of Himachal Pradesh. After passing leaving Paonta Sahib, Yamuna flows along the boundary of Haryana and Uttar Pradesh and after leaving Haryana, it continues to flow till it merges with the river Ganga (Ganges) at Sangam or Prayag in Allahabad (Uttar Pradesh). The total length of the river is 1,370 km. Its major tributaries are the Chambal and Betwa rivers.

Religious Importance : The rivers Ganga and Yamuna, along with the now dried Saraswati, are the most sacred rivers of India. Yamuna, according to the legends, is the daughter of the Sun God, Surya and the sister of Yama, the God of Death. According to ancient beliefs, it is said that those who take a dip in the holy waters of the river, do not fear death. This river is also closely connected to Mahabharata and Lord Krishna. Lord Krishna's father, Vasudeva, crossed the Yamuna with baby Lord Krishna for a safer place. It is said that Lord Krishna played along with his cowherd friends on the banks of river Yamuna during his childhood in Nandgram, Mathura.

Saraswati: River Saraswati is believed to have drained the north and northwest region of India, including Haryana and Punjab, in ancient times. It is also believed to be supporting a large number of settlements during those times. There are numerous references to the river Saraswati in the ancient Indian literature of the Vedic and post-Vedic period. *Rig-Veda*, the most ancient of the four Vedas, describes Saraswati as a mighty river with many individually recognized tributaries. The sacred book calls Saraswati as the seventh river of the Sindhu—Saraswati river system, hence the name Saptasindhu for the region bounded by rivers Saraswati in the east and Sindhu (Indus) in the west. *Rig Veda* hymns also describe life and times of the people residing in the Saraswati river valley. *Rig Veda* describes Saraswati as *Ambitamé*, the best of the mothers; and *Devitamé*, the best of the goddesses. Ancient sites in Kunal and Banawali, in district Fatehabad, has been found on the banks of the dried river bed of Saraswati.

Saraswati is believed to have originated from the Har-ki-Dun glacier in West Garhwal. It flowed parallel to the river Yamuna for some distance and later joined it, the unified river proceeding toward south as the Vedic Saraswati. The seasonal rivers and rivulets, including Ghaggar, joined Saraswati as it followed the course of the present river through Punjab and Haryana. River Sutlej, the Vedic Shatadru, joined the river Saraswati as a tributary at Shatrana, at a distance of approximately 25 kilometres south of Patiala. Saraswati, then followed the course of Ghaggar through Rajasthan and Hakra in Bhawalpur before emptying into the Rann of Kutch via Nara in Sindh province, running parallel to the Indus River. It has been established that the river Saraswati, carrying the waters of three perennial and numerous seasonal rivers, was a mighty rivers during the Vedic times.

Ghaggar: As of today, a part of the river exists as Ghaggar in Haryana; the rest of it has disappeared in the fringes of the desert of Rajasthan and Sindh. The perennial rivers Sutlej and Yamuna were once the tributaries of the Saraswati. It is believed that subsequently, some tectonic movements may have forced the Sutlej and Yamuna to change course and hence, Saraswati dried up in a period spread over a few hundred years, possibly between 2000 and 1500 BC. It is probable that desertification of Rajasthan would have taken place at that time. The present dried bed of Ghaggar was thus, a part of a major river, anciently known as Saraswati. Analysis of satellite imagery supports the hypothesis regarding the course of the 'lost' Saraswati.

This river enters Haryana near Pinjore. After passing through Ambala and Hissar, it reaches Bikaner in Rajasthan and runs a course of 290 miles before finally disappearing in the deserts of Rajasthan.

Markanda: The Markanda river's ancient name was Aruna. A seasonal stream like the Ghaggar, it originates from the lower Shivalik hills and enters Haryana near Ambala. During monsoons, this stream swells up into a raging torrent, which is notorious for its devastating power. The surplus water is carried on to the Sanisa lake where the Markanda joins the Saraswati. Its important tributary is the Tangri.

Sahibi: The Sahibi originates in the Mewat hills near Jitgarh and Manoharpur in Rajasthan. Gathering volume from about a hundred tributaries, it reaches voluminous proportions, forming a broad stream around Alwar and Patan. After reaching Rohtak, it branches off into two smaller streams and finally reaches the outskirts of Delhi. Then, it flows into the Yamuna. There are three other rivulets in and around the Mewat hills—Indori, Dohan and Kasavati; all of these flow northwards from south.

RAINFALL

Haryana receives, less rainfall each year. During the monsoons (from June to September), the plains receive rainfall. The Shivalik range receives 216 cm of rainfall (maximum) each year. The Aravalli region gets scanty rainfall. During the winter season, rainfall occurs from December to February. The districts of Ambala, Kurukshetra, Karnal, Jind, Panipat, Gurugram, Rohtak, Sonepat and Faridabad receive good rainfall. But the Mewat region of Gurugram and Faridabad does not get good rainfall. The average rainfall in the State is 45 cm. The south-western parts of the state (including Sirsa, Bhiwani, Hissar, Rewari, Rohtak, Gurugram, Faridabad and Mahendragarh) receive less rainfall. The north-eastern parts (including Ambala, Yamunanagar, Kurukshetra, Kaithal, Karnal, Jind, Sonepat and Panipat) get plenty of rainfall.

SOIL

The hilly areas of the State are limited. Most of the terrain is used for agricultural production. Rivers of the area bring fertile soil along with them from the mountains and deposit it in the plains. This soil is very useful for cultivation.

There are three types of soil in Haryana, which depend upon three types of terrain of the state. These three types of the terrain are—hilly, plain and sandy. The soil of the hilly terrain is rocky. The terrain of the plains has fertile soil. The colour of this soil is yellowish grey. It has been deposited here by the rivers Yamuna and Saraswati. The terrain of the sandy tracts of the State has sandy soil. The colour of the soil is light grey. It is brought into the state by the high-speed warm winds of Rajasthan. It is not fertile. The hilly areas of the State have thin but rock-solid soil.

The rivers of the state deliver fertile soil along their valleys. This soil has fine grains. In Yamunanagar, various types of soil are found. One type does not have nitrogen and phosphorus in abundance. Further, red chestnut soil is also found in this area. In the sub-hilly region of the

Shivaliks, *domut*, grey and sandy soils are found. The terrain has ample quantities of small pebbles and stones.

In Rohtak district, the soil is fertile. In most of the areas of Jhajjar district, one can find sand dunes. The soil here is of light grey colour; it lacks nitrogen. The soil of Sonepat district is sandy and *domut*. In Sirsa district, red soil is found. In Hissar, Bhiwani and Fatehabad, sandy *domut* soil is in abundance. In this soil, crops can be grown, if water is supplied to the same.

The soil of Gurugram district is of two types. In the uneven tract of the district, sandy and *domut* soil is found. It is found in Sohna, Gurugram and Punhana. In the plain-cum-sandy tract, the soil found is sandy. It is found in Ferozepur-Jhirka, Nagma, Tavadu and Pataudi. But at the same time the plain-cum-sandy tract also has *chikni* soil, which is found in Nuh and Ferozepur Jhirka. But it is found only in a few parts of these two towns.

In Jind district, soil has been brought by rivers Ghaggar and Yamuna. It is also called alluvial soil. The soil of Ambala and Kaithal district is yellowish-grey in colour. But in some parts, rocky terrain is also found. The soil of Faridabad is fertile, its colour is yellowish-grey. The soil of districts Kurukshetra, Panipat and Karnal is yellowish-grey and fertile. The soil of district Mahendragarh and Rewari is predominantly sandy; it is not very much fertile. The colour of this soil is light grey.

CANALS

There are four major canal systems that irrigate the agricultural land of the State.

Western and Eastern Yamuna Canal: It is the oldest canal of the state. It emerges from the Tajewala barrage, which is located on Jagadhari—Paonta Sahib road. The western canal as well as the eastern canal starts from Tajewala. There are several branches of western Yamuna canal. These branches feed water, for irrigation purposes, to the land areas of Karnal, Panipat, Sonepat, Jind and Rohtak districts. The river Yamuna feeds water to this canal.

Gurgaon Canal: This canal has been drawn at the Okhla barrage from the Yamuna. With the waters of this canal, the districts of Gurugram and Faridabad are irrigated.

Bhakra Canal: This canal has been drawn at a place near Nangal from the Sutlej. The fields of Sirsa, Rohtak and Hissar districts are supplied water through this canal.

Bhiwani Canal: This is a small canal. It has been drawn out of Bhakra Canal. The district of Bhiwani is fed water through this canal.

Jawahar Lal Canal: This canal has also been drawn from Bhakra Canal. The fields of Mahendragarh district are fed water through this canal.

LAKES

There are five lakes in the State. Four major lakes, Damdama, Khalilpur, Sultanpur and Kotla, are located in Gurugram district. The Sultanpur lake, which has become a world famous bird sanctuary, is located in the Farukhnagar division. Our readers can read more details about it in the chapter on tourism. Badkhal lake is located on the western side of Faridabad district. This area has a rocky terrain; the lake is located almost in the middle of this terrain. It is at a distance of 31 kilometres from Delhi. On the Delhi-Mathura highway, a motorable road moves to the right due west, which is 3 kilometres long. It leads us to the Badkhal lake resort. The lake was built in 1947 when two small hillocks were joined and a dam was constructed to check soil erosion. The dam has a length of 644.5 metres and a width of 6 metres. This site is an attractive tourist spot too.

CHAPTER 5

HISTORICAL PLACES

INTRODUCTION

The state of Haryana is believed to be the birthplace of the first anecdotes of history. According to a legend, nature came into being at this place because of the boon given by Brahma. The first ever dynasty (of Kurus) was established here. The great war of Mahabharata was fought here. Besides, several civilisations were born here. They faded into the oblivion with the passage of time. But nevertheless, they left their indelible marks on the culture, soil and moments of the state. Several artifacts and ancient monuments have been discovered (or unearthed) in the state. These discoveries show that several towns and villages of the state were cradles of ancient human settlements during the pre-historic and historic periods. In this chapter, we shall discuss some towns and places of Haryana where the ancient civilisation had developed and reached their respective pinnacles. Some historic towns have also been discussed in this chapter, which narrate the tales of some famous communities of India.

NAURANGABAD MOUND

It is near the village of Naurangabad, at a distance of about 10 kilometres from the Bhiwani town in Bhiwani district, Haryana. This mound came to the notice of the Government in the early eighties when children playing there found old coins after rains washed away the top soil. Some of these coins were thought to be of Kushan and Gupta periods; the same have been displayed in a museum in the Jhajjar Gurukul. In 1985, this mound was taken over by the government and handed over to the Archaeological Department. The total area of the mound taken over by the government is 58 acres. The mound is now maintained by a sub-office of the Archaeological Department situated in Hissar.

Digging was started on the mound in February, 2001; it continued for about three months.

In this preliminary digging, artifacts of ages up to 2500 years have been found. Among the artifacts found, are coins, tools, sieves, toys, statues and pots. According to the archaeologists, the presence of coins, coin moulds, statues and design of the houses suggests that a town existed here during the Kushan, Gupta and Youdheya periods till 300 BC. During the Youdheya period, the coins had seals of religious figures and these coins were cast in moulds.

Remains of houses made of mud bricks as well as baked bricks have been found. The walls have thickness varying from 18 inches to 24 inches. The floor is lined with baked bricks and the size of the bricks is approximately 18 inches by 9 inches by 3 inches. People from the nearby village have been using these bricks for constructing their own houses. This practice was stopped after the mound was declared as reserved in 1985. Kunal Mound is a small rural site, a village is compared to towns like Lothal and Kalibangan and cities like Rakhi Garhi. It is located on the bank of the dried river, Saraswati, in Fatehabad district earlier.

KUNAL

The artifacts unearthed at Kunal were not seen earlier at a pre-Harappan site. These include seals, terracotta cakes, scripts and natural motifs. Kunal's pottery depicts Harappan letters. Natural motif with both monochrome and bio-chrome have also been found. This implies a transition from the pre-Harappan culture to the fully mature Harappan culture. Some archaeologists think that the pre-Harappan culture of Kunal and the Vedic culture are one and the same. They give the example of the triangle-shaped terracotta cakes, which, they say, are the symbol of fertility in Rig Veda. A painting with a horse and pipal motif, found in Kunal, are also associated with the Vedic culture. Further, Kunal is situated on the banks of the dried Saraswati river which has been mentioned in the Rig Veda.

Kunal has three distinctive phases of pre-Harappan culture. During the earliest phase people used to live in pits. During the second, moulded mud bricks were used to line the dwellings. During the third phase bricks were used to make square-shaped and rectangular houses.

Two silver crowns have also been found at Kunal—one a little smaller than the other. They may have been used by the king or an elected headman and his consort. Other jewellery found there includes two tiaras, an armlet, a necklace, copper bangles, six disc-shaped gold beads and more than 10,000 beads of semi-precious stones, like carnelian, agate, steatite and lapis lazuli. Agroha mound is situated in Hissar district of Haryana. The remains of the Capital of the Agroha state, consisting of 18 state units, are buried here. The residents of these states, were known as Yodhya and Agraya. Some of the writings on the coins that have been excavated from the site of ancient Agroha read as Yodhyanam Bahu Dhanya Kanam, Yodhya Ganasya Jaya and Yodhyanam Jaimantra Shalinam. According to Dr. Satyaketu Vidyalankar, the ancient Agroha town existed nearly 100 years before the Kushan dynasty. The Agroha state was renowed for its prosperity. However over time, it could not bear the brunt of invasions of Hunas, Greeks and Yavanas, who invaded northern India. Their attacks led to disintegration of various kingdoms of Punjab. The disintegration of Agroha state led to the migration of the residents of Agroha to other parts of the country, like Rajasthan, Uttar Pradesh, Punjab and Malwa. However they got a common name, Aggarwals, which means *Agrohawale*. It is quite apparent from the excavations that below the mounds, existed a big, well planned and progressive town. The excavation was restarted in the year 1938-39, though this could not be carried out for a long time period due to World War II. However provided major input about Agroha's existence.

In 1978-79 the Archaeological Department of Haryana Government began excavation work under the guidance and supervision of Mr. J.S. Khatri and Mr. Acharya. The Agroha mound now has the Agroha Temple Complex on one side and the Sheela Mata Temple on the other. The Agroha Medical College faces it across the road.

Some of the materials collected from the excavated site are as follows :

(A) Coins : Large numbers of coins have been found at the excavated site. The coins are mostly made from silver and bronze in different shapes and sizes. The script and signs on these coins depict that they belong to different periods. The bronze coins have Agadke, Agach, Janpads in Prakrit language inscribed on them. A coin dated 200 BD (called die struck or counter struck) has been found besides coins Roman, Kushana, Yodhaya and Gupta dynasties.

(B) Seals : The seals that have been found at Agroha have been inscribed with words like of *Pitradutt*, *Sadhu Virdhasya, Shamkar Malasya*, *Madrsya*, etc.

(C) Artifacts : From the excavation site, many statues made of stone and sand have been unearthed. Masks, terracotta, animals and toys have been also been found. Utensils belonging to the second century B.C. and having black, brown and red polish, have also been discovered.

AGROHA

Agroha was the prosperous and illustrious kingdom of Maharaja Agrasen about 3,000 years back. The Agroha Mound or *Ther*, as it is locally called, is about 1.5 km away from the present Agroha village. Buried under this mound, are the remains of an ancient town; its excavation was started in the year 1888-89. It was at that time people came to know about this great kingdom. Agroha is located at a distance of 20 km from Hissar city in Hissar district and is 190 km away from Delhi on the Delhi-Fazilka national highway.

The development process at Agroha after the excavation was slow. It was only in 1976 that a need for a concerted group effort was felt at the convention of All India Aggarwal Representatives. This realization led to the establishment of Agroha Vikas Trust in 1976. These efforts were supplemented by the Late Master Laxmi Narain Gupta who donated 27 acres of land to Agroha Vikas Trust.

Since then, all the development process at Agroha has been planned and implemented by Agroha Vikas Trust. The developments at Agroha received a major boost from 1985 onwards. The Agroha Dham construction was planned again, with special emphasis on the temple complex and the Shakti Sarovar. Functionally, Agroha Dham has been planned as a centre of learning, philosophy and spirituality. It will also have a *Vridh Ashram* (Old Age Home), a health centre and a research centre.

The total area under the trust for the development of Agroha Dham is 27 acres. The developments have taken place in the form of a temple complex, dedicated to goddess Mahalaxmi and Saraswati. It also hosts the memorial temple of Maharaja Agrasen. The beauty of the place is exemplified by Shakti Sarovar and the well maintained lawns.

Just opposite to the trust compound is Agrasen Medical College and Research Centre. This medical college is one of the most prestigious education centres for medical studies. It is gearing up to become one of the biggest medical research centres. Less than a kilometre away from the trust compound, is the ancient Temple of Sheela Mata, which has become a major tourist attraction.

Just opposite to Agroha Medical College, stands the temple complex. The temple complex consists of three wings; section is graced with the presence of Kuldevi Mahalaxmi. The temple complex is one side of the Agroha mound while Sheela Mata Temple is situated on its other side.

Mahalaxmi Shakti peeth was resurrected on 30th October, 84. The dome of the temple is very big and is at a height of 180 ft. from the ground. The main *Kalash* of the temple is gold-plated. The idol of the goddess, seated on a lotus flower, has both aesthetic and spiritual appeals. It is believed that since the time Maharaja Agrasen was bestowed boon from Devi Mahalaxmi, the wish of every person is fulfilled at this place.

On the north-western end of the temple complex, is Saraswati Temple. Saraswati Ji is the goddess of knowledge and patience. Knowledge and adequate patience are the keys to wealth generation and business acumen with which, Aggarwals are synonymous. The eastern wing of the temple complex hosts the memorial temple of Maharaja Agrasen. In the main hall, beautiful scenes have been sculpted out which represent the ideals of Maharaja Agrasen and important events of his life. One of the scenes shows how a newcomer to the state of Agroha was given a one rupee coin and brick to give a new start to his life. Besides, there are some scenes depicting the myths from our Vedas and Puranas.

In front of the main temple, is a big Satsang Hall of area 120 × 160 sq. ft. It can accommodate approximately 5,000 people at a time. This hall, built with concrete, is the biggest hall in India, without the support of any pillars. It is an architectural wonder. At the main gate of the temple complex, are two beautifully sculpted elephants.

A big chariot depicting the scene from the great epic Mahabharata, where Sri Krishna gives sermons to Arjuna in the battle field of Kurukshetra, has been built on the canopy over the main gate of the temple complex. This is the reflection of the belief of Aggarwals in the philosophy of Karmyoga. The ramps adjacent to the stairs leading out of the main hall (Satsang Bhawan) have white statues of Ganga and Yamuna stationed on them (with coloured fountains).

Located at the back of the temple complex is a big sarovar (pond) called Shakti Sarovar. The sarovar is spread over an area of 4 acres and is surrounded by a two-storey rest house comprising of 136 rooms. On 23rd Jan. 1988, the sarovar was filled with water brought from 41 prominent rivers of India. People can have a dip in the pond, which is cleaned regularly. A platform has been built from the north-western end of the sarovar; it extends up to the middle of the sarovar on which, Samudra Manthan scene has been sculpted along with the arrangement of coloured fountains around it. An amusement park, spread over an area of 2 acres, has been developed on the eastern end of the trust compound. The park has many swings and joy rides for children and adults alike. There is more fun waiting children at the boating site where they can paddle around in a lake spread over an area of 1.5 acres.

A Bhojanalya (restaurant) is located on the eastern end of the trust compound in between the administrative block and amusement park. The bhojanalya serves free food (Bhandara) everyday to all the visitors.

Agroha has a naturopathy centre, which operates in the building surrounding Shakti Sarovar. Naturopathy is a treatment that is done with the help of five basic elements of nature *i.e.,* sky, air, fire, water and earth. Through these elements and in accordance with the rules of nature viz. the diet, environment, control over five senses and rest, an individual attains a healthy body, based on his physical and mental faculties. Yoga is one of the ways for the treatment of ailments. It believes in treatment of the person through five elements of nature.

Sheela Mata Temple is located on one side of the excavated Agroha Mound while the Agroha Temple Complex is situated on the other side. The temple has been built over the ancient Madhi of Sheela Mata. Agroha Medical College is situated right across the road.

Story of Sheela Mata : Seth Harbhajan Shah of Agroha married his only daughter Sheela to the minister of Sialkot state, Mehta Shah. Sheela was very beautiful and became the talk of the town. Even king Risalu of Sialkot heard about her beauty. He sent his minister Mehta Shah to another state for official work. Back home, he himself went to meet Sheela and made an attempt to spoil her chastity. However, Sheela fought the king bravely and protected herself. The unsuccessful king asked her maid to keep his ring under the bed sheet of Sheela's bed. On returning from another state, Mehta Shah discovered the ring on their bed and thought that Sheela had lost her moral character. He abandoned Sheela who returned to her father at Agroha. After many years, the same maid made a confession to Mehta Shah of her mistake and vouched for the morality of Sheela. Mehta Shah was grief-struck on the injustice done to his wife. He rushed to Agroha to seek pardon from his wife but died near Agroha before he could meet Sheela. When Sheela came to know about the demise of her husband, she too died. A memorial temple with a Madhi of Sheela Mata was built at the site of her death.

The construction of the temple started in 1983 and it was completed in February, 1992. The temple was renovated by the Agroha Vikas Sansthan. The temple has been constructed with red and pink stone. It has been designed on the Rajasthani architectural pattern. The main dome of the temple is 85 ft. above the ground. Under the main dome, is the Madhi of Sheela Mata. The temple has sections devoted to all main Hindu Gods viz. Radha-Krishna, Sita-Rama, Durgaji, Shankar-Parvati, Hanumanji, Ganeshji etc. This temple holds great importance among the north Indian temples due to its architectural design.

Sheela Mata Mandir is now a major tourist attraction because of its beautiful temple complex, beautiful lawns and fountains. The nicely maintained landscape in the backdrop of Agroha Mound and Agroha Temple Complex is a feast to the eyes.

Every year, during Bhadra Pad Amavasya, a big fair or mela is organised in the temple area, wherein thousands of pilgrims come, many of them visiting the temple for the Mundan (head shaving) ceremony of their kids.

Agrasen Medical Research Centre and Engineering College at

Agroha, district Hissar, Haryana are being developed to train doctors and engineers of India.

Agrasen Medical and Research College is spread over an area of 270 acres. The Agroha Temple, Agroha Mound and Sheela Mata Temple face the college across the road. Maharaja Agrasen Medical Education and Scientific Research Society was set up in 1988 to look after the affairs of the college. The first phase of the construction activity has been completed in which, around Rs. 25 crore have been invested. It is expected that the complete building of the college shall be ready very soon.

The medical college has a total of 35 seats. Admissions are granted on the basis of PMT results and are supervised by the Haryana Government. The course spans a period of five years. Out of 35 seats, 5 seats are reserved for the NRIs and 18 seats are reserved for SC, ST and OBC categories.

The medical centre has a capacity to hold 1,000 beds. At present, 250 beds have been made available. It is equipped with latest machines and equipment. The aim of Agrasen Medical Research Centre is to become one of the best centres of treatment of chronic and terminal diseases. Research activities shall be conducted at this centre for deadly diseases like cancer, AIDS and chronic diseases like Asthma, heart failure etc.

RAKHI GARHI

Rakhi Garhi is about to rewrite the 5,000 years old history of our civilisation. Recent excavations at Rakhi Garhi in Hissar district of Haryana may push the history of the civilisation back by over a thousand years. It could change the commonly held view about the Indus Valley civilization. Archaeologists and historians are already excited about the findings from Rakhi Garhi—the largest Indus Valley site next only to Mohenjodaro. Senior archaeologists consider this to be no ordinary Harapan site and state that it is the most important of all the archaelogical and sites of India. The unearthed clues may yield answers to many questions that have remained unanswered so far. They also state that their findings have already started showing new civilisation contours.

Firstly, the area of dimensions of the site are far wider than those assessed by archaeologists Raymond and Bridget Allchin and J.M. Kenyer. Its area is 224 hectares, the largest in the country and next only to that of Mohenjodaro. In terms of size, dimensions strategic location and unique significance of the settlement, Rakhi Garhi matches Harappa and Mohenjodaro at every level. Three layers of Early, Mature and Late phases of the Indus Valley Civilization have been found at Rakhi Garhi. What has so far been found uncannily, indicates that Rakhi Garhi settlement had witnessed all the three phases. The site has thick deposits of Hakra Ware (typical of settlements dating back before the early phases of Indus Valley) and also, Early and Mature Harappan artifacts.

The solid presence of the Hakra Ware culture raises the important question : "Did the Indus Civilisation come later than when it was recorded?" The Hakra and the Early phases are separated by more than 500-600 years and the Hakra people are considered to be the earliest Indus inhabitants. Although the Carbon-14 radioactive dating results are awaited, based on the thick layers of Hakra Ware of Rakhi Garhi, yet it has been opined that the site may date back to about 2500 BC to 3000 BC. This pushes the Indus Valley Civilisation history by a thousand years or more.

While this site came to be known in 1963, excavations at Rakhi Garhi started only in 1997. Had they been unearthed 70 years earlier, when Harappa and Mohenjodaro were uncovered, the story would have been different. Fossils indicate that the Harappan man reared cattle. These findings are startling. Rakhi Garhi was located on the banks of the river Dhrishdwati, which was a tributary of the river Saraswati. Copper fishing hooks and woven nets found at the site confirm the river's existence. It is believed that people living in this city traded with other people using this river for navigation purposes.

The site's antiquities, drainage system and signs of a small-scale industry are in continuity with other Indus Valley sites. All this adds one more dimension to the whole debate on Indus Civilisation. Further, many scholars had started finding the predominance of Harappa and Mohenjodaro in history books as "dead boring." But many others stand against any revision of the currently held views. All this only adds to the enigma called Indus Civilisation, rich in facts, richer still in speculation. What stands out from the churning debate is the fact that much more perhaps still remains shrouded in the annals of history. The real and very important part played by Haryana in India's history is yet to be fully understood.

Excavations done so far reveal a well-planned city 1.92 metres wide roads. Pits surrounded by walls have been found, which are thought to be sacrificial pits or areas for some religious ceremonies. They testify that fire was used extensively in their religious ceremonies. There are brick-lined drains to handle sewage from the houses. Among other things that have been found, some include, terracotta statues, weights, bronze artifacts, combs, needles and terracotta seals. A bronze vessel has been found, which is decorated with gold and silver. A gold foundry, with about 3,000 unpolished semi-precious stones, has also been found. Many tools used for polishing these stones and a furance were found at the site of foundry. A burial site has been found with 11 skeletons with their heads towards the north direction. Near the heads of these skeletons, utensils for everyday use were found. The three female skeletons have shell bangles on their wrists. Closer to one female skeleton, a gold armlet has been found. In addition, semi-precious stones have been found lying near the head, proving that they were a part of some type of necklace.

BANAWALI MOUND

The Banawali Mound, previously called Vanawali, lies 14 km. due north-west of Fatehabad on the right bank of the Rangoi Nala at 29° 37" 5' north latitude and 75° 23" 6' east longitude. This ancient mound, spread over an area of one square kilometre, rose to a height of about 10 meters due to successive settlements on the earlier rubble.

The archaeological excavations done here by the Department of Archaeology, Haryana have revealed a finally constructed fort town of the Harappan period overlying an extensive proto-urban settlement of the pre–Harappan culture. If the discovered ancient relics are arranged together, a fairly coherent picture emerges and it can be concluded that if Kalibangan was a metropolitan town in the lower middle valley of the river Saraswati, Banawali was possibly one along the upper middle course of that river.

The era of the pre-Harappan period (2703 B.C.-2300 B.C.) is characterized by the typical pottery, settlement patterns and architecture.

A rich variety of shapes and designs speaks highly of the level of their socio-economic existence and aesthetic tastes. The houses built roughly along cardinal directions, thus indicating definite town planning. Constructed usually of mould-made bricks, there are structures made of kiln-baked bricks. The civilization seems to have been conversant with the technology of copper smelting. Among personal ornaments, beads of gold, semi-precious stones, terracotta and steatite as well as bangles of clay, shell and copper have been recovered during the course of excavation. The overall picture presents a fair degree of advancement achieved by the pre-Harappans by the middle of the third millennia B.C.

While the pre-Harappan culture was still young, a new set of people occupied Banawali. They soon built a well-planned and fortified township in the classical chessboard pattern. The broad arterial streets, running from north to south, have been found to be straight and uninterrupted whereas those, running from east to west, were usually narrow and staggered. This planning perhaps protected the town from the blistering winds of the west and severe monsoon, rains of the south-west. The town seems to be divided in two sub-joined fortified areas, one separated from the other by thick wall running centrally across the mound from north to south. The thickness of the wall is 6-7 metres. A narrow opening, provided thought the defence wall in the centre of the mound was perhaps meant for communication between the two parts of the city blocks of which, the better fortified western side was dominated by the elite. The commoners and business communities lived in the eastern wing. This gate was guarded by a massive square shaped bastion.

Planned mud-brick houses with several rooms, a kitchen, a toilet, etc. are found to be built on both the sides of the roads and lanes. Their sanitary arrangements depended upon use of sanitary pottery jars, which served as washbasins; they were also used for soaking purposes. Except at a few places, which demanded constants use of water, structures were usually made of sun-baked bricks, which were meticulously molded into various sizes. Numerous household items like ovens, hearths, tandoors and blades made of chert and other stones and sophisticated, ceramics known for their fanciful shapes, have been excavated. The principal types of pottery recovered include vases, fruit stands, S-shaped jars, perforated jars, cooking handis, beakers, basins, rooters etc.

Among painted motifs, peacocks, pipal and banana leaves, trees, deer, stars, fish, flowers, intersecting circles and honeycomb patterns are of special interest. The pre-Indus ceramic tradition continues here throughout whereas at Kalibangan, it dies out half-way through. The Harappan seals recovered here depict a rhinoceros, ibex, wild goat, unicorn (a composite animal with a tiger's body and horns). Further, cubical weights and gamesman weights made of stones and ivory or bones reveal a great degree of precision and superb craftsmanship of the Harappan artists. Gold, copper and bronze pieces found here indicate that they had a profound knowledge of metallurgy. Ornaments have been found that include beads of gold, copper, agate, carnelian, Lapis lazuli, faience shell, bone and clay, bangles of copper, faience shell and terracotta and pipal –leaf–shaped ear rings of faience.

Certain figurines of Mother goddess and the like suggest that the Harappans were very fond of decorating their persons with elaborate headgear, ear rings, necklaces, garlands etc. Copper and bronze were used for making weapons and tools as also for making ornaments and items like arrows, spearheads, razor blades, chisels, fish hooks, beads, rings, bangles, antimony rods, wires and hair pins. Iron, however, was not known to them, Terracotta figurines of bulls, buffaloes, deer, dogs, rhinoceros and birds are not only the evidence of their folk art tradition, but also throw light on the fauna of those bygone days.

This site is one of most important archaeological sites of Haryana. It has attracted the attention of the Indian archaeologists and in importance, it rivals Kotdlil and Chanhuo (Sind Pakistan), Kalibangan (Rajasthan), Surkotda and Lothal (Gujarat), Rakhi Garhi (Hissar district) and Mittathal (Bhiwani district). His grave is a simple affair, just a rectangular block on a high platform approached by a flight of steps made of lakhori bricks. The tomb was renovated by the British and an inscription mentioning Ibrahim Lodhi's defeat at the hands of Babur and the renovation was included by them in 1866.

CHAPTER 6

ADMINISTRATIVE SET-UP

INTRODUCTION

Haryana was created as an independent state of India on 1 November, 1966. It was carved out of the erstwhile PEPSU, which had the areas of Punjab and Haryana as its essential components. The state

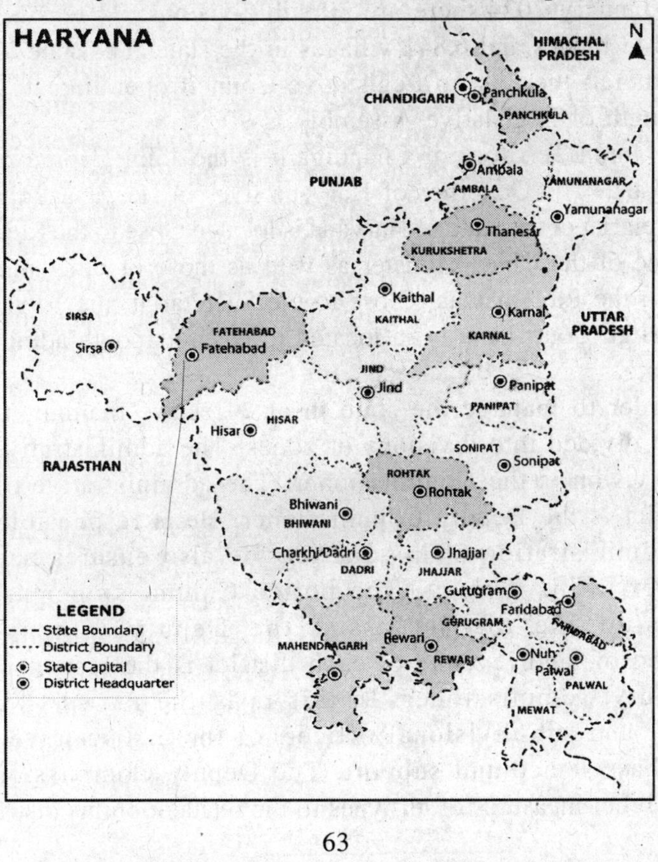

has emerged as one of the best states in terms of governance. We shall briefly study the administrative set up and polity of the state in this chapter.

THE LEGISLATURE

The state of Haryana has a population of 2,53,51,462 persons as per Census (2011). It has 1,34,94,734 males and 1,18,56,728 females as its citizens. The population density of the state is 573 persons per square kilometre. Its Capital is Chandigarh. The Punjab and Haryana High Court (at Chandigarh) has the Jurisdiction over the entire state. There are 22 districts in the state. The information and data about the same can be read in the chapter on Districts in this book.

Till January 2024 there are 80 sub-divisions, 94 tehsils, 49 sub-tehsils, 143 blocks and 6,841 villages in the state. The state legislature is unicameral; there is no Legislative Council operating in the state. The strength of Legislative Assembly is 90.

The Union Territory of Chandigarh is the Joint Capital of Punjab and Haryana. The Governor of Haryana lives in Haryana Raj Bhawan. The Secretariat of the state of Haryana is located close to the Raj Bhawan. The office of the Chief Minister as well as those of other ministers is located in the Raj Bhawan. Close to the Secretariat, the Vidhan Sabha and the High Court have been located to ensure smooth administration of the state.

In order to manage the state in an effective manner, the same has been divided into divisions or zones. The administrative officer of the division is the Commissioner. The administrative officer of the district is the Deputy Commissioner. He is responsible for the actual administration of his district. He also ensures peace, law and order in his district. The police Commissioner and other officials of the district assist the Deputy Commissioner. Collection of land revenue of each district is the responsibility of the Deputy Commissioner. In this task, the *patwari kanungo, tehsildar* and sub-divisional officer, of the district give him all types of assistance and support. The Deputy Commissioner also provides relief measures of all types to the resident on his district at the time of deluge, drought, famine etc. He also ensures that elections are held in a fair manner in his district. He also directs his juniors in respect of various tasks related to development that may be going on in his district.

There are 80 sub-divisions in the entire state. The administrative officer of each sub-division is Sub-Divisional Magistrate (SDM). Panchayats look after the land disputes of their respective villages. Some disputes are sorted out in District Courts. The Sessions Judge or District Magistrate is the top-ranking official of the district. He ensures law and order in his district. The court cases related to revenue are sorted out by the Deputy Commissioner and SDM.

There are government hospitals or health centres in all the major cities and tehsils of the state. Besides, some villages also have primary health centres. There are primary, middle, high and senior secondary schools (run by the government) throughout the state. The Block Education Officer and Sub-Divisional Education Officer look after these schools in their respective areas. All the schools in a district are looked after by a District Education Officer. This officer also works according to the instructions of the Deputy Commissioner.

Executive engineers have been appointed in the State to look after the vital public works like irrigation, road construction, building construction, electrical power, water supply etc. These executive engineers also give assistance and advice to the Deputy Commissioner of their district.

Besides the aforementioned officials, there are many other officials working in each district. They are district agriculture officer, district industry officer, district public relations officer, district welfare officer, district adult education officer, district forest and district pisces (development) officer etc. These officers are engaged in the tasks of development in their respective districts. They also apprise their seniors about such tasks and their progress.

PANCHAYATI RAJ

The Panchayati Raj Bill was passed by the Indian Parliament in 1992. According, a three tier Panchayati Raj System was established in each district of Haryana. It has three vital elements—gram panchayat,

panchayat samiti and zila panchayat. The tenure of gram panchayat as well as that of city committee is five years. After every five years, these self-governing institutions elect members for themselves under the watchful eye of the election Commission of the state. The self- governing institutions of villages and cities make plans for the economic development of the residents. These make plans for delivering social justice to the masses and also implement them. These have the rights to impose some taxes and fees on the citizens as well as collect the same from them. The state Government also gives grants to such institutes.

Every village has a village panchayat, called *gram panchayat.* The voters of each village alert the members of their gram panchayat through direct elections. These procedure is carried out in the presence of the representatives of the election commission of the state. The *gram panchayat* works for a period of 5 years. There are provisions to include women, STs and SCs in the *gram panchayat* of each village. One-third of the seats to be filled by direct elections on every gram panchayat are reserved for women. At least one-third of the such seats are reserved for women as are reserved for the SCs and STs. So much so, there is also reservation for the post of Chairman of the gram panchayat. There is a provision to make a member of SC or ST or a woman as the Chairman of the panchayat. Every gram panchayat makes plans for the social and economic development of the villagers whom it represents. It has, the right to levy some taxes or fees on the villagers. The state Government also gives grants to *gram panchayats*. Some issues or areas of operation of *gram panchayats* are: land reforms; small canals; khadi and village industries; fuels; roads, *ghats*; education; health; elimination of poverty; chakbandi (land demarcation); animal husbandry; potable water; cattle feed; bridge; rural electrification; local fairs; family welfare; and public distribution system.

Effects of Addition of Eleventh and Twelfth Schedules to the Panchayati Raj System

The following changes have been effected :

1. Elections shall be held for all the seats of the panchayat.
2. One-third of the seats shall be reserved for SCs and STs.
3. One-third of the seats shall be reserved for women.

4. Out of the seats reserved for SCs and STs, one-third of the seats shall be reserved for women of these very categories.
5. There shall be reservation of seats for the SCs and STs for the post of the chairperson of the panchayat.
6. There shall be reservation of seats for women for the post of the chairperson of the panchayat.
7. SCs and STs shall not be debarred from contesting elections for such seats as are not reserved.
8. Women shall not be debarred from contesting elections for such seats as are not reserved.

Panchayti Raj Institutions

Panchayati Raj Institutions are operating at the grassroots levels in Haryana. Their performances are commendable. Some of the features of the Panchayati Raj in the State are as follows :

1. The Haryana Panchayati Raj Act has been modified to make such institutions efficient.
2. According to the modified Act, *gram sabha* must be held at least twice a year—on 13 April and on 2 October.
3. The post of Sub-Sarpanch has been quashed. The provision of bringing a no-confidence motion against the Sarpanch has also been quashed.
4. The Sarpanch has to give up his charge (duties) within 7 days from the date of publication of the election schedule.
5. If a Sarpanch keeps a cash amount that is 21 per cent in access of the stipulated amount, then he would be liable to pay punitive interest at the rate of 21 per cent.
6. If a Sarpanch or panch is reluctant to appear in a court case, then he may be suspended for a period of six years.
7. Lavatories are being constructed in rural areas. The rates of subsidies for general persons and STs are 50 per cent and 90 per cent respectively. STs give 10 per cent as the unskilled labour put in by them to make such lavatories.
8. The State Government gives loans to dig well, install tubewells, construct shops and erect staff quarters.

CIVIC INSTITUTIONS

Urban Local Bodies are important institutions of self-governance, providing physical infrastructure and civic amenities in urban areas. Haryana's steady transformation into a predominantly urban society is now a demographic, economic and political reality. With over 35% people living in urban areas, the state is one of the highly urbanized states in the Indian Union. As with any urbanized and industrialized economy, the urban centres are the hubs of activities and growth.

There are *Nagarpalikas*, Municipalities and Municipal Corporations for small, medium-sized and large cities, respectively. The elections of members for these institutions are carried out through the direct election method. Such elections are organised under the watchful eye of the Election Commissioner of the state or his representatives.

In all these organs of the local government, there are provisions for reservation of seats for women, SCs and STs. One-third of the seats have been reserved for women. The seats for SCs and STs have been reserved in the ratio of their respective populations. There are reservations (for the posts of Chairpersons) for women, SCs and STs as well.

The tenure of each *Nagarpalika*, Municipality or Municipal Corporation is 5 years. Elections are held after every five years. These institutions have been entrusted with the tasks of making plans for the development and implementing them (in the areas of their jurisdiction). These institutions have also the rights to impose some taxes, duties and fees on the people of the areas under their jurisdiction. The state Government also gives them grants.

The subjects or areas given to these institutions are : city planning; bridges; hygiene and cleanliness; improvement of dirty colonies; socio-economics development plans; education; street light systems; environment improvement; roads, provision of potable water; fire-fighting services; plans for removal of urban poverty, medical facilities; birth and death records; transport facilities; and maintenance of parks and gardens.

THE CAPITAL

General Information : Chandigarh is bound on all sides by the states of Haryana and Punjab.

Capital : Chandigarh, Area : 114 sq. km. Population : 10,55,450 Principal Languages : Hindi and Punjabi, Urbanization rate : 97.24% Literacy rate : 86.0%, City : Chandigarh, Airport : Chandigarh Airport

INFRASTRUCTURE

Number of Bank Branches : 420 (2020-21)

Railway Route Per '000 Sq. of Area : 110 Km.

Major Industries/Crops/Minerals

State of Economy: The territory has 1727.17 hectares of cultivable land. The irrigated area is about 212.89 hectares. Wheat, maize and paddy are the major crops. The forest covers 20.07 per cent of the area. The length of the national highway in the territory is 128.79 km. There are 15 large and medium scale industrial units in Chandigarh. 2,950 units are registered in the small scale sector. As of August, 2022 Chandigarh had a total installed power generation capacity of 227.41 MW.

Universities: Panjab University, Chandigarh: Post Graduate Institute of Medical Education and Research, Chandigarh.

Places of Tourist Attraction: Rose Garden, Rock Garden, Shanti Kunj, Lake, Museum, Art Gallery, Capital Complex and National Gallery of Portraits.

MAJOR INDUSTRIES AND CROPS

Industries : Electric Meters, Bicycles, Free Wheels and Rims, Antibiotics, Hosiery and Knitting Machines, Needles, Wool Tops, Consumer Goods.

Crops : Wheat, Maize and Paddy.

LAW AND ORDER

On the pattern of the colonial Irish constabulary, Sir Charles Napier established a police system in Sindh in 1843. The British Army Officers closely supervised and controlled forces, which were resultantly more disciplined, efficient and not corrupt. Influenced by the success of Napier's police, the Court of Directions of the East India Company suggested that a common system of police be established of the pattern of Irish Constabulary. The British Indian Government set up a Police Commission headed by H.M. Court in 1860. One of the policy directives to the Police Commission of 1860 was, "....Though the duties of the police should be entirely civil, not military, the organisation and discipline of the police should be similar to those of a military body." The present police system in our country has been established under this Charter. The Punjab Police Rules were framed in 1934, which still govern the police organizations in the north Indian states of Punjab, Himachal Pradesh, Delhi, Chandigarh and Haryana.

The state of Haryana was carved out of Punjab on 1 November, 1966. At that time, it comprised one Police Range and 6 districts and had a strength of 12,165 personnel. Today, the state is divided into 5 Ranges 3 police commissionerates—Gurugram, Faridabad, Panchkula and 20 districts besides the Railway Police district. Till January 2023 Haryana Police has a total sanctioned strength of 73,391 (Gazetted Officers-470, Inspectors-1086, Sub-inspectors-3680, Assistant Sub-inspectors-6182, Head Constables-12,778, Constables-49,195).

HARYANA SHEHRI VIKAS PRADHIKARAN (HSVP)

Haryana Shehari Vikas Pradhikaran (HSVP), formerly Haryana Urban Development Authority (HUDA), is the urban planning agency of the state of Haryana except Gurugram and Faridabad which has Gurugram Metropolitan Development Authority and Faridabad Metropolitan Development Authority respectively. It was established in 1977. The Minister of Town and Country Planning Department, Haryana is the chairman of the authority. The headquarters of the authority is located in Panchkula, Haryana. The main functions of Haryana Shehri Vikas Pradhikaran are as under:

(A) To promote and secure development of urban areas in a systematic and planned way with the power to acquire sell and dispose off property, both movable and immovable.

(B) Use this so acquired land for residential, industrial, recreational and commercial purpose.

(C) To make available developed land to Haryana Housing Board and other bodies for providing houses to economically weaker sections of the society, and

(D) To undertake building works.

Administrative Set up of HSVP

The Authority consists of a Chairman, a Vice Chairman, a Chief Administrator and such other members (not more than 12 but not less than 6) appointed under notification issued from time to time, provided that the number of non-official members shall not, at any time exceed three.

Zonal Administration

The entire state is divided into 30 Urban Estates. The work of these Urban Estates is being supervised and monitored by 5 Zonal Administrators assisted by 18 Estate Officers. The main functions of these Estate Officers are to manage the estates by selling developed and undeveloped plots/properties of all categories of land and realize the revenue. All the financial receipt of transactions are looked after by the Estate Officers and channelized through the accounts branch of Head Office for expenditure on development activities. The Estate Officers are also responsible for pursuing the matters relating to the construction activities within the framework of construction and building byelaws applicable thereto. The Zonal Administrators acts as co-coordinators between various wings at Zonal level engaged in the planned urban development of the respective areas and are responsible for the implementation of various schemes/projects being executed in these areas.

The zonal Administrators are located at following places:

(*a*)	Administrator, HSVP, Faridabad	HSVP Complex, Sector 12, Faridabad
(*b*)	Administrator, HSVP, Gurugram	HSVP Complex, Sector 14, Gurugram
(*c*)	Administrator, HSVP, Hisar	HSVP Complex, Urban Estate II, Hisar
(*d*)	Administrator, HSVP, Panchkula	C-3, Sector-6, Panchkula
(*e*)	Administrator, HSVP, Rohtak	Sector 1, Rohtak

Functions of Various Wings of HSVP

Engineering Wing : Engineering wing is headed by a Chief Engineer. As soon as land is acquired and handed-over to HSVP, infrastructural development works are taken up by the Engineering wing as per approved layout plan/demarcation plan of the area and after providing the basic infrastructural facilities, possession of the plots is handed over to the Estate Office, who in turn offers the possession to the respective allottees.

Finance Wing : Finance/Accounts Wing is headed by the Chief Controller of Finance which comprises of One Senior Accounts Officer at the Head Quarter and One with each of the Administrators, and their supporting staff posted in all the Estates, Circles, Divisional offices etc. This wing is responsible for the financial management of the Authority. The Haryana Shehri Vikas Pradhikaran is working on "No Profit No Loss" basis and carrying out its activities by circulation of funds.

Town Planning Wing : Town Planning Wing established at Head Quarter to look after the work of perspective planning for establishment of new Urban Estates. The Planning Wing is headed by a Chief Town Planner with supporting staff for town planning works and entrusted with the job of designing and issue of advertisements in the news papers regarding sale of sites in City Centers, Shopping Centers and Residential/ Industrial Sectors in all the Urban Estates.

Architecture Wing : Architectural Wing is headed by a Senior Architect with supporting staff and entrusted with the job of preparation of architectural controls and Architectural designs of all buildings constructed by HSVP. There is also one Land Scape Architect for designing parks, open spaces and gardens.

Some other wings of HSVP are:

Legal wing, Monitoring wing, Enforcement wing, Vigilance wing, Establishment and Authority wing, Policy wing, Land acquisition divisions and Information technology wing (IT Wing).

CHAPTER 7

DISTRICTS

INTRODUCTION

Till January 2024 Haryana has a total of 22 districts. It has a total of 80 sub-divisions and 94 tehsils. There are 143 blocks in the State. The total number of villages in the State is 6,841. There are 154 cities in the state. The Capital of the State is located at Chandigarh.

District-wise information has been appended in the text that follows: Refer map given on next page.

AMBALA

The district headquarters is situated in Ambala city. Other towns are Ambala Cantonment, Barara, Naggal, Mulana, Saha and Shahzadpur. The total area of Ambala district is 1,574 square kilometres and its population is 11,28,350. It is famous for its army cantonment, air force base and railway junction.

There are many stories regarding the name Ambala. According to one of those this town was founded in the fourteenth century by one Amba Rajput.

According to another, the town is named after the Goddess Bhawani Amba. Yet another story claims that the town was originally called Amb Wala (Place of Mangoes). Over a period of time, this got corrupted into present name Ambala.

After an outbreak of malaria, the British abandoned the cantonment at Karnal in 1841. In its place, a large army cantonment was founded in Ambala in 1843. Ambala district is now famous for its industries, especially those of scientific instruments, metal casting and kitchen mixer grinders.

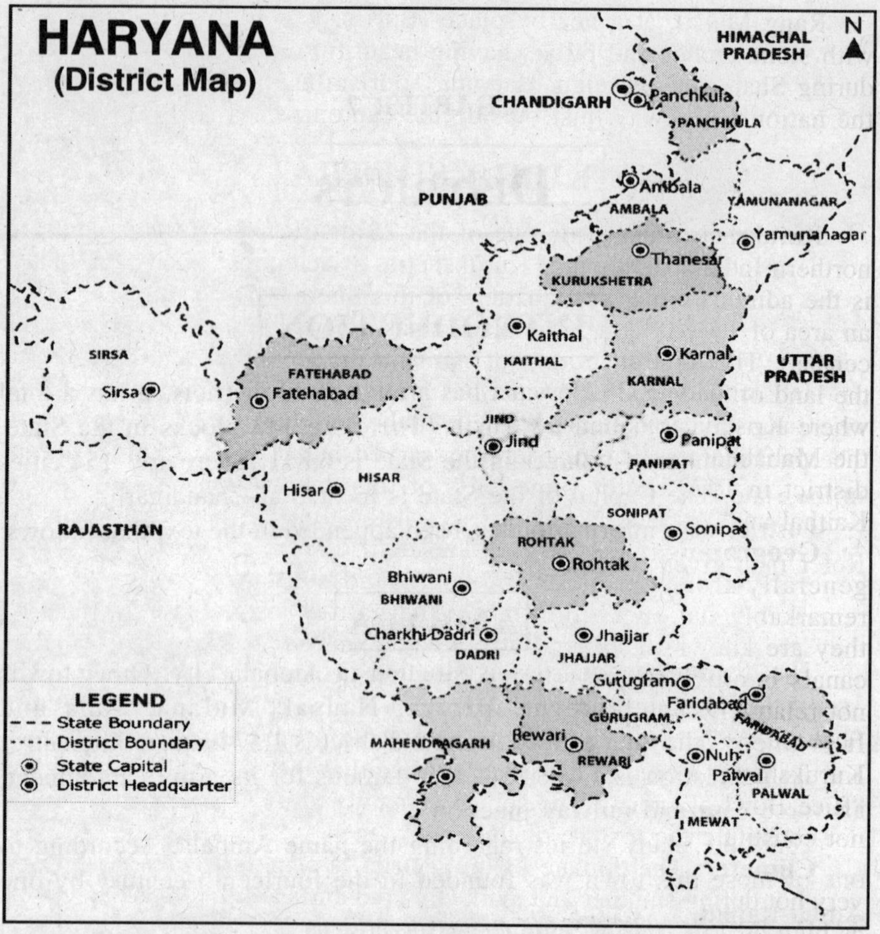

There are many shrines in and around Ambala city. There is a temple, Bhawani Amba Temple, named after the Goddess Bhawani. The Badshahi Bag Gurdwara, Sis Ganj Gurdwara, Manji Sahib Gurdwara and Sangat Sahib Gurdwara are the historical gurdwaras of the city. These are associated with Guru Gobind Singh, Guru Tegh Bahadur and Guru Hargobind. Besides, there are popular Muslim shrines of Lakhi Shah and Taqwal Shah. Further, Saint Paul's Church and an old British Christian cemetery are also located here. Patel Park in Ambala Cantonment and City Park in Ambala city are two beautiful gardens.

Rang Mahal, at a nearby place (Buria), is a finely crafted palace with stone arches and pillars having beautiful carvings. It was erected during Shah Jahan's reign. Haryana Tourism has Kingfisher Resort on the national highway, just outside the cantonment.

KURUKSHETRA

Kurukshetra district is one of the 22 districts of Haryana state in northern India. The town of Kurukshetra, a sacred place for the Hindus, is the administrative headquarters of this district. The district occupies an area of 1530.00 km². The district has a population of 964,655 (2011 census). This district is part of Ambala division. Kurukshetra is also the land of Srimad Bhagawad Gita. Jyotisar is the place in Kurukshetra where Krishna is believed to deliver the sermon of Gita to Arjuna in the Mahabharata. The district was carved out of the erstwhile Karnal district in 1973. Later some parts of this district were transferred to Kaithal and Yamuna Nagar districts at the time of their creation.

Geographical Features : The district is a plain, which slopes generally from north-east of south and south-west. The plain is remarkably flat and within it, are the narrow low-lying flood plains; they are known as either Betre Khadar or Naili. A good network of canals is providing irrigational facilities. Underground water level is not relatively high. Tubewell irrigation is also common in the district. It is one of the prosperous districts from agricultural viewpoint. Kurukshetra, along with Karnal and Kaithal districts, is known as the "Rice Bowl of India." The soil is generally alluvial; loam and clay do not constitute the texture of this soil.

Climate : The climate of the district is of polarised character *i.e.*, very hot during summer and markedly cold during winter. It may become as high as 46°C during summer and as low as 2°C during winter.

Kurukshetra is a place of great historical and religious importance. It is revered all over the country for its sacred associations. It was here that the Battle of Mahabharata was fought and Lord Krishna preached his philosophy of *Karma* as enshrined in The Bhagwad Gita, to Arjuna at Jyotisar. In the very first verse of Bhagwad Gita, Kurukshetra is described as *Dharamkshetra i.e.* 'Region of righteousness'. According to Hindu mythology, the name Kurukshetra applied to a circuit of about 48 *kosas* or about 128 kilometres, which includes a large number of holy places, temples and tanks associated with the ancient Indian traditions and the Mahabharata war as well as the *Kurus*, the ancestor of Kauravas and Pandavas.

Places to Visit : There are about 360 *tirthas* of religious and historic importance. The foremost among the Kurukshetra *tirthas* are the Brahmasarovar or Kurukshetra Tank, Sannihit Tank, Sthaneshwara Mahadev Mandir, Jyotisar, Baan Ganga, Bhishma Kund (Narkatari), Chandrakupa, Nabhi Kamal, Bhadrakali Mandir, Arnai Temple, Prachi Tirtha (Pehowa), Saraswati Tirtha (Pehowa), Prithduk Tirtha (Pehowa), Rantuk Yaksh Bir (Pipli), Karna Ka Tila, etc. A few sites of archaeological interest have yielded various objects of antiquarian interest and a distinctive class of pottery, known as the Painted Grey Ware. These sites are Raja Karna Ka Tila, Asthipura, Bhor Saidam, Bhagpura and Daulatpur.

Kurukshetra is one of the very few places visited by all the Sikh gurus and Gurdwaras have been constructed to commemorate their visits. The most prominent among them is the Gurdwara Sixth Patshahi, which is dedicated to the sixth Guru—Shri Hargobind Ji. Hundreds of devotees visit this shrine every day. Its architecture is marvellous. The eighth Sikh guru, Shri Harkishan Ji, performed a miracle of making a deaf and dumb boy recite verses from The Bhagwad Gita. The ninth guru, Shri Teg Bahadur Ji, set up a camp near Sthaneshwar *tirtha* where a gurdwara stands even today. Gurdwara Rajghat, the biggest of all the Kurukshetra gurdwaras, is located near the main bank of the Kurukshetra tank. This was built in the memory of Guru Gobind Singh who had visited this place.

The tomb of Sufi saint, Sheikh Chilhi Jalal, is a fascinating monument. It is octagonal in shape and crowned with a dome of white marble. It is surrounded by a white marble courtyard. Chini Masjid and Pathar Masjid, two outstanding monuments of the Mughal architectural style, are also located in the same area.

KARNAL

Karnal district has an area of 2,520 square kilometres and its population is 15,05,324. The district headquarter is situated in Karnal city. Karnal was founded by the Kauravas around the time of the Mahabharata for King Karna. It is at a distance of 123 kilometres from Delhi on the National Highway NH1, also called the GT Road. It is at a distance of 126 kilometres from Chandigarh. Other towns are Assandh, Nilokheri, Gharuanda, Indri and Taraori. It is known world over for shoes, basmati rice and agricultural research institutions.

Karnal, called the "city of Daanvir Karna". In 1739, the Persian King, Nadir Shah, defeated the Mughal ruler Muhammed Shah in the Battle of Karnal; was annexed by the Raja of Jind in 1763 A.D. and was taken from him by George Thomas in 1797. The British established a cantonment in 1811 but abandoned it after 30 years due to the outbreak of malaria. Karnal district lies on the western bank of river Yamuna, which forms its eastern boundary of the district. Yamuna separates Haryana from Uttar Pradesh. The Karnal district, including Panipat, lies between 29°09'50" and 29°50' north Latitude and 76°31'15" and 77°12'45" east Longitude. Its height from mean sea level is around 240 metres. Karnal is surrounded by Kurukshetra district on its north-west, and Jind by Kaithal districts on its west. Panipat district on its south and Uttar Pradesh is on its east. The district is a part of the Ganga-Saraswati-Indus plains and has a well-spread irrigation network of western Yamuna canal. Its geographical area has been divided into three agro-climatic regions, called Khadar, Bhangar and Nardak belt. Khadar starts from Indri-Karnal road, one mile away from Karnal and covers the area between the Yamuna river and National Highway No. 1 up to Patti-Kalyana village. Bhangar area starts from the western side of Khadar area and covers Gharaunda development block. The Nardak area lies in Nissing, Nilokheri and Assandh blocks. However, its water is saline and not fit for irrigation. Karnal is the centre of National Dairy Research Institute (NDRI), CSSRI, Wheat Research Directorate, National Bureau of Animal Genetics Research and Sugarcane Breeding Institute. People desiring to learn flying can do so at the Karnal Flying Club.

JIND

The district headquarters is situated in Jind town. Other smaller towns are Narwana, Safidon and Uchana. The total area of Jind district is 2,702 square kilometres and its population is 13,34,152.

The town headquarters of the district is situated on the Ferozepur-Delhi section of Northern Railway, 123 kilometres away from Delhi and 57 kilometres away from Rohtak. It is also connected by road to Delhi, Patiala, Chandigarh and other important towns of the state.

The town has Arjun stadium, milk plant, cattle feed plant, Bulbul restaurant and a large grain market. There are facilities for the stay at PWD rest house, canal rest house and market committee rest house. The town has schools, colleges, hospitals and other basic amenities. Jind is noted for its numerous temples for the worship of Lord Shiva.

The town dates back to the Mahabharata period. According to the legend, the Pandavas built a temple in the honour of Jainti Devi (the Goddess of Victory) at this place. They offered prayers for success in their battle against the Kauravas. The town grew up around the temple and was named Jaintapuri, (the above of Jainti Devi). In course of time, the name was corrupted to become Jind.

Raja Gajpat Singh seized a large tract of the region including the present districts of Jind from the Afghans in 1755. He made Jind the Capital of the state in 1776. He also built a fort here in 1775. Later, Sangrur was chosen as Capital of Jind State by Raja Sangat Singh (1822 A.D. to 1834 A.D.).

SONEPAT

The district headquarters is situated in Sonepat. Other smaller towns are Gohana, Ganaur, Murthal and Rai. The total area of Sonepat district is 2,122 square kilometres and its population is 14,50,001.

PANIPAT

Panipat is situated on the banks of the river Yamuna. The famous three historical battles were fought in and around this city.

The First Battle of Panipat fought in AD 1526 in which, the invader (Babar) defeated Ibrahim Lodhi, the Sultan of Delhi, on April 26. In the Second Battle of Panipat, on November 5, 1556, Akbar's guardian, Bairam Khan defeated the Hindu ruler, Hemu. Ahmad Shah Abdali, the Afghan ruler, defeated the Marathas in the Third Battle of Panipat that took place on 14 January, 1761.

Today, Panipat is an industrial town, which is known for its handloom products. The districts headquarter is situated in Panipat town. Other smaller towns are Israna., Naultha and Samalakha. The total area of Panipat district is 1,268 square kilometres and its population is 12,05,437.

Ibrahim Lodhi's Tomb : This king who was defeated by Babar in 1526 in the First Battle of Panipat, lies buried here in a tomb. His grave is a simple affair; just a rectangular block on a high platform approached by a flight of steps made of lakhori bricks. The tomb was renovated by the British in 1866.

Kabuli Shah's mosque was built by Babar after his victory over Ibrahim Lodhi. He named the mosque after his wife Kabuli Begum. Six years later, when Humayun defeated Salim Shah, he got a platform called Chabutara Fateh Mubarak made around the mosque. The mosque has chambers on two sides and an inscription in Persian runs along the parapet.

Hotels : Midtown hotel, a/c rooms and restaurant. Skylark motel, a/c rooms as well as a dormitory and restaurant; Blue Jay and Kala Amb are also decent places for short stays. Many smaller hotels and guest houses are located on GT road. There are Jain temples in Holi Mohalla and a shrine of the Muslim saint, Abu Ali Kalandar. A fort also exists at Panipat. There is also a park named after the famous Urdu poet and critic, Altaff Hussein Haali who was born in Panipat in 1837.

ROHTAK

The district headquarters is situated in Rohtak town. Other smaller towns are Meham, Sampla, Kalanaur and Hasangarh. The total area of Rohtak is 1,745 square kilometres and its population is 10,61,204. Rohtak district is also known as the Political Capital of Haryana.

Rohtak is said to be a corruption of Rohtasgarh, a name still applied to the ruined Khokrakot sites of two cities, one lying to north of Rohtak town and the other about 4 kilometres to the east. It is believed it was named after Raja Rohtas, in whose days, the city was built. It is also claimed that the town drives its name from the Roherra tree called *rohtika* in Sanskrit. It is said that the town was built by clearing a forest of *rohtika* trees and hence its name Rohtak.

Another version connects Rohtak to Rohitaka, which has been mentioned in the Mahabharata.

It was quite possibly the Capital of Bahudhanyaka. In the Vinaya of the Mulasarvasti-vadins, Jivaka has been shown as undertaking a journey from Taxila to Bhadramkara, Udumbra, Rohitaka and Mathura in the Ganga doab. The ancient road carried the trade of the Ganga valley to Taxila, passing through Rohitaka to Sakala. The Rewari and Gajjak of Rohtak are famous all over India as well as at many places abroad.

The ruins of the ancient town are found at Khokrakot or Rohtasgarh. Some experts opine that the town is probably as old as the Indus Valley

Civilisation. Some minor finds at Khokrakot are typical of the Indus Valley sites. Clay moulds of coins discovered here have thrown light of the process of casting coins in ancient India. The existence of the town during the rule of the Kushanas has been testified by the recent recovery of a Kushana pillar, decorated with carvings of winged lions and riders. An example of a lion of the first/second century AD, it resembles the lion in the British museum at London, which has stupas famous for its inscriptions. The riders on it are similar to the riders on elephants at Karle Cave and figures at the Sanchi gateway. It is a significant example of the sculptural art of Haryana towards the beginning of the Christian era. The coin moulds of the later Yaudheyas of the third/fourth century AD have been discovered by the Archaeological Survey of India in large numbers here. Of the same and subsequent dates, are several clay seals. A Gupta terracotta plaque and a head of a later date have also been discovered. The town continued to flourish till the tenth century AD, as coins of Samanta Deva, the Hindu king of Kabul, have been found here. The town is said to have been rebuilt during the reign of Prithviraj Chauhan. In 1828, General Mundy wrote about the "ancient and consequently ruinous town of Rohtak. The wide circuit of its dilapidated fortifications and the still elegant domes of many time-worn tanks tell melancholic tales of gone-by grandeur."

At one time, the town had a wall all around, with gates at regular intervals. Only three gates can now be seen which are in a dilapidated condition. The town has a number of old mosques, some of which, remind us of elegant Muslim structures. Dini Mosque or Adina Mosque is the oldest among these. At the north end of this mosque, was a *tehkhana* (underground cell). Over its arch, is an inscription of Ala-ud-Din Khilji, dating back to 1308. There is an old and mythical tank with *ghats* on three of its sides, known as Gaokaran tank. Its complex includes Shiva, Devi and Hanuman temples in addition to a park and a baradari.

FARIDABAD

The district headquarters is situated in Faridabad city. Other smaller town is Ballabhgarh. The total area of Faridabad district is 741 square kilometres and its population is 18,09,733. Faridabad city is the most populated and industrialized in whole of Haryana.

GURUGRAM

The district headquarters is situated in Gurugram city. Other smaller towns are Sohna, Badshahpur, Manesar and Pataudi. The total area of Gurugram district is 1,258 square kilometres and its population is 15,14,432.

During the Mahabharata times, Gurugram was a thick forest in which, the ashram of Guru Dronacharya existed. It was here that Pandava and Kaurava princes got their training in warfare. Because of Guru Dronacharya's ashram, people started calling in the Gurugram, which changed into Gurgaon later on. In 2017 BJP government renamed it again Gurugram from Gurgaon. This place had been gifted to Guru Dronacharya by Yudhishthira as *guru-dakshina*.

Today, Gurugram has become one of the most important corporate and industrial hubs of Haryana. The office and manufacturing plant of India's largest car maker, Maruti Udyog Limited, in addition to many other small and large industries. Another area in which Gurugram is excelling in the IT industry and software development. In order to cater to the corporate clientele, hotels have been built in Gurugram, including The Radisson and 32 Milestone.

MAHENDRAGARH

Mahendragarh district was formed in 1948 by grouping different tracts of the erstwhile Princely States—Narnaul and Mahendragarh tehsils from Patiala State, Dadri (Charkhi Dadri) from Jind State and a part of Bawal Nizamat from Nabha State. The headquarters of the district is at Narnaul.

Location : The district lies between North Latitude 27°47' to 28°26' East Longitude 75°56' to 76°51'. It is bounded on the north by Bhiwani and Rohtak districts, on the east by Rewari district and Alwar district of Rajasthan, on the south by Alwar, Jaipur and Sikar districts of Rajasthan and on the west by Sikar and Jhunjhunu districts of Rajasthan. It has 5 tehsils—Narnaul, Nangal Chaudhary, Ateli, Kanina and Mahendragarh. Its total area is 1,899 square kilometres and its population is 9,22,088.

Origin of the Name of the District : The Mahendragarh town was previously known as Kanaud, which took its name from the Kanaudia group of Brahmins. It was founded by Malik Mahdud Khan who was a servant of Babar. There is a fort at Mahendragarh, which was built by

Maratha Ruler, Tantia Tope during the seventeenth century A.D. The fort was named as Mahendragarh in 1861 by Narendra Singh, the then ruler of the erstwhile Princely State of Patiala, in honour of his son, Mahendra Singh. Subsequently, the town came to be known as Mahendragarh. The name of Narnaul Nizamat was changed to Mahendragarh Nizamat.

BHIWANI

Bhiwani district came into existence on July 22nd, 1972 and is named after the Administrative city Bhiwani. Bhiwani is situated between 28.19 deg. & 29.05 deg. North latitude and 75.26 deg. and 76.28 deg. East Longitude. Bhiwani district has been divided into 4 sub-divisions, 5 Tehsils, 1 sub-Tehsil and 7 Blocks.

The district headquarters is situated in Bhiwani town. Other smaller towns are Loharu, Bawani Khera and Tosham. The total area of Bhiwani district is 4,778 square kilometres and its population is 16,34,445. (The data of Charkhi Dadri district is included in it). Bhiwani district has many places worth visiting. Among these, are the Star Building, Loharu Fort, Tosham Hill etc.

An archaeological site, called the Naurangabad Mound, at a distance of 10 km from Bhiwani town, is now being excavated.

CHARKHI DADRI

Charkhi Dadri was formed as the 22nd district of Haryana on December 1, 2016. It was carved out from Bhiwani district. Charkhi Dadri comprises of two sub divisions namely Charkhi Dadri and Badra. It has been divided into 2 Tehsils Charkhi Dadri and Badra, 1 sub-Tehsil Bhaund Kala and 4 blocks Charkhi Dadri, Badra, Bhaund Kala and Jhounjhu. Charkhi Dadri was made by joining the villages of Charkhi and Dadri after urban development. NH 148 B (Narnaul - Bathinda) pass through the city. There are some locally places in the city which include Shyamesar Johar (pond) and Dayal Temple to name a few.

HISSAR

Hissar district, also called Hissar, has an area of 3,983 square kilometres and its population is 17,43,931. The district headquarters is situated in Hissar town. Hissar is one of the important districts of Haryana, if viewed from a political angle. Other smaller towns are

Hansi, Uklana, Adampur, Agroha and Barwala. Hissar town was one of the prime centres of Harappan culture. The area has been associated with ancient Vedic tribes such as Bharatas, Purus, Kurus, Mujavatas and Mahavrishas. During medieval times, it went through upheavals and conquests and gained importance for its strategic location with regard to Delhi. Feroze Shah Tughlaq constructed a fort here and called it Hissar-e-Firoza (the Fort of Feroze) and dug canals from the Yamuna and Ghaggar rivers to irrigate the dry land. It is a grand structure, which has a basement and a mosque. He built a mosque called Lat ke Masjid. Humayun built a Masjid at Fatehabad near Hissar town. Emperor Akbar made Hissar the headquarters of the district, which was earlier controlled by Feroze Shah. During the early nineteenth century, the British took Hissar under their charge along with the rest of Haryana. Hissar is now an important industrial centre of Haryana having lots of steel and cotton industries. Chaudhary Charan Singh Agriculture University, also called Hissar Agricultural University, is one of the foremost educational institutions dedicated solely to agriculture. Beside the above, there are many other monuments like Jahaz Kothi, Gujri Mahal and Jain pillar.

Ancient Sites : Two sites from ,the pre-Harrapan and Harrapan periods can be found at Rakhi Garhi and Agroha Mound.

SIRSA

Sirsa district has an area of 4,277 square kilometres and its population is 12,95,189. The district headquarters is situated in Sirsa town. It is located at a distance of 255 kilometres from Delhi and at a distance of 280 kilometres from Chandigarh. Other smaller towns are Dabwali, Ellenabad, Rori and Rania. The district lies between 29°14' and 30° north Latitude and 74°29' and 75°18' east Longitude, forming the extreme west corner of Haryana. It bounded by the districts of Faridkot and Bhatinda of Punjab in the north and north-east, Ganga Nagar district of Rajasthan in the west and south and Hissar district in the east.

Sirsa district has been divided into four sub-divisions and six tehsils. There are a total of 323 villages in the district. About 75 per cent of the population lives in rural areas. Sirsa gets an annual rainfall of about 26 cm. The district excels in the production of cotton and citrus fruits. In 2006 the Ministry of Panchayati Raj named Sirsa as one of the country's 250 most backward districts (out of a total of 640). It is one of the two districts in Haryana that used to receive funds from the Backward Regions Grant Fund Programme (BRGF).

The Delhi territory along with districts of Bhattiana and Hissar was transferred to Punjab in 1858 and the district of Bhattiana was renamed as Sirsa. The Sirsa district, which comprised three tehsils of Sirsa, Dabwali and Fazilka, was abolished in 1884 and Sirsa tehsil (consisting of 199 Villages) and 126 villages of Dabwali tehsil formed one tehsil and the same was merged in Hissar district. The rest of the portion was transferred to the Ferozepur district (Punjab). On 1 September, 1975, Sirsa and Dabwali tehsils of Hissar district were constituted into a separate Sirsa district with headquarters at Sirsa. Chaudhary Devi Lal's birthplace, the village of Chautala, falls in this district.

The terrain of Sirsa may be classified into three types—the Haryana Plain, alluvial bed of Ghaggar or Nali and sand dune tract. The Haryana Plain is a vast surface of flat to rolling terrain and extends due south to the northern boundary of the bed of river Ghaggar. It covers over 65 per cent of the area of the district. The elevation of the surface varies from 190 to 210 metres. The palaeo channels set the occurrence of sand dunes in this terrain apart from those in the dune tract. The plain is traversed by dune complexes and shifting sands. Alluvial bed of Ghaggar (Nali) is a clayey surface of a flat plain bordered in the north and west by the Haryana Plain and in the south along the sand dune tract.

REWARI

The district headquarters is situated at Rewari. Other smaller towns are Bawal, Dharuhera and Kosli. The total area of Rewari district is 1,594 square kilometres and its population is 900,332.

KAITHAL

The district headquarters is situated at Kaithal. Other smaller towns are Guhla, Pundri and Cheeka. The total area of Kaithal district is 2,317 square kilometres and its population is 10,74,304.

YAMUNANAGAR

The district headquarters is situated in/at Yamunanagar. Other smaller towns are Jagadhari, Radaur and Sadhaura. The total area of Yamunanagar district is 1,768 square kilometres and its population is 12,14,205.

PANCHKULA

Panchkula is a well planned city of state of Haryana. Panchkula city, was established in the year of 1995 as district. It is a satellite city of the Union Territory of Chandigarh. The prestigious Chandimandir Cantonment Headquarters of the Indian Western Command, is also located in Panchkula city. There are five towns in the district named Panchkula, Barwala, Pinjore, Kalka, and Raipur Rani. The only Hill station in Haryana called Morni is also in this District. In 2011, Panchkula had a population of 561,293 of which male and female were 299,679 and 261,614 respectively. Panchkula and Mohali (in Punjab) are two satellite cities of Chandigarh. These three cities are collectively known as Chandigarh Tricity.

Physical Aspects : Panchkula is surrounded by Himachal Pradesh in the north and north-east, by Ambala district in the east, by Kurukshetra district in the south and by Punjab and Union Territory of Chandigarh in the west.

Panchkula district has a sub-tropical continental monsoon climate where we find seasonal rhythm, hot summer, cool winter, unreliable rainfall and great variations in temperature. During winter, frost sometimes occurs during December and January. The district also receives occasional winter rains due to the western disturbances. The rainfall is generally restricted to rolling plain in north and north-east in Pinjore area and the flood plain along the Ghaggar river. Morni hills constitute the highest point of the district as well that as of Haryana. The important rivers/streams of the district are Ghaggar, Sirsa Nadi, Kaushalya etc. Generally, the slope of district is from north-east to south-west. In this direction, most of the rivers and rain-fed torrents flow down and spread gravel and pebbles in their beds. Only the Sirsa Nadi, in Kalka *tehsil*, flows towards north-west through a arrow halt of the Shivalik tract. The district is devoid of any perennial river. The soils in the district are mainly light loam (*seoti*) piedmont (*ghar and kandi*), Shivalik (*pahar*), silt clay (Naili and Chhachhra dakar), etc.

The underground water in the district occurs under confirmed and semi-confirmed conditions; it is generally fresh and suitable for domestic and irrigation purposes. The underground water level is generally high in the southern parts and low in the northern and northeastern areas, which have hilly tracts. The district lies in a region where earthquakes of moderate to high intensity had been felt in the past. Being situated near the Himalayan boundary fault zones, it is prone to earthquakes. The district has a favourable climate for the growth of rich and abundant vegetation due to reasonably good rainfall and elevation. Shisham (*Dalbergia sissoo*), Kikar (*Acacia nilotica*) and Mango (*Mangifera indica*) are the important tree species grown in these plains. Safeda (*Eucalyptus hybrid*) has been introduced since 1963 in forest areas as well as on private lands. The natural vegetation mainly comprises forests. Tropical dry deciduous forests and sub-tropical forests are found here.

The Economy of Panchkula District: The present district of Panchkula has a mixed type of economy. Out of a total population of 5,61,293, about 31.03 per cent have been identified as main workers in the district against 28.64 per cent for the State as a whole at the time of 2011 census. In the district, 29.78 per cent of its main workers are engaged in agriculture activities, which include cultivation and agriculture against the figure of 37.54 per cent for the State as a whole. The proportion of the main workers engaged in the household industry is 1.83 per cent in the district against 2.18 per cent for Haryana. The percentage of main workers in manufacturing, processing servicing and repairs (other than those for household industry) is 13.26 per cent in Panchkula district against 9.60 per cent for the State. The proportion of main workers in construction, trade and commerce, transport, storage and communications is relatively higher in the district than the State figures.

Princely State of Nahan and the stream, which supplied water to the pilgrims visiting the temple, was cut off by some hill people, thus causing great distress to pilgrims. The goddess appeared in the dream of Gurbax Singh, the ruler of Mani Majra and asked him to construct a temple for her at this place. This temple contains thirty-eight panels of wall paintings besides floral designs painted all over the ceiling and the arches leading into the temple. The drawings of the temple are not of a high standard but a great variety of themes has been illustrated in the same. The other temple is said to have been constructed by Maharaja Karam Singh of the erstwhile Patiala State in 1861 AD to commemorate his success in the battle against the Gurkhas. The fairs are held twice a year in March-April (Chaitra Shudi Ashtami) and September-October (Ashwina Shudi Ashtami).

Pinjore is an ancient historical and religious place. It is said that the earliest man lived in the Pinjore region around Chandigarh, one and a half crore years ago. Tools of Tower Paleolithic period, fabricated on quartzite, have been found in the region stretching from Pinjore to Nalagarh. The place is associated with Mahabharata as five Pandavas stayed here for sometime during the period of their exile. The place was then known as Panchpura, which was corrupted to become Pinjore. The name Panchpura was deciphered from the Pinjore Baoli inscription found from here. Important sculptures and other antiquarian remains recovered from the place can be assigned to be period ranging between 9th century A.D. to 12th century A.D. Pinjore is famous for the beautiful Mughal Garden, now called the Yadavindra Garden.

Morni Hills are offshoots of the Shivalik range, which run in two parallel ranges. The village of Morni (Bhoj Jabial) lies on the mountainside, at 1220 metres above the mean sea level. Traditions assign the name of Morni to a queen who is believed to have ruled this area. Among the spurs of hills, lie two lakes; the larger one is about 550 metres long and 460 metres broad and the other one is about 365 metres either way. A hill divides these two lakes but there is some hidden channel linking them as the level of two lakes remains the same. The Haryana Government has developed this hill resort and provides facilities to tourists. A motorable road was constructed to connect the Morni hills with the Haryana state Highway near Panchkula. A forest tourist hut "Lal Munia" and a PWD rest house were also constructed to the district serves as important link between the hills and the plains. The present district of Panchkula remained industrially backward particularly till the beginning of the twentieth century. Its manufacturing units were far and few and unimportant. The Panchkula town of the district had made rapid progress in the field of industrial development since it came into existence on 3rd July, 1989. The district now has a prominent place in the industrial map of Haryana. Panchkula Urban Estate, H.M.T., Pinjore and Surajpur are important industrial centres. It also keenly promotes animal husbandry, fisheries and forestry, which plays a subsidiary but an important role in agriculture economy. Irrigation in the district depends on tube wells. The percolation wells are also located in plain areas where sub-soil water level is not too low. Kuhl irrigation is also prevalent in hilly tract of the district. The major Kharif crops are sugarcane, paddy and maize while minor or subsidiary crops are chillies, pulses, vegetables, etc. The major Rabi crops are wheat, gram, barley and oilseeds while minor Rabi crops are barseem, *methi*, onion and other winter vegetables.

Places of interest in Panchkula : The Panchkula district comprises a region, which is located in the valley of the Rigvedic Saraswati river. The district abounds in many ancient sites, the antiquity of which, has been established by archaeological explorations. Some other places have now acquired importance on account of their economic and industrial significance. Still other places have been developed as tourist spots, like Morni hills and Pinjore complex.

Mansa Devi temple lies in Bilaspur village, about three kilometres east of Mani Majra (Chandigarh UT). There are two temples here. The older one is said to have been built by the ruler of Mani Majra (1815 AD).

FATEHABAD

The district Fatehabad was formed on 15 July, 1997. The district headquarters is situated in Fatehabad town. Other smaller towns are Tohana, Ratia, Bhuna and Bhattu. The total area of Fatehabad district is 2,538 square kilometres and its population is 9,42,011. There are facilities for stay at PWD rest house, HSEB rest house, market committee rest house and *dharamsalas*. The town has schools, colleges, hospitals and other basic amenities.

The Fatehabad town was founded by the emperor Firoze Shah Tughlaq and named after the name of his son, Fateh Khan, in 1352 A.D. The site on which, the town was founded, was previously a hunting ground. Firoze Shah Tughlaq got a channel dug from the river Ghaggar in order to supply water to the town. He also built a fort, which is now in ruins; however the walls can be seen on the east of the town. He also built three forts in the neighbouring villages after the names of his three sons. The old town was surrounded by a wall, which has been dismantled to a great extent except the part near the fort.

Formerly, Fetehabad was an important trade centre for the export of surplus grains but with the construction of Rewari-Bhatinda railway line (which runs about 20 kilometres to the west of the town), the trade shifted to Bhattu. But the town assumed greater importance after independence when metallic roads provided important links for transport.

The two important monuments in Fatehabad are the Lat and Humayun's mosque. Lat is a stone pillar measuring about 5 metres in height and 1.90 metres in circumference at the base. It was erected in the centre of an Idgah. The lower portion of the pillar is a monoblock of light buffed sandstone and is possibly the remaining part of the pillar that lies in the mosque at Hissar. It is more than likely that both these pillars once made a single monolithic pillar, which was possibly erected by Ashoka at Agroha or Hansi. Firoze Shah Tughlaq had a craze for taking away such columns and transplanting them at his favourite complexes. The Ashokan epigraph that was once engraved on the pillar was systematically chiselled off for writing the Tughlaq inscription recording the genealogy of Firoze Shah in beautiful Tughra Arabic characters carved in high relief.

There are two inscriptions, one on a light coloured rectangular sandstone studded into the left part of the screen wall of Idgah, immediately behind or to the west of the Lat, praising emperor Humayun. The other one is on a rectangular sandstone placed on the outer wall on the mosque's enclosure and contains a well-known invocation to Ali in Arabic. The mosque can still be seen in good conditions but is not in use.

Humayun's mosque is a small and beautiful mosque. The legend assigns the association of the mosque with the Mughal Emperor Humayun who, on his flight after his defeat at the hands of Sher Shah Suri, happened to pass through Fatehabad on Friday and is said to have prayed at this mosque. The inscription praising Emperor Humayun was originally found here, which was studded into the screen-wall of the Idgah at a later stage. The mosque is said to have been repaired by one Nur Rehmat in the early eighties of the last century.

Two important archaeological sites have been found in this district. They are the Kuna Mound and the Banawali Mound. The ancient mound of Banawali, previously called Vanawali, lies at a distance of 14 kilometres due north-west of Fatehabad on the right bank of the Rangoi Nala at 29°37"5' north Longitude and 75°23"6' east Longitude. This pre-historic mound, spread over an area of 1 square kilometre, rose to a height of about 10 metres due to successive settlements on the earlier rubble.

JHAJJAR

Jhajjar district was carved out of Rohtak district on 15 July, 1997. This district headquarters is situated in/at Jhajjar town at a distance of about 65 kilometres from Delhi. The town is said to have been founded by one Chhaju and Chhajunagar was changed to Jhajjar later. Its name may also have been derived from Jharnaghar, natural fountain. A third derivation could be from Jhajjar, a water vessel, because the surface drainage of the area around this town runs into it, thus making it a water sink. Other towns in the district are Bahadurgarh and Beri. Bahadurgarh was founded by Rathi Jats and was formerly known as Sharafabad. It is situated at a distance of twenty-nine kilometres from Delhi and had developed into an important industrial centre.

The total area of Jhajjar district is 1,834 square kilometres and its population is 9,58,405. The district consists of 2 industrial areas, which have 2408 plots. The basic industries are ceramics, glass, chemicals, engineerings, electrical and electronics. The culture of Jhajjar which is a part of Haryana is a mixture of Punjabi and Haryanvi culture. Here Haryanvi as well as Punjabi festivals are celebrated with equal enthusiasm. The customs of yoga, meditation and Vedic mantras are observed by many. The language that is mostly spoken in this region is "Jatu" or "Haryanvi".

NUH

Nuh (Mewat) district was carved out from erstwhile Gurugram (Gurgaon) and Faridabad districts, which came into existence on 4th April 2005 as the 20th district of Haryana. Nuh comprises of four sub-divisions namely Nuh, Punhana, Taoru and Firozpur Jhirka. The district headquarter is located at Nuh. Total area of Nuh is 1507, square kilometres.

Geographically, Nuh district is situated between 26-degree and 30-degree North latitude and 76-degree and 78-degree East longitude. Gurugram district bounds it on its North, while Rewari district lies to its West and Faridabad district to its East. On South, the district shares its boundary with Rajasthan. NUH district is largely comprises of planes. Inconsistency in Mewat topography is evident from its patches of land with hills and hillock of the Aravali Mountain on the one hand and plains on the other.

Nuh, land of the Meos, has its genesis in its tribal inhabitants, the Meo tribals, who are agriculturalists. The area is a distinct ethnic and socio-cultural tract. The Meos, who trace their roots to the early Aryans of North India, call themselves Kshatriyas and have preserved their social and cultural traits to a surprisingly large extent, unlike the other tribes of nearby areas. During the regime of the Tughlak dynasty in the 14th century A.D., these people embraced Islam but till today, they have maintained their age-old distinctive ethno-cultural identity.

According to the Census of India 2011, the total population of Nuh district was 10,89,263 of which 1,24,106 (11.40%) lived in urban areas and the major chunk 9,65,157 (88.60%) of the population lived in rural areas. Out of the total population of 10,89,263, the district has 5,71,162 males and 5,18,101 females. The total numbers of households are 1,42,822 out of which 1,35,253 (95%) are in rural areas and remaining 7569 (5%) are in urban areas.

The main occupation of the people of Nuh district is agriculture and allied and agro-based activities. The Meos are the predominant population group and are completely agriculturalists.

PALWAL

Palwal is a city and a municipal council and is the 21st district of Haryana in the Indian state of Haryana. The new district of Palwal is carved out of the Gurugram division. Most of the areas are from the Faridabad and Nuh districts. The addition of the city to the districts of Haryana has been a significant achievement for which the citizens of the city were thriving and thus shows the result of hardship of people's efforts. It is situated at a distance of 60 km from Delhi on the Delhi-Mathura highway. The latitude of the town is 28° 40' N and longitude is 76° 59' E. The new district has 282 villages, a total area of 1,359 square kilometres and a population of 10,42,708 people.

It is a place of great antiquity, supposed to figure in the earliest Aryan traditions under the name of Apelava, part of the Pandava kingdom of Indraprastha, which was later restored by Vikramaditya.

Its importance is mainly historical, but it is a centre for the cotton trade in the area. It is the site of a Hindu temple called "Panchvati" which is a great symbol of the religion. Mahatama Gandhi was arrested for the first time at the Palwal station. There are many hospitals like City hospital, Bagla Nursing Home, Manav Kalyan Ultrasound Centre etc.

CHAPTER 8

PEOPLE

INTRODUCTION

Haryana has always been the hub of social and cultural activities in India since times immemorial. Being a gateway to North India, the State of Haryana has witnessed the invasions of the Muslim rulers, battles of the Marathas and incursions of the Sikhs. Several Hindu saints and Sikh gurus have also traversed this and spread their messages of universal love and brotherhood.

The people of Haryana are simple, straight-forward, enterprising and hard-working. Since ancient times, they have survived many upheavals' and upheld the traditional glory and greatness of the land to this day. They have preserved their old religious and social traditions. They celebrate festivals with great enthusiasm and traditional fervour. The region has its popular folklores, folksongs and musical instruments. The women are devoted and diligent and assist men on the farms. The people have simple food habits.

Religion has always provided the main basis for the structure of this society. During ancient times, the people followed the Vedic religion. Later, Buddhism, Jainism and Islam came and influenced the people. In the present-day Haryana, Hindus form about 87.5 per cent of the population, Sikhs 4.9 per cent, Muslims 7.0 per cent and Christians 0.2 per cent. The Hindus are divided into a number of castes like Jats, Brahmins, Ahirs, Aggarwals, Gujars, Arora Khatris, Sainis, Rajputs and Rors. Among them, the Jats occupy a pre-eminent position in Haryana, being the largest group in the State. The artisan castes such as Sunars (goldsmiths), Lohars (blacksmiths), Telis (oil traders), Nais (barbers) and Dhobis (launderers) are found throughout the State and especially, in villages.

More than 75 per cent of the population is dependent on agriculture for livelihood. People speak several dialects of Hindi. The most important dialect is Bangaru. The people of Haryana are taller, stronger and healthier than the average Indian due to hard work and the inclusion of lots of dairy products in their diet. The main languages spoken by the people are Hindi, Punjabi, Urdu and English.

JATS

Although the Jats are not a single socio-religious group, as the term is commonly understood today, they live in Haryana, western Uttar Pradesh, Uttarakhand, Rajasthan, Punjab and Delhi in north India. Though the common definition refers to only the Hindu Jats, a significant number of Jats are Sikhs and Muslims. The Jats are not a homogeneous ethnic group. They are the people who live scattered around the world among several ethnic groups but retain their own identity. This distinction is often based on occupation and heritage. The Jats are primarily located in north-western India and southern Pakistan, though there are also some Jat communities in Maldives, Russia and Ukraine. They are said to be of Indo-Aryan (or Indo-Scythian) descent. History proves that they had reached Egypt along with the Muslim conquerors, lived in Afghanistan before the Muslims and invaded China along with the Mongol army. They had also proved to be a threat to Timur the Lame in Persia and Uzbekistan.

There are different opinions as to the origin of the Jats but the most of these recognize them to be of Indo-Aryan descent. There is also a theory suggesting that they may be the processors of Gypsies. Whatever their origin, in the eighteenth century, the Jats became a force that could not be ignored. Jats are a brave, hardworking and independent people. Primarily agriculturists, the Jats led a fairly autonomous political life. Even during the Mughal period, the rule of their state was under their control. With the exception of Bharatpur, no Jat kingdoms were founded. As per the Varna (caste) system, the Jats are Kshatriyas or warriors. As they are outside the rigorous brahmanical social order, this position was not emphasized till the growth of the Arya Samaj among the Jats. They have a very good self-image. They are brave and hardworking people who possess both the desire and ability to rule. It has been said that no Jat wants to be ruled. Rather, he desires to have power over a group, if not over an area.

The first opposition to Aurangzeb's autocratic rule came from the Jats of Mathura. In 1669, the sturdy and hard-working peasantry of Jats, under the leadership of Gokla, the landlord of Tilpat, rose against and killed the imperial Faujdar, Abdun-Nabi. It took more than one year for the powerful Mogul forces to subdue the Jats. Gokul was killed and his family forcibly converted to Islam. But this did not deter the Jats and they once again rose in 1685 under the leadership of Raja Ram. Akbar's tomb in Sikandra was plundered by them in 1688. Finally, the Jats were defeated and Raja Ram was slain in 1691. But the brave Jats organized once again under the leadership of Churaman and revolted. They continued a strong armed resistance against the Mughals after Aurangzeb's death.

Towards the end of Aurangzeb's region, predatory bands of Jats under individual leaders like Raja Ram Bhajja and Churaman carried out depredations around Delhi and Agra. They slowly increased their power.

But whatever they had achieved was lost when Sawai Jai Singh II captured Churaman's stronghold of Thun in 1721. Till this time, Jats where never united and followed their individual village headsmen. But all this was changed by Badan Singh, the son of Churaman's brother, Bhao Singh. Even in the face of great difficulties, Badan Singh established his authority over almost of Agra and Mathura by wisdom, versatility and marriage alliances with powerful Jat families. Badan Singh died on 7th June, 1756. His adopted son and successor was suraj Mal.

Suraj Mal has been variously described as "Plato of Jat Tribes" and "Jat Ulysses" because of his sagacity, intellect and clear vission. Suraj Mal extended his kingdom to Agra, Mathura, Dholpur, Mainpuri, Hathras, Aligarh, Etawah, Meerut, Rohtak, Farukhnagar, Mewat, Rewari and Gurugram. He has been dscribed as the greatest warrior the ablest statesman that the Jats have ever produced. Suraj Mal died on 25th December, 1763. Such was the might of the Jats that Bharatpur came to be known as the impregnable city. The beautiful palace and gardens at Deeg and the Bharatpur fort, both built by Suraj Mal, symbolized the coming of age of the Jat State. Soon, nobody dared question their prowess in battle. A british general, Lord Lake, through otherwise and paid dearly with his life due to his decision to besiege the Lohagarh fort. At Deeg, the Maharaja's men successfully took on the might of a combined Mughal and Maratha army of 80,000. Growing from strength to strength, the Jats even dared to attack the Red Fort in Delhi, the ultimate icon of Mughal power.

Known for their military prowess, many Jats were recruited in the British India army during World War I. Before that, they served as fighters in the Persian army. A large number of Jats serve in the Indian armed forces and form one of the largest ethnic groups in the army. The Green Revolution brought considerable prosperity to the Jats during the late sixties and early seventies of the last century. Jat regions in India are among the most prosperous ones. Today, many Jats are well and some occupy high positions in academic and technical arenas. Conservative by nature, the Jats rarely marry poeple from other ethanic or Muslims. The Jats living in Pakistan are primarily Muslims.

The religious beliefs of Hindu Jats are usually non-orthodox. A large number of people came under the influence of Arya Samaj during the early part of the twentieth century. The influence of Arya Samaj played a significant role in shaping their socio-religious identity. Until recent times, the Sikh Jats seemed to be the least meticulous in their observance of Sikh traditions; they had leaned more towards Hinduism. The Muslim Jats are sunnis, belonging to the Hanafi school but are known to have a strong trandition of worshipping many local saints. Sir Chhotu Ram and Chaudhary Devi Lal are the two most famous Jat leaders from Haryana.

RAJPUTS

The word 'Rajput' indicates that they are descendents of rulers who ruled a large part of India particularly after Harshvardhan. They are known for their valour, chivalry, loyalty, horsemanship, swordsmanship and friendship.

A number of theories have been put forward regarding their origin. They had a higher social status only next to Brahmins. However, in Haryana, they are considered next to Jats. They are chiefly concentrated in Bhiwani, Rohtak, Hissar, Sonepat, Gurugram and Mohindergarh. In general they are a land-owning class and many of them opt for military service. Panwar, Chauhans, Tanwars, Bhatis, Bachhas, Badgujars and Jatus are the prominent class of Rajputs found in this region. Muslim Rajputs are known as Ranghars. It is significant that the practice of Sati was not much prevalent among the Rajput of this region. However, widow-marriage was not popular.

They are tall, fine, brave men and retain the feudal instinct more strongly developed than any other non-menial castes; the heads of the people wield extra-ordinary authority. They are very tenacious of the integrity of their communal property in the village land and seldom admit strangers to share in it. They are generally regarded as brave and proud, look upon manual labour somewhat derogatory.

BRAHMINS

The Brahmins of Haryana are divided into four main groups : Gaurs, Saraswats, Khandelwals and Dhimans. The Gaurs claim that they had come originally from Bengal. But it is believed they had come as Purohitas of various immigrant farming tribes. The Saraswats are the original settlers of this region, taking their name from the Saraswati river. The Khandelwals and Dhimans came to this region much latter, most probably from neighbouring Rajasthan. The Brahmins themselves had a ranking system among them, with Gaurs being on the top, followed by Saraswats, Khandelwals and Dhimans. Brahmins have lived in every village and town of Haryana. During earlier times, most of them were working as Purohitas (priests), though some of them were also engaged in agriculture. The Brahmins were held in high esteem by people due to their high socioreligious status. In the pre-independence dayts, they formed about 8 per cent of the total population of the region.

AHIRS

Ahirs, Yadavs or Yadavas are found throughout the country, especially in Haryana. They includ the Abhiras or Ahirs of northern India, Raos of Haryana, Gwalas of Uttar Pradesh, Mandals of Bihar, Pradhans of Odisha, Ghoshals of Bengal, Gopas and Reddis of Andhra Pradesh and Wodeyars of Karnataka. Yadavas call themselves Somavanshi Kshatriyas. Their contribution to the composite culture of India is immense : thenomadic art forms, the Abhira language (Apabhramsa), the Raslila and certain ragas, like Ahir-Bhairav, Abhirika, Gopixa, Kannadaguala and the Krishna cult.

Although the Ahirs andYadavas form one group, yet former (the Ahiras or Abhiras) are an important community of Haryana. But numerically, they constitute less than 10 per cent of the total population. Most of them live in the region around Rewari and Narnaul, which is known as Ahirwal or the abode of Ahirs. Some historians hold that they were a powerful race of nomad cowherds from eastern or central Asia who had entered India from the Punjab in large hordes at about the same times as the Sakas and the Yuehchis during the first or second century BC and gradually spread over large parts of northern, eastern and central India. Other views are that they had come from Syria or Asia Minor in the beginning of the Christian era; were Dravidians; had originated from the Ayars of Tamil Nadu; lived in India long before the Aryan invasion; were descendants of the Yadavas of the lunar family of Pururavas Aila; and their original habitat was the region between the Sutlej and the Yamuna from where they had migrated beyond Mathura in the east and beyond Gujarat and Maharashtra in the south.

The Ahirs of Mathura and Braja regions where known to be peace-loving cowherds whereas the Abhirs of Haryana and Mahendragarh who, later on, where called Ahirs, where powerful and accomplished warriors. Out of these Yadavas, many have been categorized into backward classes whereas the rest of them are flourishing farmers in Haryana, Uttar Pradesh and Bihar.

The name of the state of Haryana may have been derived from its ancient inhabitants : Abhirayana led to Ahirayana, which led to

Hirayana, which finally led to the present name-Haryana. The name Abhira may stem from a-bhira—a meaning not; bhira meaning fear—fearless. The Ahir's hold over Haryana must be have remained intact for centuries after the Battle of Mahabharata. At the beginning of the Christian era, the invading Scythians and Kushans forced most of them out of their land of lower Rajasthan in the Arbuda (Aravalli region). In Marubhumi (Marwar), Saurashtra and Maharashtra, they served the local rulers and established their own kingdom. Ishwar Sena, a great Ahir general, became the master of western Deccan by replacing the famous Satavahanas. He took the title of Rajan and an era was named after him. his descendants continued to rule for nine generations. For centuries, the Ahirs were eclipsed as a political power in Haryana until the time of the Pratihara dynasty, With the passage of time, they became independent rulers of south-western Haryana.

Rao Tula Ram was the most well known of Ahir leaders. He fought against the British in the 1857 Revolt.

MEOS

Meos inhabit a territorial region that falls between important urban centres of Delhi, Agra and Jaipur. Mewat, consisting of some adjoining parts of Haryana, Rajasthan and Uttar Pradesh, where the Meos have lived for a millennium, was a terrain of peasant radicalism during the pre-independence period. It saw intensive work by the communist leaders such as the historian-activist Kunwar Mohammad Ashraf and others who were then working with the Indian National Congress. There was a close inter-community relationship between the Meos and other peasant-pastoral castes such as the Jats, Ahirs and Gujars. In Haryana, the Mewat region falls in the Nuh district.

Meo men are all tall and dark, with ponderous turbans woven around their heads, dressed in long flowing robes. The Meos are about a million-strong tribe, a Muslim Rajput community living in southern Haryana and north-eastern Rajasthan known for its admixture of Hindu and Islamic customs, practices and beliefs. Only one in ten

Meos is able to properly read and write. The Meos have two identities both of which, they are equal proud of. On the one hand, they claim to be Muslims, tracing their conversion to various Sufi saints who began settling in their territory from the eleventh century onwards and whose shrines or 'dargahs' today dot the entire Mewati countryside. On the other hand, they also claim to be Rajputs and believe that they are the direct descendants of Krishna and Rama. These Hindu deities are respectfully referred to by the Meos as 'dadas' or 'grandfathers.'

AGGARWALS

Aggarwal claim themselves to be the followers of Maharaja Agrasen, the King of Agroha. Agroha is located at a distance of about 20 kilometres north-west of the city of Hissar and was once a very prosperous city. However, it has changed a lot due to the ravages of time. Agroha village is about at a distance of 2.5 kilometres from the Agroha Mound, the remains of the old Agroha City. Maharaja Agrasen proceeded to conduct 18 *Maha Yagnas*. He divided his kingdom among his 18 children and established the 18 gotras after the guru's of each of his children. These were: Garg, Mangal, Kucchal, Goyal, Bansal, Kansal, Singhal, Jindal, Thingal, Airan, Dharan, Madhukul, Bindal, Mittal, Tayal, Bhandal and Naagal. The neighbouring kings were envious of Agroha because of its prosperity. So they frequently attacked it. Because of these aggressions, Agroha faced numerous plights. In due course, the strength of Agroha was sapped. A huge fire engulfed the city causing the citizens to flee and disperse into various areas of Bharata. Today, these people are known as Aggarwals. They still have the same 18 gotras that were given to them by their gurus. They carry on the fame of Maharaja Agrasen. As per Maharaja Agrasen's guidance, the Aggarwals are in the forefront of social service. The Agroha Temple Complex and Agroha Medical Colleges are being built near Agroha with generous donations from the Aggarwal community.

MIRASIS

The Mirasi community of India and Pakistan are the genealogists and traditional singers and dancers of a number of communities. The word "mirasi" is derived from the Arabic word miras, which means inheritance or sometimes heritage.

Some Mirasi groups are from the Hindu caste system of the 'low caste' and accepted their religion as Muslim, while others claim to have originally belonged to the Hindu Charan community. They are said to have accepted Islam at the hands of Amir Khusro, the 13th-century Sufi poet.

The North Indian Mirasis are divided into five main subgroups:

Abbal, Posla, Bet, Kattu, and Kalet. In customs, they are similar to the Muslim Raibhat, another community of genealogists. Also related to the Mirasis are the Kingharia, another community that was once employed as musicians and entertainers. They are also known as Pakhwaji due to the pakhwaj, a timbrel that they play.

The Mirasis maintained pedigrees of their patrons and were often involved in negotiations of marriages. As genealogists, the Mirasis were also styled Nasab khwan, or the keepers of the family tree.

The Mirasis were found throughout Northern India. They were traditionally ballad singers, and would often sing at weddings. The community were also connected with the manufacture of paper flowers. They can be seen performing in fairs in the rural area. As an urban community, found at the edges of towns, many are now employed as wage labourers. Some Mirasis have migrated to neighbouring states: Rajasthan, Bihar, Gujarat, Punjab, and Western Uttar Pradesh.

GURJARS

Gurjar or Gujjar are a simple, thrifty and industrious group with populations in India and Pakistan and a small number in north-eastern Afghanistan. Alternative spellings include gurjara, Gurjjar, Gojar and Gujar. Although they are able to speak the language of the country where they live, Gurjars have their own language, known as

Gujari. The Gurjars are classified as Other Backward Class (OBC) in some states in India; however, Gurjars in Jammu and Kashmir and parts of Himachal Pradesh are categorised as a Scheduled Tribe. Hindu Gurjars were assimilated into various varnas in the medieval period.

The Gujjars basically belong to the north-western regions of India like that of Gujarat, Rajasthan, Himachal Pradesh, Jammu & Kashmir, Uttar Pradesh, Uttarakhand Haryana and Punjab. It is also said that Gujarat is said to be named after them as they settled there in the 6th century AD. Originally Gujjars are through to be an Aryan tribe that entered India in parts of Gujarat and Rajasthan from the North West.

Gujjars in Haryana are mostly settled in Faridabad and Panchkula districts and also in the Samalkha segment of Panipat district. The population of Gujjars in Haryana is relatively big. Here the Gurjars are also hugely concentrated in Ambala, Kurukshetra, Yamunanagar, Karnal, Panipat, Kaithal, Hisar, Gurugram and several other cities. The Gujjar community in Haryana also decided in a 'mahapanchayat' (also means 'the great panchayat') that those people who wanted dowry would be excommunicated from their society.

CHAPTER 9

CULTURE, FAIRS, ART AND CRAFTS

INTRODUCTION

Haryana is proud of its unique and rich cultural heritage. The State has an ancient tradition of folklore. The centuries old customs are still observed by the masses. The seasonal and religious festivals glorify the culture of this region. The dance is said to be the mother of all the arts. Music and poetry exist in tune, painting and architecture in space. The creator and the creation, the artist and his work are one and the same thing. The dance is just not a form of recreation but something needed to release the physical and emotional energy. Folk dances, like any creative art, helps in sublimating the performer's worries and cares.

Haryana has always remained a State of diverse races, cultures and faiths. It is on this soil that they met, merged and crystallized to form a unique cultural ethos. The people of Haryana have preserved their old religious and social traditions. They celebrate festivals with great enthusiasm and traditional fervour. Their culture and popular art are expressed in folk dances, dramas, ballads and songs in which, they take great delight.

Along with Hindi, Punjabi, Urdu and English as the main languages, of the State, there are numerous dialects, which are spoken throughout the length and breadth of Haryana. However, almost all of them have their lingual base in Hindi with a few selected words drawn from Urdu and Punjabi. In towns and cities, English is still to be adopted as the household lingo but it is spoken in a hazy mixture of Hindi, The most striking feature of Haryana is its language itself or the manner in which, it is spoken. Popularly known as Haryanavi (or Bangaru or Jatu), it is perhaps a bit crude.

DANCES

Ras Leela : This dance is common among the people living in the Faridabad district. In this dance, Gopis form a circle around Lord Krishna.

Phag Dance : This is seasonal dance of the farmers usually performed in the month of Phalguna. This is a mixed dance but sometimes performed by men only. Women wear colourful traditional clothes and men display gay colourful turbans. The dance is accompanied by the beats of Tasha, Nagada and Dhol.

Loor Dance : It is a well-known dance of Haryana. It is performed around the Holi festivals and is very popular in the Bangar. Girl usually participate on this dance wearing their traditional dress of Ghagra, Kurti, Chundri and Chunda.

Dhamal Dance : This is an ancient dance, which is quite popular among the Ahirs of Gurgaon and Mahendragarh. The dance is performed outdoors by men on moonlit nights of Phalgun. They sing and dance to the sound of the Dhamal beats. At the beginning of the dance, a long tune of a *been* is played. It is said that people perform this dance whenever their crops is ready for harvesting.

Gugga Dance : Gugga Pir is worshipped all over Haryana by both Hindus and Muslims. The dance is performed in a procession, which is held about a week before the Gugga Naumi. The devotees sing and dance in praise of Gugga Pir. The dance is accompanied by musical instruments like Deru, Thali and Chimta.

Jhumar Dance : This dance is exclusively by women. It takes its name from Jhumar, an ornament commonly worn on the forehead by young married women. The dance is performed on the beats of dholak and thali.

Ghumar Dance : It is a Rajasthani dance, which is also popular in the area of Loharu, Dadri, Sirsa and Hissar. It is religious dance and is performed by women devotees on their way to the temple. Women start dancing a circle and then form two rows. Finally, they end up dancing pairs within a circle.

Khoria Dance : This dance is popular in the central areas of Haryana. This dance is performed by women at the house of bridegroom on the night on which, the marriage party goes to bride's house, Through this dance, women ask for the safe and sound return of the marriage party along with the newly wed couple. By staying awake for the whole night for this dance, they also protect their house since the men folk are all away to the bride's house. Due to the rough nature of this dance, children are generally kept away from it.

Gangore Puja : With brass plates in their hands, girls make a circle, sing and dance.

Holi Dance : This dance is connected with the Holi festivals of spring. It is performed along with drums and pipes. Both men and women participate in this dance. This dance is popular in the areas of Faridabad, Palwal and Ballabhgarh.

Chhathi Dance : On the birth of a male child, this dance is performed on the sixth day of the birth by women. It is romantic dance and performed at night. At the end of the celebration, boiled wheat and chana are distributed.

Sang : This is performed by a group of ten or twelve persons. They sing religious stories and folk tales in open space. It can be called open air theatre too. The performance can continue for five hours. Some of the men dress as women to act and dance. Sang or Swang means a disguise or impersonation. This form of dance or drama was started in its present form in about 1750 AD by Kishan Lal Bhaat.

Chaupaiya Dance : This dance is performed by men who wear dhoti, kurtas and colourful turbans. They dance to the beats of *manjiras, chimtas, and nagadas.* It is performed while harvesting crops. It is based on songs having four lines or tetrameter, hence called Chaupaiya.

POTTERY

Haryana mainly has a rural economy and pottery is one of the main occupation. The potter's wheel, dating back to pre-Aryan times, is the most common feature of any village of India. Although numerous types of wheels are used throughout India, yet its kick-operated type is common in the State of Haryana. The actual wheel may be either of cement or of stone. Pottery is essentially a village craft; and Haryana is essentially a State of villages. While the potter works on the wheel, he has a helper (usually his son or a relative) who mixes clay, a woman (his wife or a sister) makes intricate designs on the finished vessel or toy. From utensils to toys to decorative pieces, clay forms the most essential ingredient on which, the potter literally survives. During festival seasons, he has to make hundreds of toys, like miniature cows, horses, people, houses and sepoys, which are sold in brightly decorated stalls along dusty lanes.

EMBROIDERY, WEAVING AND HANDLOOMS

Haryana, is quite famous for its woven work, be it shawls, durries, robes or lungis, The Haryana shawl is known as *Phulkari.* It is an offshoot of the shawl from Kashmir. It is spectacular cloth, full of magnificent colours and intricate embroidery. Worn with a tight-fitting choli (blouse) and Ghagra (long skirt), it forms the basic winter wear for the women of Haryana, A deviation from the *phulkari* is the *bagh* (garden). In this case, the entire cloth is covered with embroidery. The *phulkari* is made by female members of a house and takes a long time to make; sometime even a few years may be needed to complete one piece. Traditionally, work on a *phulkari* commences from the time a daughter is born on the family and is given to her at her wedding. Against a red background, motifs of birds, flowers and human figures are stitched into the cloth. The *bagh* design almost always follows a geometric pattern, with green as the basis to colour probably because mainly Muslims used to work on them. Although lacking in technical finesse, it makes up for the loss by a colourful display of its design. One can see the rich diversity of patterns and designs of such items at the Surajkund Crafts Mela or in various shops dotted throughout the state. Haryana's durries are rather coarse, though spectacular geometric designs adorn the entire rug. The Jats of Haryanas are known to make durries with white triangles set against a blue background. In Haryana, durrie-making is concentrated in and around Panipat. Karnal is a hot spot for bright robes and *lungis* (a skirt-like garment worn by men and originally invented by Gautama Buddha), a common garments worn by inhabitants of rural India.

PAINTING

Haryana was always been a rendezvous for various tribes, invaders, races, and faiths since 2500 B.C. It has witnessed the merging of numerous styles of painting. Discoveries of earthenware and designs painted on them in black-and-white in Siswal district in Haryana are the first impressions of art in this state. Mittathal and Banwali districts have also revealed that art did exist here but definitely on a much smaller scale than that in the Deccan and southern India. The drawings are mainly in horizontal and vertical lines, with a little more creativity allotted to floral art. During Harsha's reign, art and painting received special attention for some time as the king himself was a painter of sorts.

In the past, the rich *jagirdars* (landlords), who liked paintings, engaged artisans and painters to do up their houses, ceilings and walls. Temples were other buildings for which, painters were engaged. The painters of those times painted everything within their reach with landscapes, dances, hunting expeditions, wrestling bouts, birds, bees and love scenes. Come the eighteenth century and Rewaris made sure that painters got enough work, albeit under a Rajput style. Lord Krishna was painted mostly villages; walls, doors windows etc. bore his image and the Mughal and Kangra styles of painting merged with the Rajput style.

The walls of the palace of Maharaja Tej Singh of Mirapur (in Gurgaon) are adorned with paintings, which follow the Rajput pattern. The patterns on the walls express scenes from the Ramayana. The Asthal Bohar paintings are also in the Rajput style and their influence can be seen even in Shiva temples in Panchkula and Pinjore, Venumadhava temple in Kaul, the temples in Kaithal and Pabnama, Kapil temple in Kilayat and Sarsainath temple in Sirsa. The Rang Mahal at Pinjore is also decorated with wall paintings, which are the creative legends of Mughal painters. The samadhis of Lala Balak Ram and Jamuna Das in Jagadhari in Ambala are famous for their wall paintings from Hindu mythology. The entrances to both of these *samadhis* are flanked by heavily painted dwarapalas.

Kurukshetra's Bhadri Kali temple has religious themes and frescos running out its structure. The second floor at covered with murals.

Further, the *haveli* (house) of Rani Chand Kaur is Pehowa, the temple of Shri Ram Radha at Pehowa and the temple of Baba Shrawan Nath also have mural-covered floors. In fact we shall find similar painting in temples and holy Hindu places throughout Haryana. The Persian style, infused with script. also gains prominence, especially with murals in which, the Persian script has been used. Mughal paintings entered into Hindu temples, especially in Kaithal, Kalagat and Rohtak. In Rohtak, paintings have been found, which are now under the control of the Manuscript Department of Kurukshetra University. Liberal use of blue, pink, green, orange and red hues enhances the beauty of these paintings, which represent Lord Vishnu and His incarnations.

SCULPTURE

Rock and stone were the most common for the development of art, right from the Maurya period to the era of Harshavardhana to the reign of Mughals and finally to the rule of the British. Many Hindu gods formed the basis of sculpture in ancient Haryana. Sculpture in Haryana was concentrated around central and northern parts and was basically religious in content. Lord Vishnu was the most important God. He and His incarnations were the subjects of creation for sculptors. A figure of Lord Vishnu, found in Kurukshetra, is a remarkable piece of art; it shows Him with four arms, gracefully reclining on the coils of Anantnag, the snake with multiple heads. This stone figure was probably made during tenth century A.D. Sandstone was widely used, be it green, buff, grey or black. But besides the images of Hindus gods and goddesses, Jain image from the Pratihara period (ninth century) have also been found; all of these are made of sandstone. Lord Buddha is also found at some places. In Rohtak, he was found seated cross-legged on a lotus pedestal and made entirely of grey stone.

MUSICAL INSTRUMENTS

Dholak : It is small percussive instrument often used by women and professional musicians. The main body of the dholak is a shell made of wood and the heads are mounted with skin. A rope or thread is passed around the shell and over braces to adjust the pitch of sound produced by striking the faces of the skin. Hands are used produce beats. Sometimes, two sticks are tied to a finger or a ring is put around the thumb to produce an additional musical effect.

Dhol : An instrument similar to dholak but bigger than it is the dhol. It is played by men by using two sticks. The dhol is slung in the front from the neck using a string. The loud sound of a big dhol can be heard from a great distance.

Damru : It is small palm-held-drum with strings attached to beads, which strike the sides when shaken with fingers.

Deru : Deru is percussive instrument like dholak made of wooden shell and skin—mounted on both of its sides. Infact, it is a large damru, which is struck with sticks to produce rhythmic beats. It is used by folk performers as well as by wandering devotees.

Chimta : It is tong-like instrument made of two long metallic strips which are joined on one side. The strips are often embellished with rings, which produce tinkling sounds when the chimta is played. To produce percussive sounds, one holds the joint in one hand and plays strips between the fingers by striking one with the other. The chimta is used as an accompaniment in folk musical performances.

Been : This wind driven instrument is used primarily by the snake charmers. It is said that the snake charmers charm the snakes using the *been's* haunting music. But it has found its permanent place, in Haryanavi dances too. Made from dried pumpkin, it has two joints pipes to produce different notes the player of the *been* has to produce continuous flow of air by breathing into it. It is difficult to play and requires good breath control.

Manjira : Manjiras (cymbals) are made of brass and are either flat-shaped or cup-shaped. These are used in pairs of different sizes and shapes. They are played in classical, folk and devotional music performances. Two cymbals are tied together with a long chord and are struck with each other on their front sides to produce very pleasant tinkling sounds.

Harmonium : A musical instrument with keys, metal reeds and bellows. It is played by using the bellows to force air through the reeds, which are opened by putting fingers over the keys.

Gharah : Also called the matka. It is a simple earthen pitcher and is used as an accompaniment to provide rhythm with folk singing. The open mouth is covered with stretched rubber and played with a small stick. Raagni singers often use it with Nagara and Dholak to complement the musical beat.

Saarangi : It is a type of string instrument, which is played with a bow.

Khartals : These are wooden cymbals having two pieces of hard wood, which are made flat on one side and round on the other. Fixed in the fingers of one hand, the flat surfaces are struck with each other to produce, percussive. Sometimes, small bells or metallic rings are also fixed at the back of each khartal to produce a tinkling effect.

Shehnai : It is flute-like instrument, which is played mainly at weddings.

Bansuri : It is flute-like wind instrument consisting of a cylindrical bamboo tube. It is played by blowing across a hole near one end. The tune is played by closing the holes and key's along its length with the help of fingers.

SURAJKUND MELA

The very first effort for organizing cultural events on a national level by Haryana Tourism was made with the launching of the annual Surajkund Crafts Mela. It was inaugurated for the first time in 1981. It gives a handsome glimpse of the finest handloom and handicrafts traditions of our country. It is a fortnight-long even that embodies the spirit running through the people of India and her rich culture. It is held from first to fifteenth day of February. The Surajkund Crafts Mela is held just 8 km from south Delhi.

Beneath thatched roof platforms, master crafts persons display the finest of handlooms and handicrafts from all over the country. The event is so colourful and rich in experience, that many a tourist has returned to visit it again and again. The Surajkund crafts mela is more than a celebration of crafts. At the fan-shaped open-air-theatre called Natyashala, rich folk dances and musical evenings are organised throughout the mela fortnight.

How to Reach Surajkund: Surajkund is 8 km from South Delhi. The mela ground had been linked to major bus stops in Delhi, Gurgaon and Faridabad. The mela begins from 9.30 a.m. and closes at 5.30 p.m. evening from 1st to 15 February every year.

REWRI AND GAJJAK

Rewri of Rohtak is known and famous for its distinct flavour and crispness. Rewri is sweet delicacy made from Gur (jaggery) and Til (sesame). The reputation of Rohtak's rewri has not only crossed Haryana's borders, but also reached the markets of Europe and the Middle East. Rewri of Rohtak was made famous by Jamini, a Muslim halwai, who had a shop at Barra Bazaar during pre-partition days. It is said that rewri came into existence during the later Mughal period. Jamini's legacy has now assumed the status of a flourishing cottage industry in Rohtak. During the winter months, people on North India enjoy eating the crispy rewri and gajjak products. Most households buy it as a seasonal delicacy for self consumption and also, for gifting it their friends and relatives.

The total production of rewri in Rohtak alone during the winter is nearly 3,000 tons. The rate of this product depends upon the quality and freshness of the product. The shelf life of these products ranges from two-three months.

CHAPTER 10

LITERATURE

INTRODUCTION

Haryana is a unique state in terms of literacy activities as well. *The Bhagwad Gita* was spoken and written on this land. It gives the ultimate philosophy that every human being can adopt to relieve himself off the agonies of birth and death. It is the supreme sermon of Lord Vishnu, which must be read and imbibed in letter and spirit.

During the medieval age, many literature and poets adorned the land. Similarly, during the pre-independence era, several poets and writers found their ultimate salvation through the creation of verses and prose. We shall briefly discuss the poets and writers of both these eras. Finally, we shall give brief details of poets and writers of the modern times as well.

THE MEDIEVAL ERA

It is believed that Chand Bardai and Surdas were the products of Haryana. Chand Bardai become immortal by writing *Prithvi Raj Raso*. Surdas wrote *Sur Sagar*. Further, Sant Haridas, Kavi Maldev, Veerbhan, Sant Udhodas, Pushpadant, Sant Nityanand, Banarasi Dass, Jain Poet Sunderdass, Nischal Das, Banwari Dass, Kavi Ummed and Mast Ram are the famous litterateurs of Hindi language. These sages and poets have enriched Hindi literature to the maximum extent with the help of their creative works.

Among the Muslim Saints, the names of Sheikh-u-Alishah Kalandar, Muhammed Afzal, Sheikh Abdul Qadoos, Sannat Sadullah, Sheikh Bahauddin Chishti, Gulam Nilami, Nur Mohammed and Jan Kavi Jisno may be recalled. These poets and writers wrote in *Brij* and Hindi and contributed to the world of Hindi literature.

THE PRE-INDEPENDENCE ERA

During the rule of the British, the residents of the unified State of the Punjab struggled to liberate the nation from the clutches of the British. So, literacy activities took a back seat for some time. However, one poet (of Urdu) made his mark during this period of turmoil. His name was Altaaf Hussain Haali.

ALTAF HUSSAIN HAALI

Khwaja Altaaf Hussain Haali (1837-1914), the famous poet, prolific scholar and Urdu critic, was born in 1837 at Panipat. He came from an economically backward family and lost his parents by the age of nine years. He was brought up by his elder brother and sisters. Even though he was not properly educated, he managed to get good knowledge of Urdu, Persian and Arabic. He was married, against his wishes, to his cousin Islam-ul-nisha at the age of seventeen years. After marriage, he went to Delhi and got himself enrolled in Huseen Baksh's Madrassa near the Jama Masjid. There, he studied languages like Urdu, Persian and Arabic and got interested in poetry. He started frequenting the Mushairas (gatherings of poets) and gradually became very popular.

Haali returned to Panipat in 1855 and remained there for one year. In 1856, he got a job in the office of Deputy Commissioner, Hissar. After the Revolt of 1857, he left the government job, returned to Panipat and studied there for four more years. But his deteriorating financial position forced him to look for a job. In 1861, Nawab Shefta of Jahangirbad employed him to teach his son. Shefta was a skilled poet and critic of Urdu and Persian. Haali too got associated with poetry under his influence. Till 1869, he remained in Delhi and continued writing poetry. Then, he met legendary Urdu poet, Mirza Ghalib. Ghalib was not in the habit of encouraging each and every budding poet. But when he heard Haali's *shers* (Urdu couplets), he liked them a lot and encouraged Haali to continue writing poetry. In one of his *shers*, Haali wrote that though he respected Mirza Ghalib and was guided by Nawab Shefta, he benefited most from Mir, whose style he deeply admired.

From Delhi, Haali shifted to Lahore and got a job as a supervisor in the government book depot. There, he had to give assistance in rectifying

Urdu books, which were translated from English. During this period, he got good working knowledge of English and was also exposed to the modern literary activities of Europe. Thereafter, his poetry started taking a new shape and form; which was hither to unknown to Urdu literature. He continued in this job for 4 years. Then, he returned to Delhi and took up a job as a teacher in an Arabic school. There, he met the famous Sir Sayyed Ahmad Khan, the founder of Aligarh Muslim University. They became close friends within a short time period.

When the Prime Minister of Hyderabad visited the university in 1888, Sir Sayyed requested him to offer a fellowship to Haali. This was granted, keeping in mind Haali's contribution towards the enrichment of Urdu literature. Haali began on an allowance of Rs. 75, which was increased to Rs. 100 per month. Haali was a person, who was satisfied with limited means. On receiving the fellowship, he left for Panipat and devoted himself completely to the service of Urdu. The Government of India recognized his contribution and he was honoured with the highest title-Shamshulmaan.

His simplicity, honesty and religiosity were exemplary. He never gave pain to others but was very concerned for the progress of his fraternity. He did not touch wine nor was he attached to love and beauty. However, he wrote *ghazals* due to his association of all time greats, like Ghalib and Shefta. He was concerned about the miseries faced by nobles, during and after he sepoy mutiny. His prose and poetical works are as follows : *Tiriya ke Masmoom*, *Majaalis Ulnisa*, *Mazaamine-e-Haali*, *Hayaat-e-Saadi*, *Muqadam-e-Sher-o-Shairi*, *Yaadgar-e-Ghalib*, '*Hayaat-e-Javed*', '*Masnaviyaat*', *Manajaatebewa*, '*Chupki Daad*, *Shikwaye Hind*, *Musaddase Haali*, *Deewan-e-Haali* and *Roobaiyaat*.

His most important work was *Muqadma-e-Sher-o-Shairi*, written as a preface to his collection of poetry. Ahmed Sarwar called it "the first manifesto of Urdu poetry." There are about 116 ghazals composed by him, which consist of about 1300 *shers*. Haali was known for his love for and welfare of Muslims. His death on September 30, 1914, was a serious loss to the world of Urdu. A school was established in his memory at Panipat. His centenary was celebrated in all the big cities in 1935.

THE MODERN ERA

Deedar Singh, Bhai Santokh Singh, Sahib Singh Mrigendra, Bagg Singh, Ujjwal Singh and Joginder Singh are some of the literacy personalities of modern Haryana. They wrote in Hindi and Punjabi. Joginder Singh, an educationist and litterateur of Shahabad, contributed effectively to the literature of three languages—Hindi, Punjabi and Urdu.

In the field of Hindi literature, Balmukund Gupta, Madhav Prasad Mishra and Radhakrishna Mishra are the names worth mentioning. Bishambhar Nath Kaushik was born in Ambala Cantonment. But he migrated to Kanpur. Pandit Neki Ram Sharma was from Bhiwani. He had started a magazine (*Sandesh*), which was in Hindi. Tulsiram Sharma Dinesh, the famous poet from Bhiwani, wrote *Shyam Satsai*, *Satyagrahi Prahlad* and other landmark books of poetry (in Hindi). Ayodhya Prasad Goyaliya was born in Badshahpur, a village in Gurgaon district. He introduced Urdu poetry (*Shairi*) to Indian audience. He remained an office-bearer of Bhartiya Gyanpeeth for many years.

The first ever state poet of Haryana was Uday Bhanu Hans. On 31 March, 1967, Anupchand Aftab was also honoured (as the state poet in Urdu) along with Uday Bhanu Hans. Khushiram Sharma was the next state poet. Mr. Sharma has written *Rana Nimantrana*, *Guru Gobind Singh* and *Yuddha Charita*.

Bhai Parmanand, the renowned poet from Hissar, also took active part in Bhoodan Movement. He used his sonorous songs to deliver the message of Vinoba Bhave to the masses. Ishwar Chandra Panday and Leeladhar Dukhi were also the famous poets of the State.

Many sons of Haryana contributed to theatre too. Jaswant Singh Tohanvi, Bastiram, Lakshmi Chand Sangi, Dhanpat Singh and Rajaram Shastri are the prominent names. These writers used drama and *sang* to mesmerise their readers. They contributed to the Hindi literature through their unique literary creations and mass-based activities. Further Dr. Ranjit Singh is a famous Hindi (prose) writer of Haryana.

Geminy Haryanvi contributed to Haryanvi literature. He wrote couplets and poems, which fall under the gamut of humorous literature. Other poets, like Om Prakash Aditya, Baldevraj Shant, Deepchand Nirmohi and Vishnudatt Kaviratna also made contributions to the vast literary ocean of the State.

CHAPTER 11

Religious Festivals

INTRODUCTION

Hindus are in majority in the State. But Christians and Muslims are also the residents of many parts of Haryana. All these communities celebrate their respective religious festivals or days with devotion and unflinching commitment. We shall discuss the major religious festivals being celebrated in Haryana in this chapter. These are, in fact, in perfect tuning with those celebrated in the northern parts of India.

FESTIVALS OF THE HINDUS

DEEPAWALI

Diwali or *Deepawali* is a festival of lights, which symbolises the victory of righteousness and the end of spiritual darkness. The word *Deepawali* literally means rows of *deepaks* or *diyas* (clay lamps). It is celebrated 20 days after Dussehra on the thirteenth day of the dark fortnight of the month of Ashwina (October-November). Continuing the story of Lord Rama, this festival commemorates His return to His kingdom (Ayodhya) after completing His fourteen-year exile. Twinkling *diyas* and candles light up every home. Firework displays are common all across the country. The goddess Lakshmi, who is the symbol of wealth and prosperity, is also worshipped on this day. Lord Ganesha, the symbol of auspiciousness and wisdom, is also worshipped in most Hindu homes on this day. The occasion of *Diwali* is also apt for cleaning and white-washing of houses. Decorative design or rangolis are painted on floors and walls. New clothes are bought and family members and relatives gather to offer prayers, distribute sweets and light up their homes.

DUSSEHRA

It is one of the important Hindu festivals, celebrated with much fervour in the entire country. The occasion marks the triumph of Lord Rama over the demon king, Ravana. The destruction of the demon king is deemed the victory of good over evil. Brilliantly decorated tableaux and processions, depicting various facets of Lord Rama's life, are taken out. On the tenth day, the Vijayadashmi day, huge effigies of Ravana, his brother Kumbhakarna and son Meghanatha, are constructed in an open ground. Rama, accompanied by his consort Sita and his brother Lakshmana, arrives and shoots arrows of fire at these effigies; these effigies are stuffed with explosive material. The result is a deafening blast, enhanced by the cheers from spectators. In burning the effigies the people are asked to burn the evil within them and therefore, follow the path of virtue and goodness. People recall that Ravana, despite all his might and majesty, was destroyed because of bad deeds (*kukarmas*).

JANMASHTAMI

This festival is celebrated in the month of August every year. It is the birth anniversary of Lord Krishna, the incarnation of Lord Vishnu.

The temples of the State witness an extravagant and colourful celebration on this occasion. Raslila is performed to recreate incidents from the life of Lord Krishna and commemorate his love for Radha. The image of infant Lord Krishna is bathed at midnight and placed in a cradle. Devotional songs and dances mark the celebration of this festive occasion all over northern India. This festival is celebrated with a special fervour by people of Brij Bhoomi area of Faridabad district.

BAISAKHI

Baisakhi, celebrated with music and dances, in New Year's Day for Punjabis. It falls on April 13, though once in 36 years, it occurs on 14 April. It was on this day that the tenth Sikh Guru, Guru Gobind Singh, founded the Khalsa in 1699. Sikhs visit gurdwaras and listen to kirtans. After the prayer, *kadah prasada* (sweetened semolina) is served to the congregation. The function ends with langar, the community lunch. Processions are taken out, at the heads of which, are the

Panj Piaras. Mock duels and bands, playing religious tunes, are a part of these processions. School children also enthusiastically take part in them. For people living in villages, this festival is the late opportunity for relaxing before they start the harvesting of wheat. Processions and feasts follow oration of the holy scripture of the Sikhs, *Shri Guru Granth Sahib*.

Mansa Devi Mela is held in Bilaspur village near Manimajara (Chandigarh). There are two temples dedicated to the goddess. The fairs are held twice a year—the first one in March-April (*Chaitra Shudi Ashtami*) and the other one in September-October (Ashwina Shudi Ashtami).

LOHRI

Lohri marks the culmination of winter and is celebrated on the 13 January, a day before *Makar Sankranti*. For Punjabis, this is an important festival. Lohri celebrates fertility and the spark of life. People gather round bonfires and throw sweets, puffed rice and popcorn into the flames. They dance, sing songs and exchange greetings with one another. The *prasada* comprises things like *til*, *gazak*, *gur*, *peanuts phuliya* and *popcorn*. There is puja involving parikarma around the fire and distribution of *prasada*. This symbolizes a prayer to Agni, the spark of life, for abundant crops and prosperity. The first Lohri of a bride is extremely important. The first Lohri of a newborn baby, especially that of a boy, is also equally important. Children go from door to door, singing and asking for the *Lohri Prasada*.

HOLI

Holi is a spring festivals. It is celebrated in the month of Phalgun, as the lunar month is locally known. The main event of Holi is indeed a carnival of colours. On this day, children, friends and neighbours come out on streets. And the exciting spree of colour-anyone-you-see takes over. Coloured powders or gulal was earlier made out of dried seeds of some tropical flowers like the *Palash* and also, from dried silt of the riverbed. This has now given way to dyes, which are available in as pigments. People throw these coloured powders in the air as they shout *Holi Hai*. They also smear one another with this coloured powder. They also met one another with coloured water from *pichkaris*, which are type of water gun. Coloured water is prepared by mixing the pigments of dyes. These dyes are available in a range of shades. Also water-filled balloons are used these days to charge the target with a splash of colour.

BASANT PANCHAMI

Basant Panchami, the Festival of Spring, is celebrated mainly in Haryana and Punjab during the month of February-March. It is celebrated at the end of winter to welcome spring. *Basant Ritu* means the spring season. It is during this time when in Haryana, the mustard fields are in full bloom, giving the impression of yellow carpets laid out on acres of land. People welcome this change of season by wearing yellow clothes and flying kites.

Kite flying is the major and most colourful event of this festivals. The sky is covered with different colourful kites. New clothes are made and purchased for this festival and many delicious dishes are also prepared for this particular occasion. In Haryana, sweet yellow rice is prepared especially for this occasion.

Kite flying or *Patang Baazi* is a cultural sport in Haryana. Kite flying is mostly done on the Basant Panchami, Raksha Bandhan, Makar Sankranti and Independence day. However, kites can be flown any time throughout the year. It is a fun sport for all times.

SANJHI

Sanjhi is worshipped as the Mother Goddess by unmarried girls of Haryana in order to make the image of Sanjhi, malleable mud is moulded into various shapes. These shapes of stars, moon, sun, face of the goddess etc. are given different colours. The star-studded collage is fixed on the wall of a dwelling, preferably facing south, in the later half of the Ashwin month in Shukla Paksh, *i.e.,* early October or late September. At some places, the images of Sanjhi is painted on the wall.

This art form is now again becoming popular and finds a place in the famous Surajkund Crafts Mela. The images of Sanjhi are suggestive of Goddess Durga, Uma and Katyayani. In the recent past, people have tried to keep this ancient custom alive. The presence of intellectuals amongst them has encouraged the rural folk.

Apart from the various forms of Sanjhi which the virgin girls create on the first day of the moon in Kartika, there are some other rituals observed by the girls during the Navaratras. Devotional songs are sung just after dusk. A few lighted earthen lamps are held by adolescent girls who assemble around Sanjhi. They sing chorus songs that are centuries old and hence, please the goddess.

GANGORE

Gangore is celebrated on Chaitra Sudi in March-April every year. Idols of Ishar and Gangore are taken out in a procession and songs in their praise are sung till they are immersed in water. This spring festivals is held in the honour of Gauri, the goddess of abundance. Girls dress up in their finest clothes and pray for getting a spouse of their choice. Married ladies do the same for the happiness of their husbands. Girls worship the goddess throughout the preceding fortnight. Colourful images of Gauri, beautifully dressed and bejewelled, are taken out in procession with the town band. Thousands of people take part in the procession of the Gangore image.

TEEJ

Teej is celebrated on Shrawan Sudi (July-Aug.). It is celebrated to welcome *sawan* or rainy season. After the first showers of *sawan* a, small red insect, called teej in Haryana, comes out from the earth's soil. Swings are set up in the open courtyards and teej gets the first swing of the season. Girls apply henna on their hands and feet and are given a break from the household chores on this day. On the *teej,* girls receive new clothes from their parents and the mother also sends a *baya* or gift. Puja is performed in the morning. The *baya*, which consists of a variety of foodstuff, is placed on a *thali* at the place of worship where a *chowk* (square) has been decorated. A idol or a picture of Parvati is also installed at the *chowk.* The evenings are set aside for singing and dancing.

KARTIK FAIR

The Kartik Cultural Festival of Haryana is the result of the consolidated effort of Haryana Tourism and a number of allied agencies. Prominent among those were Ministry of Tourism and Department of

Culture of the Government of India, Department of Youth Affairs and Sports of the Government of India, Department of Cultural Affairs (Haryana), Development Commissioners-Handlooms and Handicrafts, North Zone Cultural Centre, North Central Cultural Centre, Nehru Yuva Kendra Sangathan and Ballabhgarh Development and Beautification Society.

Kartik Cultural Festival Mela : It was planned with the express view of promoting fort ambience, martial arts and the rich repertoire of both classical Indian music and dance, matching it with an equally rich variety of folk theatre. The festival has given a new life to dying folk arts, martial arts and worked to bring traditional folk dances and music on the national stage.

The Kartik Cultural Festival was held at Nahar Singh Mahal that lies on Ballabhgarh town. The fort, the venue of the festival, was built by the forefathers of Raja Nahar Singh in around 1739 AD. Raja Nahar Singh, after whom, the palace is named, ascended the throne in 1829 AD. The Raja was a young king of the empire of the last Mughal emperor, Bahadur Shah Zafar. He gave up his life fighting for the cause of the nation in the First War Independence .

The Palace of Nahar Singh was identified for beautification by the Government of Haryana and restored to its original glory by a well-known team of experts—Francis Nacziarg and Aman Nath. They had worked on many such restoration projects. The palace is an outstanding specimen of architectural design. In terms of architectural pattern, the palace carries a reflection of the finesse of other palaces and forts of Bharatpur.

Chaitra Chaudas Mela

It is held annually in Pehowa, which has the holy Saraswati tank, also called Saraswati Teertha or Prithudak Teertha. The Teertha also finds mention in the ancient Hindu texts. At this place, the Chaitra Chaudas Fair is held during the spring season. Pilgrims, both Sikhs and Hindus, flock to this place to offer *pindas* for their ancestors. It is claimed that at in this holy spot, Yudhishthira had offered *pindas* in memory of all those relatives who were killed in the Mahabharata war. Pilgrims take bath in the Saraswati tank during this fair.

Sili Sate Fair

It is held to worship Sitamata.

Nirjala Akadashi Fair

It is organised in the month of Jaishtha. The women keep fast and abstain from drinking water.

Madlia Navami

It is celebrated at the beginning of the rainy season.

FESTIVALS OF THE MUSLIMS

Eid-ul-Zuha

It is celebrated by the Muslim brothers and sisters of the State with fervour and delight.

Eid-ul-Fitr

It is celebrated after the month of Ramzan by the Muslim residents of the State.

Muharram

It is observed every year to mourn over the death of Hazrat Hassan Hussain, the brother of Hazrat Imam Hussain.

FESTIVALS OF THE SIKHS

Guru Parvas

The Sikh community celebrates many *parvas* in Haryana. The birthdays of Guru Nanak, Guru Gobind Singh and Guru Arjan Dev are celebrated with devotion and religious fervour. Processions are taken out in various cities and townships of Haryana on such occasions. The *paath* of *Shri Guru Granth Sahib* starts early in the morning. Sikh devotees listen to the paath. At 12 p.m. in the noon, the *bhog* ceremony is held. Later, in the evening, people visit markets and their relatives in a bid to sustain the supremacy of the religious devotion of the Gurus. Sweets, *langars* and other religious processions are common. In many cities, processions are also taken out on the eves of such birthdays.

The martyrdom days of Guru Tegh Bahadur and Guru Arjan Dev are also celebrated in the entire State. *Akhand Paath* and processions are common on such occasions. Further, some devotees Organise *Chhabils* and *langar* and serve sweetened milk and food to the masses. The cities and towns of Panipat, Kurukshetra, Rohtak, Ambala cantonment, Jind and Sonepat are the major centres of attraction on such occasions, though such ceremonies are organised by the Sikhs throughout the State.

FESTIVALS OF THE CHRISTIANS

Christmas

The limited number of Christians does not deter them from celebrating Christmas in the State. These brothers and sisters pray in the churches and seek the blessings of Jesus Christ on twenty-fifth day of December every year. Mass is held in churches on twice a day.

Good Friday

This day is celebrated in the month of April by Christians of Haryana. Mass and fasting are two main events of this day.

CHAPTER 12

FAMOUS PERSONALITIES

INTRODUCTION

Haryana has given birth to famous leaders, scientists, politicians and social workers during the recent times. Since the days of the Mahabharata, this land has given famous thinkers, warriors and statesmen who changed the course of history during their respective eras. Among the ancient personalities, Karna, Bhishma, Arjuna, Yudhishthira are particularly noteworthy. During the modern times, several personalities of Haryana affected the national and global history with their sagacity, wisdom and dedicated actions. The lives of few of them are being discussed in this chapter.

CHAUDHARY DEVI LAL

Chaudhary Devi Lal was born to Shugna Devi and Chaudhary Lekh Ram on Sept. 25, 1914 in Teja Khera village of Sirsa district. Chaudhary Lekh Ram was a wealthy landlord of Chautala who owned 2,750 bighas of land. Chaudhary Devi Lal, whose original name was Devi Dayal, received education up to middle standard and then got training in wrestling from 'Akhara' of Badal village in Punjab.

On 8 Oct., 1930 he received rigorous imprisonment for one year for taking part in Salt Movement. He was sent to Hissar Jail and Lahore Jail. He took part in the movement of 1932 and was kept in Sadar Delhi Thana. In 1938, he was selected as a delegate of All India Congress Committee. In March, 1938, his elder brother, Chaudhary Sahib Ram was elected as an M.L.A. in a by-election on the Congress party's ticket. In January, 1940, Chaudhary Sahib Ram courted arrest as a *satyagrahi* in the presence of Chaudhary Devi Lal and over ten thousand people. He was fined Rs. 100 and sentenced to a nine-month imprisonment.

Chaudhary Devi Lal was arrested on 5th October, 1942 and kept in jail for 2 years for taking part in Quit India Movement (1942). Therefore, in 1942, Chaudhary Lekh Ram's both sons, Chaudhary Sahib Ram and Chaudhary Devi Lal, were in Multan jail for taking part in the freedom struggle. Chaudhary Devi Lal was released from prison in October, 1943 and he got his elder brother Chaudhary Sahib Ram released on parole. In August, 1944, Sir Chhotu Ram, the then revenue minister, visited Chautala village. He, along with Lajpat Rai Alakhpura, made efforts too woo both Chaudhary Sahib Ram and Chaudhary Devi Lal to desert the Congress and join the Unionist Party. But both the workers refused to leave the Congress party. After independence, he started farmer's movement and was arrested along with his 500 workers. After some time, the then Chief Minister, Dr. Gopi Chand Bhargava, made an agreement and the Muzzara Act was amended.

He was elected as a member of Punjab Assembly in 1952 and as Congress President of Punjab in 1956. He played an active and decisive role in forming Haryana as a separate state. In 1958, he was elected from Sirsa. In 1971, he left the Congress after being its member for 39 years. He was elected in 1974 from Rori constituency against the Congress. In 1975, Indira Gandhi declared emergency, and Chaudhary Devi Lal, along with all the opposition leaders, was sent to jail for 19 months in Hissar Jail and Mahendragarh fort. In 1977 emergency ended and general elections were held. He was elected on Janata Party's ticket. He became the Chief Minister of Haryana. He remained a member of Parliament from 1980 to 1982 and also Member of the State Assembly from 1982 to 1987. He formed Lok Dal and started Nyaya Yuddh under Haryana Sangharsh Samiti and became popular among masses. In state elections (1987), the alliance led by Chaudhary Devi Lal won a record victory winning 85 seats in the 90 member house. Congress was routed in the State winning only 5 seats. Chaudhary Devi Lal became the Chief Minister of Haryana for the second time. In parliamentary elections (1989), he was elected from Rohtak. Consequently, he became the Deputy Prime Minister of India. He was elected to the Rajya Sabha in

August, 1998. He died on 6 April, 2001.

Mr. Devi Lal fought against the British rule. After independence, he matured as a leader of farmers of India. During his tenure as Chief Minister of Haryana, he made several decisions, which showed how much close he was to the masses. He was so much popular among people that they used to call him *Tau*. Haryana's economy is continuously gaining strength and his heading towards new heights of development. The Gross State Domestic Product (GSDP) in real terms had recorded a growth of 6.0 per cent during 1998-99, which was mainly due to recovery in the agriculture sector. The structural composition of economy has witnessed significant changes since the formation of Haryana as a separate State. There has been a considerable improvement in manufacturing sector, which occupies the second important place in the economy next only to agriculture and allied sectors. Its contribution to the economy has increased from 18.9 per cent during 1993-94 to 21.3 per cent during 1998-99, reflecting healthy signs of industrialization in the State. The share of secondary sector, which includes manufacturing, has also increased from 24.3 per cent during 1993-94 to 26.3 per cent in 1998-99.

It is a matter of pride that today it ranks first in the whole country in the production of passenger cars, motor cycles, tractors, sanitary wares, GI Pipes and scientific instruments. During the last three decades, the number of large and medium units has gone up in the State from 162 to 1023. The State has been able to attract sizable investments from multinational companies, large business houses, foreign investors, Non-Resident Indians etc. The State has become the home of more than 530 projects with foreign technical/financial collaborations. Some of these are Maruti Udyog, Hero Honda, Alcatel, Escorts, Sony India, Whirlpool India, Pro-agro PGS India, Bharti Telecom, Perfetti India, TDT Copper, Carrier Aircon etc. Some major units in the public sector are HMT Ltd., National Fertilizers Ltd., Bharat Electronics Ltd., IDPL etc. The latest addition to this clique is the Rs. 6000-crore oil refinery set up by Indian Oil Corporation in Panipat district.

Since the commencement of economic liberalization and de-licensing policy of Government of India in the year 1991, 2313

Industrial Entrepreneur Memoranda (IEMs) have been filed for setting up industrial units in Haryana. These projects would mobilise an investments of Rs. 24021 crore. Out of these, 1128, IEMs have been implemented and 140 projects are at various stages of implementation. Despite recession in the industry, Haryana is at sixth position in the country, so far as filing of IEMs is concerned. Only five states of Maharashtra, Gujarat, Uttar Pradesh, Tamil Nadu and Andhra Pradesh, which are very big in size and have plenty of natural resources, are ahead of Haryana. The percentage of implementation of IEMs in Haryana is about 48 per cent against an all-India average of about 35 per cent. Haryana has also made remarkable progress in the field of exports. Exports from Haryana have increased from Rs. 4.5 crore in 1967-68 to more than Rs. 68,032 crore in the year 2013-14.

LALA LAJPAT RAI

Lajpat Rai was born on 28 January, 1865 at village Dhudike in Ferozepur district of Punjab. His father, Munshi Radha Krishan Azad, was a great scholar of Persian and Urdu. Lalaji's mother, Shrimati Gulab Devi, a strict religious lady, inculcated strong morals values in her children. Lalaji was brought up in a family background that allowed freedom of having different faiths and beliefs. Since childhood, he had a desire to serve his country and her people. So, he took a pledge to liberate her from foreign rule.

In 1884, his father was transferred to Rohtak and Lala Lajpat Rai came along with him. He became the Secretary of Arya Samaj in Rohtak. In 1886, he passed the law examination and started his practice in Rohtak. Then, he moved to Hissar where some of his friends were also practising law. Lalaji's early legal practice at Hissar was very successful. He was elected to the Hissar municipality as a member and later, as its Secretary. Besides practising, Lalaji collected funds for Daya Nand College and attended Arya Samaj functions. After the death of Swami Dayanand, Lalaji, along with his associates, toiled to develop the Anglo-Vedic College. He came in contact with all the important Arya Samajis there.

In Hissar, Lalaji started attending the meetings of the Congress Party and became its active worker in the Hissar-Rohtak region. When the Lieutenant Governor visited Hissar, Lalaji pleaded that the welcome address be presented to him should be in Urdu. To satisfy the British officer, a speech had already been prepared in English. Lalaji's suggestion made everyone nervous. But without a trace of fear, he presented the address in Urdu and thereby, invited the wrath of the British.

Lala Lajpat Rai shifted to Lahore in 1892. He provided service to the famine relief efforts during the famines of 1897 and 1899. He mobilized the students of DAV College and went to Bikaner and other areas of Rajasthan to rescue destitute children, he brought such children to Lahore. He believed, "A nation that does not protect its own orphan children cannot command respect at the hands of other people." When people fleeing the famine reached Lahore, they spent their first night at Lalaji's house.

In 1898, Lalaji curtailed his legal practice and vowed to devote all his energy for the nation. The Kangra district of Punjab suffered destruction in the earthquake of 1905. Lalaji was there once again, organizing relief programmes to take people out of debris.

His activities were multifarious. He was an ardent social reformer. He founded the Indian Home Rule League of America in October, 1917 in New York. A year later, he also set up, with himself as the Director of the Indian Information Bureau in New York, which aimed to serve as a publicity organization for India. Lala Ji returned to India on 20 February, 1920 as a great hero.

He joined Gandhi's Non-Cooperation Movement. In Punjab, under Lajpat Rai's leadership, this movement spread like wild fire in the province. Soon, he came to be known as 'The Lion of Punjab' or *Punjab Kesri*. He travelled far and wide in India and his eloquence brought hundreds of people to the Congress fold. His writings and speeches were both hard hitting and effective. He was a crusader, who had no fear and championed every worthy cause with great zeal.

His love for service was insatiable. He founded educational institutions. He befriended the suppressed classes. In the political field, he was indispensable. Lala Lajpat Rai's supreme sacrifice came when he led a procession in Lahore on 30 October, 1928 to boycott the Simon Commission. The procession was sought to be broken up by the police the police and Lajpat Rai received lathi blows. While Lalaji tried his level best to keep the demonstration peaceful, the police targeted him and wounded him on his chest. The people were enraged at this insult and held a meeting the same evening. Lalaji, though in intense pain, gave a speech and declared "...every blow aimed at me is a nail in the coffin of British Imperialism..."

He recovered from the wounds left by the British but he remained emotionally scared at the brutality of the civilized British. Why had he been specifically targeted by the British? Why had they lathi-charged against a peaceful gathering? These thoughts tortured his spirit till the very end. Lalaji died on 17 November, 1928 of heart failure.

OM PRAKASH CHAUTALA

Mr. Om Prakash Chautala is the former Chief Minister of Haryana. He had assumed the office of Chief Minister of Haryana record five times. Born on 1 January, 1935 at village Chautala in Dabwali tehsil of Sirsa district, he had his education at his village and later on at Sangria and Dabwali. Being a son of Chaudhary Devi Lal, he developed a passion for politics at an early age.

Mr. Chautala successfully organized *Nyaya Yuddh* the call for which was given by Chaudhary Devi Lal under the aegis of the Haryana Sangharsh Samiti. Its aim was to provide justice to people. He also organized huge public meetings like Haryana Bachao, Samast Haryana and Kisan Rally in different parts of the State to protest against lawlessness and corruption prevalent in the state.

Mr. Chautala was elected to the State assembly seven times in 1970, 1990, 1993, 1996, 2000, 2005 and 2009. He resigned from Haryana Legislative Assembly on 1 November, 1995 in protest against the failure of the erstwhile to safeguard the interests of people of Haryana on the issues of Yamuna water and pumping of flood affected areas. He defended Haryana's case in the Ravi-Beas water and territorial disputes.

Mr. Chautala had served the state five times as Chief minister. He become the Chief Minister on 2 December, 1989 and on 12 July, 1990. He became the Chief Minister again on 22 March, 1991, 24 July, 1999 and finally on 2 March, 2000.

He also remained a member of the Rajya Sabha from 1987 to 1990. He became the leader of opposition on 24 May, 1996 in the ninth Haryana Vidhan Sabha. He was elected as the President of the Haryana unit of Indian National Lok Dal in 1999. He remained the President of Haryana state Janata Dal and National General Secretary of the Samajwadi Janata Party. He also served as Secretary General of the Samjwadi Janata Party and Chief of the Kisan Kamgar Cell of All India Lok Dal.

Mr. Chautala has also attended several national and international conferences. He has toured extensively in the country and abroad. The countries visited by him include the United States, the UK, Germany, France, Spain, Portugal, Australia, Japan, Holland, Pakistan, Canada, New Zealand, Singapore, Greece, etc.

During his all tenure from as Chief Minister, Mr. Chautala had laid emphasis on transforming the economy of Haryana and made it free from floods. His government had also taken steps in evolving progressive policies concerning the industry, particularly in the field of Information Technology.

RAM LAL KAPIL DEV NIKHANJ

Kapil Dev, the Haryana Hurricane, was born on 6 January, 1959 in Chandigarh. Kapil Dev played his first competitive game of cricket at the age of 13 years. In Chandigarh, he used to be a regular spectator to watch the inter-sector matches. One Sunday, the team of sector 16 fell short by one player and Kapil, who had gone to watch the match, was taken in as a replacement. The sector 16 team boasted of 3 players who had played Ranji Trophy cricket for Haryana. The young Kapil Dev impressed them with his attitude and talent and became a regular member of the side.

His family noticed his passion for the game and encouraged him to take up the game seriously. His elder brother also encouraged him. At the age 14, Kapil started playing for DAV School and College. He was coached by Desh Prem Azad who was the only well-known cricket coach in Chandigarh. At the age of 15, Kapil Dev was invited to attend a live-in coaching camp in Bombay. The camp held at the Cricket Club of India was conducted by Hemu Adhikari who also was a former Indian Test cricketer.

Kapil Dev made his first class debut in November, 1975 at the age of 17. He played for his home state (Haryana) against the neighbouring state of Punjab. His performance in this match was very impressive as he got 6 wickets for just 39 runs. In another top class performance he picked up 8 wickets for 36 runs against Jammu and Kashmir. His 7 wickets for 20 runs against Bengal and 8 wickets for 38 runs against services are considered to be one of the best bowling performances in the Indian domestic cricket.

Kapil Dev made his Test debut on 16 October, 1978 at Faisalabad against Pakistan. His bowling in the first innings was disappointing as he had figures 0/71 from 16 overs. In the second innings, he bowled better and got his first test wicket—that of Sadiq Mohammed. India was comprehensively beaten in that series but it saw the emergence of Kapil Dev as a talented fast bowler and all-rounder. He learned a lot in this series and modified his action on the advice of Sunil Gavaskar and started bowling from close to the stumps to make his out swingers more effective and lethal. He also performed with the bat and made some useful scores in the middle order. His best batting performance was the innings of 59 in 48 balls, which included two sixes and eight fours in the third Test at Karachi.

Till he retired in mid nineties, Kapil Dev was one of the leading all-rounders in the game. He held the record for the most numbers of Test and One-day wickets for quite a long time till Courtney Walsh and Wasim Akaram took over. Captaincy of India to win the World Cup in 1983 was the highlight of his illustrious career. Other highlights included leading India to a 2-0 series win against a strong English side in England in 1986.

His unbeaten innings of 175 runs against Zimbabwe in the World Cup in 1983 when India were tottering at 17 runs for 5 wickets and his 4 successive sixes of Eddie Hemmings in the first innings of the Lords test in 1990 to get the 24 runs needed to avoid the follow on are now a part of cricketing folk lore. His superhuman efforts with the ball in the Melbourne Test of 1980 against Australia in which, he bowled nonstop for 3 hours to bowl out Australia after taking pain, killing injections for a torn hamstring and a pulled groin muscle, is still remembered with awe.

Kapil Dev remained India's top strike bowler for almost 15 years. His extraordinary test match figures of more than 5000 runs, 434 wickets and 64 catches show that he was a world class cricketer and rare all-rounder. He remained away from the game for some time after he retired and concentrated on improving his golf. He became the coach of the Indian Cricket team in 1999.

RAO TULA RAM

Rao Tula Ram was one of the most important leaders of the 1857 Revolt. He was born on 9 December, 1825 in the well known Rao family of village Rampura (Rewari). His father's name was Puran Singh and his mother's name was Gyan Kaur. He was educated according to the customs prevalent customs during those times. He learned Persian, Urdu, Hindi and English. In November, 1839, Rao Tula Ram ascended the throne on the death of his father.

In 1857, on hearing the news of rebellion at Meerut and other places, the people of the Rewari rose up in revolt. In the Rewari area, Rao Tula Ram led the rebels. His cousin, Gopal Dev, also stood by him. The forefathers of the Raos had helped the Marathas in 1803 in their fight against the British and as a result, when the latter came out as successful in the struggle, they confiscated their Jagir and gave instead an *istamarari* grant of about 58 villages. This was a great blow to the Raos as this incident shattered their status and dignity and made them unhappy with British Raj. On 17 May, 1857, the Raos went to the tehsil headquarters at Rewari with four to five hundred followers and deposed the tehsildar and thanedar. They took away cash from the tehsil treasury, all the government buildings in their possession and proclaimed, under the sanction of Emperor Bahadur Shah, their rule over the pargana of Rewari, Bhora and Shahjahanpur. For their headquarters, they chose Rampura, a small fortified village, one mile south-west of Rewari. Tula Ram, the elder Rao, became Raja and Gopal Dev became his Commander-in-Chief.

After assuming charge, Tula Ram organized the revenue department and collected revenue and taxes. He took donations and loans from the mahajans of Rewari. He raised a force (about five thousand men) and set up a large workshop in the fort of Rampura where a substantial number of guns, gun-carriage, and other small arms and ammunition were manufactured. The Rao enforced law and order and defended his state from external attacks. These activities pleased Bahadur Shah and he confirmed Rao Tula Ram in his Jagirs of Rewari, Bhora and Shahjahanpur. Tula Ram, in return, rendered all possible help to Emperor Bahadur Shah and those rebels waging war against the British in Delhi. He sent Rs. 45,000 through General Bakht Khan at such a critical time when non-payment of the salaries to the sepoys had caused great insecurity and anxiety, though this small sum did not improve the situation. The Raos also supplied forces to Delhi, along with large quantities of other commodities.

But this help could not protect Delhi, which fell to the British on 20 September, 1857. Soon after, Brigadier General Showers led out a column (from Delhi) of 1,500 men with a light field battery, 18 two-pound guns and two small mortars, to attack and destroy Rao Tula Ram and his followers. The column had light skirmish with some Rewari *sowars* on 5 October at Pataudi, which is at a distance of 37 miles from Delhi. In the words of Hudson, who accompanied the column, "They fired at our advance and bolted at speed." The column's next attack was on Rewari, which was still held by Rao Tula Ram. The situation was serious and the Rao foresaw that a fight with the British forces in the mud fort of Rampura, the changed circumstances after the fall of Delhi, would result in the complete destruction of his army without any serious loss to the British. So, he left his fort before the arrival of Brigadier General.

The British column reached Rewari on 6 October. The fort of Rewari (Rampura) was taken without any opposition. Immediately after the occupation of the fort of Rewari, Brigadier General Showers sent a messenger to Tula Ram telling him that if he surrendered along with guns and arms, he would be treated on merits. But Tula Ram turned down this inducement of the British. The authorities at Delhi were alarmed by these developments. They sent a strong column comprising about 1,500 men, under Colonel Garrard, on 10 November, 1857. The column reached Rewari three days later. They occupied the abandoned fort of Rampura. Here they were joined by two squadrons of the Carabineers.

After taking rest for a few days at Rewari (Ramupra), Colonel Gerrard proceeded to Narnaul via Kanaud and reached there in the evening. In the night, he was joined by the Haryana Field Force. On 16 November, Gerrard marched to Narnaul. As the track was sandy, the column reached Nasibpur, a small village, two miles due north-west of Narnaul and halted for rest. The rebel force, having abandoned their strong fort in the centre of the town pounded on them. Rao Tula Ram's first charge was irresistible and the British forces scattered before them. The Patiala Infantry and the Multani Horse on the left side of the British were completely disheartened. The Guides and the Carabineers came to save those who were beaten.

The English fire, especially of the artillery, was too much for the rebels. The Guides and the Carabineers, under the cover of the artillery fire, launched a heavy attack. Next, the First Bengal Fusiliers, swooping upon the weak rebel artillery, captured some of their guns. This encouraged the British cavalry on the right and they pressed through the Indian ranks. Hence, they successfully overpowered them on the right and in the centre. But soon the situation took an unexpected turn when Colonel Gerrard, the British Commandant, was mortally wounded by a musket ball. As a result the British too were demoralized. Taking full advantage of the circumstances, Rao Tula Ram swooped down upon them. The British could not stand the charge and the Multani Horse fled away in bewilderment. The forces of Rao Tula Ram recaptured their guns and inflicted heavy losses upon the enemy. The right and the left wings of the British forces were thrown into chaos.

Appreciating the gravity of the situation, Major Caulfield, the officiating British Commandant, ordered his artillery to start heavy bombardment. He also order the cavalry and infantrymen to charge straight on with full force into their front ranks. Rao Tula Ram's forces fought back furiously and remained firm on their grounds. The British artillery fire broke their backbone and split their forces into two parts—one engaged in the battle and the other one fleeing to go out of the range of the British guns. Meanwhile, Kishan Singh and Ram Lal, the two best commanders, received musket shots and died. This disheartened Rao Tula Ram's forces and they retreated. The British resumed their forward movements until they came to a dry bed of a stream, which flew between Nasibpur and Narnaul. The British guns were unable to cross the stream owing to its sandy bed. Hence, they moved towards their right and took up a position near the Horse Artillery guns. The 23rd Punjab Infantry and Patiala Infantry, with other units of the cavalry, crossed the stream and advanced towards the camp.

The heavy shelling of the artillery and infantry fire confused Rao Tula Ram; his soldiers ran pell-mell in all the directions. Mostly, they retreated to the town hid themselves in the buildings. The pursuit of the fleeting soldiers was quick and inexorable and they were very soon driven out of the town after some fighting. Rao Tula Ram lost the day and when the Sun went down, there remained none in Narnaul except heaps of corpses here and there. Though Tula Ram and Abdus Samad Khan escaped, Rao Kishan Singh, Ram Lal, Samad Khan's son and many other top- ranking officers were killed in this action. The British captured nine guns and other arms. The total loss on the British side was 70 killed and 45 wounded. They lost their commander, Colonel Gerrard and Captain Wallace, while Lieutenants Graije, Kennedy and Pearse were severely wounded.

The Battle of Narnaul was undoubtedly one of the most decisive battles of the Uprising of 1857. The English felt jubilant over their success on this confrontation, for it resulted in the end of the crucial period of struggle on the Haryana region and northern Rajasthan.

After the battle, Rao Tula Ram moved into Rajasthan. Then, he joined Tantya Tope's forces for one year. After the British proclamation of promising unconditional pardon amnesty and oblivion to all offences against the British to all except those who directly or indirectly took part in the murder of British subjects (issued on 1 November 1858). He sent a petition to the Governor General, Lord Canning, on 24 December, 1858. He stated that he considered himself to be an offender but as he looked up to the government as his protector. He begged to solicit that an inquiry might be directed to be instituted and that he as well as his followers be pardoned. He was refused pardon, for he was chief instigator and prime mover of the revolt. He therefore, left India, in 1862. He went to Iran and then to Afghanistan in the winter of 1862. There, he died of dysentery at Kabul on 23 September 1863 at a young age of 38.

His cousin, Gopal Dev, also left Narnaul and took asylum at the residence of one of his relatives at Udairamsar, a village in Bikaner state. He stayed there in perfect secrecy for four years. Offers of surrender were made to him through his friends by the Deputy Commissioner of Gurgaon but he shunned all enquiries. In consequence, his jagir of 41 villages was confiscated. He died in 1862. With the end of the revolt, the vengeance of the British started. Hundreds of people were hanged or shot dead and their villages were burned. Rao Tula Ram and Gopal Dev were dispossessed of their *Jagirs.*

SIR CHHOTU RAM

Sir Chhotu Ram was born on 24 Nov. 1881 in Ghari Sampla in Rohtak district. Debts and litigation compounded the problems of his father, Chaudhary Sukhi Ram, who died in 1905. Chhotu Ram joined a primary school in January, 1891 and passed out four years later. He studied for his middle school examination in Jhajjar, which was at a distance of 12 miles from his village. He left Jhajjar to get himself enrolled in the Christian Mission School in Delhi. When the father and son approached the bania at Sampla mandi for a loan, the bania flung a fan at the father to cool his large perspiring semi-naked body. This and other humiliating incidents left an indelible mark on his personality.

He passed his intermediate examination in 1903 and then, enrolled in Saint Stephen's College from where, he graduated in 1905. It was his stay at this college that he was drawn towards the Arya Samaj. He studied Sanskrit rather than English, the preferred subject of most of the students. In 1905, he worked for Raja Rampal Singh of Kalakankar in the United Provinces, but left the job within a month. He returned to Kalakankar in 1907 and worked for a few months as the Editor of the English newspaper, *Hindustan* and then, proceeded to study law at Agra. He obtained his law degree in 1911. In an article published in the college magazine in 1907, he reflected on the ways to improve the life in rural areas and curb the monopoly of the village bania, whom he called "the incarnation of Shylock in our times."

While teaching at Saint John's High School and studying law at Agra, Chhotu Ram studied the local conditions in the divisions of Agra and Meerut. In 1911, he became the honorary Superintendent of the

Jat Boarding House in Agra. In 1912, he set up his legal practice along with Chaudhary Lal Chand. Both became involved in recruiting soldiers during the First World War. Owing to their efforts, the Jats provided about half of the total recruits in the Rohtak region. Recruitment figures rose from 6,245 in January, 1915 to 22,144 in November, 1918. Sir Chhotu Ram established the Jat Sabha at Rohtak in 1912. He founded educational institutions, including the Jat Arya Vedic Sanskrit High School in Rohtak and donated the first year's revenue of five squares of colony land to the school after the First World War; this colony land was given as a grant to him. The Jat Arya Samaj of the Rohtak-Hissar region arranged a meeting in Rohtak on 1 April, 1913 to discuss the establishment of a Jat school; the same established on 7 September, 1913.

He encouraged Jat students to join the Young Jat Association and study at the Jat School in Rohtak and at Saint Stephan's College and provided support to them. He exhorted his friends to wear the sacred thread to establish their identity. He attached most social significance to the thread and saw it as a sign of *dwija* or twice-born. Between 1916 and 1919, he wrote against the *bahis* (account books) and the cruel manner in which, moneylenders obtained decrees against poor and ignorant farmers. Sir Chhotu Ram worked as the President of the Rohtak District Congress Committee from 1916 to 1920. He resigned on 8 November, 1920 because as per his version, the Congress ignored the rights and claims of the rural population. He made it clear that if he had to make a choice between on urban Hindu and a Muslim farmer, he would always sympathize with the latter. He also thought that a disadvantaged class, like the Jats, could not afford to fight against the government (and the Congress essentially stood for anti-government movements) He emerged as the sole spokesman of Jat interests by this time.

After the war, Sir Chhotu Ram extended his activities beyond Rohtak. He set out to mobilize Jats in present-day Rajasthan and western UP, where they were already organized by the Jat Sabha. During this period, he developed links with Jat and Arya Samaji leaders such as Chaudhary Piru Singh, Manager of the Gurukul in Matindu. Soon, he became Piru Singh's legal advisor. His association with the Gurukul also brought him in contact with Swami Shraddhanand and he began visiting him in Delhi. He tried to ensure that British did not impose restriction on recruiting Jats in the army. He was convinced that recruitment to the army was economically beneficial and helped Jats to emphasize their Kshatriya status. In 1925, he organized a *Maha Sabha Jalsa* at Pushkar in Rajasthan, momentous event in Jat history. In 1934, he organized a rally to 10,000 Jat peasants in Sikar in Rajasthan to launch an anti-rent campaign. The campaigners donned the sacred thread, made of offerings of ghee and read from the Satyarth Prakash. The rally was a major event and enhanced the stature of Sir Chotu Ram.

After 1920, Sir Chhotu Ram tried to create a non-sectarian peasant group consciousness. He was associated with the Punjab Zamindar Central Association, established in 1917 to advance the interests of Hindu and Sikh Jat agriculturalists. This was the first step towards the formation of homogenous rural block based on economics rather than on religious interests. The formation of the Unionist Party (Zamindara League) in 1923, a cross-communal alliance of Hindus Jats and Muslim agriculturists (committed to the Land Alienation Act of 1900) was the culmination of this process.

He asserted that the poverty of the peasantry was the sole cause of indebtedness. He challenged official assumptions on overspending on marriage, death and festivals. He asserted that land revenue was the principal cause of indebtedness and ruin. He rejected the use of co-operatives as tool to curb moneylenders. He argued that market forces would not release the peasantry from debts. Nor did he agree with Mahatma Gandhi and Jawaharlal Nehru who regarded the peasants as a passive identity. He saw the peasant as the agent as well as the beneficiary of change.

CHAPTER 13

TRANSPORT

INTRODUCTION

The main modes of transport in the state are roads and railway tracks. Haryana does not have well-defined facilities for facilitating air traffic through its cities. Hence, people depend mostly on buses and trains for their movement as well as for the movement of cargo. Let us briefly study the main transport modes of the state.

ROADS

Roads of Haryana are a trend setter in the field of passenger transport. It has total road length of 31,422 (31-10-2023) kilometres. The remotest parts of the state are linked with metalled roads. Its modern bus fleet of 3,369 buses (31-10-2023) covers a distance of 10.57 lakh kilometres per day. About 5.88 lakh passengers travel by these buses everyday. It was the first state in the country to introduce luxury video coaches. The State Government proposes to construct an express highway and free ways for speedier vehicular traffic.

Government encourages private sector investment in this sector for upgradation of roads, construction of ROB and BOT including four-lane ROB. The length of the national highway (state PWD + NHAI) in Haryana is 3,391 km till 31-10-2023.

Details of Highway and Roads (Upto 31-10-2023)

National Highway : 3,391 km
State Highway: 1,659 km

Major District Roads: 1,375 km

Other District Roads: 24,997 km

Haryana Roadways is amongst the best run State Road Transport Undertakings of the Country. The authorized fleet of Haryana Roadways is 5,300 Buses. At present (as on 31.10.2023), it has a fleet of 3,369 buses which are being operated from 24 Depots and 13 Sub Depots. Haryana Roadways buses operate an average of 10.57 lakh kms daily and carry an average of 5.88 lakh passengers per day. The norm of drivers and conductors for ordinary buses in Haryana Roadways is 1:1.4 respectively. The performance of Haryana Roadways has been noteworthy on parameters like average age of fleet, vehicle productivity, staff productivity and fuel efficiency are amongst the best and accident rate are amongst the lowest.

Haryana Roadways has won the Union Transport Minister's Trophy and cash award of ₹ 1.50 lakh each year for lowest accident rate among all the State Road Transport Undertakings in the country during the years 2005-06, 2006-07, 2007-08, 2009-10, 2012-13 & 2013-14.

RAILWAY LINES

The total length of railway lines in Haryana is 3,224 kilometres. The major railway stations are Ambala Cantonment, Panipat, Jind, Hissar, Rohtak, Faridabad, Bhiwani and Rewari. There are broad gauge railway tracks in the state, through the Delhi-Jaipur reach also has a meter-gauge railway line. It passes through Pataudi.

Haryana is well connected through the rail network. Under the NCR, there is already a proposal to provide rail corridor connecting towns around Delhi to link the major satellite towns like Faridabad, Gurugram, Bahadurgarh, Kundli etc. Similarly, there is also a proposal to provide rapid mass transportation system between Delhi and these satellite towns. The major railway routes passing through Haryana are :

(A) Amritsar-Delhi
(B) Rewari-Ahmedabad
(C) Bhiwani- Rohtak-Delhi
(D) Ambala-Ferozpur
(E) Delhi-Ferozpur
(F) Kalka-Jodhpur
(G) Kalka-Howrah
(H) Amritsar- Howrah
(I) Delhi-Shimla

DELHI METRO ROLLS TO GURUGRAM

The 14.47-km-long Huda City Centre-Qutab Minar corridor of the Delhi Metro railway connecting neighbouring Gurugram with Delhi was thrown open to the public on June 21, 2010 ending the long wait of the residents of the millennium city for a world class transport system connecting them to the nation's Capital. The line has been extended to Central Secretariat in New Delhi and is now connected to Jahangirpuri-Central Secretariat Line. It becomes the longest metro route in NCR.

RAPID METRO IN GURUGRAM

The 5.1 km stretch of Rapid Metro Rail Gurugram Limited (RMGL), India's first fully privately funded Metro Rail system, was opened to the public on November 14, 2013 evoking a lukewarm response from the commuters. The Rapid Metro connects cyber city, National Highway-8 and the existing Sikanderpur metro station on the Yellow Line of the Delhi Metro and mostly caters to those working in the software companies and some residential areas as well.

METRO TO FARIDABAD-BALLABHGARH

Prime Minister Narendra Modi has flagged-off the Delhi-Faridabad Metro Line on September 6, 2015. The extension of the Delhi Metro connects Badarpur to Raja Nahar Singh (Ballabhgarh).

AIRWAYS

Civil Aviation Department, Haryana has 5 Airstrips in the State at Pinjore, Karnal, Hisar, Bhiwani and Narnaul. Presently two Flying Training Centres of Haryana Institute of Civil Aviation (HICA) are established at Karnal and Pinjore where flying training is provided to the boys and girls.

CHAPTER 14

FAUNA AND FLORA

INTRODUCTION

The State of Haryana is rich in terms of varieties of fauna and flora, various types of animals and birds are found here. Further, a large variety of trees, flowers and plants is also available here. These animals and birds are a delight of the veterinary doctors, scientists and researchers of the related fields. The trees, plants, shrubs and vegetation are interesting specimens for research, commercial use and parts of state's recreation. In this Chapter, we shall discuss vital parts of fauna and flora of the state.

FAUNA

MAMMALS

Primates are represented by the Bandar (rhesus macaque) and the common Langur (presbytis entellus), carnivores found in the state are Leopard (panthera pardus), Jungle Cat (felis bengalensis), the small Indian Civet (viverricula indica), the common monogoose (herpestes edwardsi), Geedar or Jackal (canis aureus) and Indian Fox. The state has deer like the Barking Deer (muntiacus muntjak), Sambar (cervus unicolor) and antelopes like Neelgai (blue bull) and Black Busk. Most of the wild life is found in the forests of Morni Hills, Kalesar Forest and the Aravali Hills region. Birds can be seen at Sultanpur Bird Santuary and Bhindawas Bird Sanctuary.

The gray musk shrew or Chachunder (suncus murinus) and two species of bats, (the common yellow bat and the tickell's bat) are usually found in the state. The Gileheri of five-strip palm squirrel (funambulus palmarum), Sahi or Indian Porcupine (hystrix indica), the Indian Gerbil, the common house rat (rattus rattus) and the common house mouse are the common rodents in the state. Sassa the Indian Hare (Lepus nigricollis) is also found in the bushes.

BIRDS

Haryana has about 350 species of birds. The Sultanpur Bird Sanctuary (Gurgaon), Bhindawas Bird Sanctuary (Jhajjar), Bir Bara Ban Sanctuary (Jind) Kalesar Forest (Yamunanagar), Morni Hills (Panchkula), the banks of the river Yamuna and the Western Yamuna Canal and its channels are the main areas where most of these birds can be found. The following list of birds is by no means complete:

Bare-headed Goose
Graylag Goose
Mallard
Pied Bushchat Grey Bushchat
Brown Rock Chat
Crested Serpent Eagle Brahminy Kite
Shikra
Common Kestrel
Long billed Vulture
White rumped Vulture
Black Drongo
Gray Winged Biackbird
Common Crow
Racket-tailed Drongo
Greater Coucal
Koel
Himalayan Bulbul
Red-vented Bulbul
Red-whiskered Bulbul
Yellow-footed Green Pigeon
Blue Rock Pigeon
Spotted Dove
Laughing Dove
Eurasian Collared Dove
Refous Treepie
Common Hoopoe
Pheasant Tailed Jacana
Bronze Winged Jacana
Cattle Egret
Great Egret
Little Egret
Little Cormorant
Indian Cormorant
Great Cormorant
Eurasian Spoonbill Purple Her
White-breasted Waterhen
River Tern
Painted Sandgrouse
Common Moorthen
Gray Francolin
Black Francolin
Jungle Bush Quali
Rain Quali

Ruddy Shelduck
Eurasian Curlew
Indian Roller
Painted Stork
Eurasian Wigreon
Gadwall
White Ibis
Common Teal
Northern Pintail
Common Pochard
Great Thick-knee
Asian Openbill
Green Bee-eater
Chestnut-headed Bee-eater
House Swift
Darter
Red Junglefowl
Common Coot
Ruff
Black-winged Stilt
Yellow-wattled Lapwing
Red-wattled Lapwing
Greater Flamingo
Common Woodshrike
Dusky Crag Martin
Plain Martin
Common Myna
Bank Myna
Asian Pied Starling
Brahminy Myna
Red rumped Swallow
Plain Prinia
Ashy Prinia
Siberian Lesser Whitethroat
Common Tailorbird
Common Chiffchaff
Large Gray Babbler
Jungle Babbler
Oriental Pied Hornbill
Purple Sunbird
Eurasian Golden Oriole
Northern Shoveler
Black Rumped Flameback
Brown-headed Barbet
Greater Short-toed Lark
Crested Lark
Rufous-winged Lark
Red Avadavati
Red-headed Bunting
Indian Silverbill
Streaked Weaver
Baya Weaver
Paddyfield Pipit
House Sparrow
Chestnut Shouldered Petronia
Large-tailed Nightjar
Spotted Owlet
White-throated Kingfisher
Yellow-crowned Woodpecker
Black Kite
Rose-ringed Parakeet
Magpie Robin and
Blue Peafowl (National Bird of India)

Game Birds

Various types of ducks and geese such as Graylag Goose, Barehead Goose, Brahminy Duck, Common Shelduck, Pintail, Common

Teal, Mallard, Gadwall, Wigeon, Blue-winged Teal, Shoveller, Common Pochard, Ferruginous Duck and Tufted Duck can be seen at the banks of river Ghaggar during winters.

Some other ducks such as Comb Duck, Cotton Teal, Spotbill Duck and Tree Duck are found throughout the year in suitable habitats. Dabchick is also a residential bird. Other game birds like Partridges (Tittar), Black Partridge (Kala Tittar) and Quails are also common. Sand Crouse has been noted as residential (Indian Sand Grouse) as well as visitor bird. Bengal Green Pigeon is found in the vicinity of villages chiefly on Ficus trees. Blue Pigeon occurs in almost all the villages. Western Turtle Dove is a winter visitor whereas some other doves are generally found in cultivated fields.

Scavenger and Predator Birds

Pariah Kite, Brahminy Kite, White-backed Vulture, King Vulture, Tawny Eagle, Greater Spotted Eagle, White eyed-Buzzard Eagle, House Crow and Indian Jungle Crow etc. keep the state cleared of dead animals by feeding on them. Scavenger vultures feed on dead animals and keep the state clean. Predators like Black-winged Kite, Indian Shikra, Lagger Falcon, Shahin Falcon, Red-head, Merlin and Kestrel are residential birds of the state. Others, like Booted Hawk Eagle, Eastern Steppe Eagle, Pale Harrier etc. visit the state during winters. These, along with Spitted Owlet and Eagle Owl, keep a check on the population of rodent pests and various insect pests.

Colourful Birds

The common colourful birds such as Blue Jay, Northern Green Barbet, Coppersmith, Northern Golden-backed Woodpecker, Indian Golden Oriole, Large Indian Parakeet, Rose-ringed Parakeet, Pied Crested Cuckoo, Koel Common Crow, Pheasant, Kingfisher such as Small Blue Kingfisher, White Breasted Kingfisher, Indian Pied Kingfisher, Red-vented Bulbul, Indian Purple Sunbird, Lal Munia, Indian Spotted Munia and Crested Bunting etc., along with National Bird of India, the common Blue Peafowl, add beauty to the varied wildlife of the State. Besides, some other birds and different types of storks, cranes, ibis, egrets and lapwings are also found in the State.

Snakes

The poisonous snakes like the common Indian Krait, Russell's Viper, Phoosra and other snakes like Blind Snake, Indian Python, John's Sand Boa, Wolf Snake, Rat Snake and Sand Snake are found in Haryana.

Lizards

The common lizards can be seen in the houses. Kirli or Girgit is found in the lawns and hedges and attracts the attention by changing its colours. Sanda is found in sandy areas. Besides, a few other types of lizards are found in bushes and areas of thick vegetation.

Tortoises

Two species of tortoises are also found in the State.

Frogs

The common frogs found in Haryana are the Indian Bull Frog, Indian Cricket Frog, Indian Burrowing Frog and Common Toad.

Fish

The different water courses of the state abound in many species of fish. The species from the view point of food and game are the featherback Fish Parri, Katla, Mrigal, Chunni, Bata, Siriha, Ghally, Mallee, and the Snake-head fish, Dolla and Curd.

FLORA

Haryana has forest-covered land, which is about 3.63 per cent of its total area. A thorny dry deciduous forest as well as pines thorny shrubs can be found all over the state. Chief trees are Kikar or Babul (Acacia nilotica), Neem (Azadirachta indica), Shisham or Indian Rosewood (Dalbergia sissoo), Pipal or Bo Tree (Ficus religiosa), Aam or Mango (Mangifera indica), Jamun to Java plum (Syzygium cumini), Imli or Tamarind (Tamarindus indica), Barh or Banyan (Ficus indicus), Sagwan or Teak (Tectona grandis), Ber or Indian Jujube (Zizyphus mauritiana), Mitha Jal or Pillu (Salvadora indica), Khara Jal or Pillu (Salvador persica), Semul, Khejri (Prosopis cineraria), Lasura or Lehswa (Cordia dichotoma), Amla Dhak (Butea frondosa) Shahtoot or Mulberry (Morus alba atropurpurea), Eucalyptus, Amrood or Guava (Psidium guajava), Pine and Poplar.

The Kalesar forest is full of Sal trees. The Ritha tree can be found in the Morni Hills as well as in the Kalesar forest.

An important shrub species of the state is the leafless Kair or Teat (Capparis decidua). Another important plant that has religious and medicinal values, is the Tulsi. A beautiful tree is the Kachnar, whose flowers are used for many purposes. Other trees that are found in Haryana are Baheda, Tun and Bel. A carpet of grass covers the Morni Hills region which makes them excellent grazing grounds for Black Buck (Antelope cervicapra) and Neelgai or Blue Bull (Boselaphus tragocamelus Pallas). A lone Leopard (Panthera pardus) or a Striped Hyena (Hyena hyena) can be spotted there, White Foxes, Wild Boars (Sus scrofa), Mongooses (Herpestes edwardsi), Jackals (Canis aureus) and Wild Dogs (Cuon alipnus) are aplenty. A large variety of birds is found in the Sultanpur Bird Sanctuary.

Kikar

Botanical Name: Acacia nilotica (L): Kikar is a thorny small tree growing to a height of 7 m. Its life is at least 60 years. It is found widely in Haryana as well as all over India.

Taxonomy, Variation and Plasticity: Nine sub-species have been recognized. Hybridization between various sub-species occurs and has been influenced by man's capacity of seed dispersal. Within the Acacia nilotica complex, the pods are very variable.

Reproductive Biology : The yellow sweetly scented flowers are nectarless and found as round heads.

Most flowers are functionally male with a few hermaphrodites and are mainly bee-pollinated. Pods are indehiscent. Seed production is high (up to 175,000 seeds/tree) and yearly provided water is plentiful like along water courses. Leaf production and fall are affected by rainfall whereas temperature affects flowering and fruiting. Most of the leaf shedding occurs during the dry period when the tree bears green pods.

Resilience and Resistance: Species is sensitive to frost but is resistant to animal grazing, drought, fire and salinity.

Environmental Requirements: It requires water for seed germination and seeding establishment. It can regenerate under pioneer woody plants in seasonally flooding habitats and subsequently, outclass them.

Products and Uses: It is extensively used as firewood and timber. Its bark and seeds are a source of tannin while its bark, roots and flowers are used for medicinal properties. The gum is also used. Its wood is suitable for paper production. It may planted for forestry or reclamation of degraded land.

Climate : Grows in areas where the mean monthly temperature of the coldest month is above 16ºC. It tolerates a wide range of rainfall from less than 350 mm to more than 1500 mm per year.

Site Requirements : A sub-species of Acacia nilotica is indica, which is commonly found on soils with a high clay content. But in areas of higher rainfall, it may grow on deep sandy loam soil. It is found growing close to waterways along side seasonally flooded rivers.

Pests and Diseases : Many wild mammals feed on seed pods and a large number of insect species attack the mature seeds.

Neem

Botanical Name : Azadirachta indica

Common Names : Neem, Nim, Indian Lilac, Nimmi, Limbo, Limda.

Neem is a native tree of India, a tropical tree especially suited to semi-arid conditions. It is now grown in many Asian countries and in tropical regions of the western hemisphere. Neem is considered to be part of India's genetic bio-diversity. Neem is a medium-sized tree having short, straight bole, furrowed, dark brown to grey bark, and dense rounded crown of pinnate leaves. Native to India and other south Asian countries, neem is widely planted and naturalized in semi-arid areas throughout Asia and Africa. In Haryana, the neem tree is found in each and every village.

Neem is an evergreen tree of the tropics and sub-tropics. It belongs to the family Meliaceae and is becoming increasingly popular for its insect repellant traits and a unique property of inhibiting the nitrification process in the soil. In India, neem grows in plains and in areas that reach an elevation of approximately 1850 metres. It is cultivated from an elevation starting from the mean sea level up to a level of 1500 metres. Neem is tolerant to most soil types including dry, stony, shallow soils, lateritic crusts, highly leached sands and clays.

With an extensive and deep rooted system, neem can grow and flourish even in marginal and leached soils and can thrive up to an elevation of 100 metres. The neem tree flowers between February and May. The honey-scented white flowers, found in clusters, are a good source of nectar for bees. Neem fruits are green drupes, which turn golden yellow on ripening in the month of June, July and August in India.

The termite resistant neem timber is used as a building material and in making furniture and farm implements. The bark yields tannin and gum. The amber-hued-gum is used as a dye in textiles and traditional medicines. Leaves are used as fodder and green manure.

Neem derivatives such as azadirachtin, nimbicidin and a host of other compounds are now used in medicines and commercial pesticides. Many bioactive ingredients have been identified and isolated, the most important ones among them being azadirachtin and meliantriol.

The most active ingredient of neem is azadirachtin. It finds applications in neem-based pesticide formulations, which are safe, natural, bio-degradable and manageable at the farmer's level and environment-friendly, unlike chemical and synthetic pesticides, which leave behind residues that pollute air, water and soil.

CHAPTER 15

Place for Tourism

INTRODUCTION

Haryana Tourist Corporation is running 42 Tourist Complexes named after birds along the highways across the whole of the State which are extremely popular among the tourists. The total availability of the accommodation with Haryana Tourism is at present 843 AC Rooms, 13 Dormitories and 56 Conference Halls/Multipurpose Halls/Banquet Halls/ Conventional Halls etc. Moreover, Haryana Tourism has 42 restaurants, 5 fast food centres and presently 31 Bars in various tourist complexes of Haryana Tourism.

It has been decided that new projects may be taken in joint venture/ collaboration with the private sector. The joint venture will created in the following areas:

(A) Setting up of hotels/motels
(B) Health resorts/spas and beauty parlours
(C) Amusement parks, including water games
(D) Multiplex complexes
(E) Golf courses
(F) Shopping arcades

Haryana has excellent golf course facilities near the industrial estates of Gurugram and Faridabad, which can be used by investors and entrepreneurs. The State is making incessant efforts to extend and upgrade the existing infrastructure to meet the ever growing demand of entrepreneurs. Haryana had good infrastructure for investment in projects for power generation, hospitals, nursing homes, polyclinics, public schools, tourism ventures like hotels, resorts health clubs, fast food restaurant and other industries. The Haryana Government offers attractive packages of financial and fiscal incentives to the entrepreneurs interested in setting up their projects in Haryana.

The Haryana Government has set to many tourist complexes, motels and camping sites in the State to promote tourism. Haryana has one of the most successful tourist development programmes led by Haryana Tourism department. Some tourist complexes, which have a large number of visitors, are named after birds found in Haryana. Some of these places have dormitories and all of them have restaurants. Hotel Rajhans (Surajkund) and Badkhal Lake are on the Delhi Agra Highway. Krana Lake (Karnal), Skylark (Panipat), Parakeet (Pipli) and Kingfisher (Ambala) are on the Delhi-Amritsar Highway (NH1). Yadavindra Gardens at Pinjore, on the Chandigarh-Shimla road, attract tourists and visitors from India and abroad. Surkhab (Sirsa) and Flamingo (Hissar) complexes are on the Delhi-Fazilka National Highway.

PINJORE GARDENS

These also called Yadavindra Gardens, are at a distance of 20 kilometres from Chandigarh, 15 kilometres from Panchkula, on the Chandigarh-Shimla road. Taxis and buses ply regularly between Pinjore, Kalka, Panchkula and Chandigarh. Pinjore lies on the foothills of lower Shivalik ranges. The fascinating Mughal Gardens are one of the most popular picnic spots. A mini zoo, plants nursery, a Japanese garden, historic palaces and picnic lawns await tourists. During weekends, fountains are switches on and after dusk, lights pick up the beauty of the places by night.

Special programmes are arranged Yadavindra Gardens for the Baisakhi (Spring) festival in April and for Mango Festival in June and July. Accommodation is available at Chandigarh but a taste or royalty can be savoured at Pinjore itself through a stay at the Budgerigar Motel at the gardens, which is run by Haryana Tourism. Bhima Devi temple and an old baoli in the Pinjore town have legendary connection with Pandavas and Mahabharata.

Nawab Fadai Khan, a great architect and foster brother of the Mughal emperor Aurangzeb, is said to have designed the idyllic gardens. He planned the gardens on the classical Charbagh pattern, giving the area a central waterway. Both sides of this waterway were covered with patches of green grass, with flowers and trees at the periphery of the grass-covered path. He supervised the construction of Sheesh Mahal (palace of glass), the Rang Mahal (painted palace) and the cube-like Jal Mahal (palace of water). After Fadai Khan's departure and the end of Mughal rule, these gardens were overtaken by the wilderness. His Highness Maharaja Yadavindra Singh of Patiala is said to have restorted Pinjore Garden to its former glory.

SULTANPUR BIRD SANCTUARY

Sultanpur National Park and Bird Sanctuary is located in Gurugram district of Haryana, at a distance of about 50 kilometres from Delhi and at a distance of 15 kilometres from Gurgaon on the Gurugram-Farukh Nagar Road. This park is best visited during winters when a large number of migratory birds also visited it. In the old map and district gazetteer of Gurugram district, this area is shown as marshy land having a salt pan where water accumulates during rainy seasons and dries out during summers. A number of organisms like crustaceans, fish and insects thrive during floods which attract a number of birds to this area. Its sanctuary potential was first identified by an enthusiastic bird watcher, Mr. Peter Jackson. He convinced Mrs. Indira Gandhi, the then Prime Minister of India, of the need for giving protection to this area. Keeping in view its importance and potential, the area covering 359 acres was declared a Bird Sanctuary in 1971 and was upgraded to the status of National Park in 1991 by Haryana Government.

The Department of Wild Life Preservation, Haryana has carried out a number of development tasks, like construction of mounds and widening of paths. Further, four tubewells have also been dug here. Efforts are being made to improve vegetation in the area by planting more trees. Trees, which are popular with birds (like Acacia Nilotica, Acacia Tortilis, Beris and Neem) have been planted here. For the benefit of bird lovers, certain facilities have been provided like an education and interpretation centre, a library having films, sides and binoculars. There are four watch towers (*machans*) located at different points. In addition, there are parking lot and facilities for toilets and drinking water. For those interested in staying for the night, there is a resort just near the entrance, which provides food and lodging.

The Educational Interpretation Centre has over 70 attractive colour photographs of different species of birds, varying from 16" × 16" to

38" × 40". The photographs are accompanied with informative write ups about birds, which will be of interest to bird lovers. The Haryana Wild Life Department has dedicated a room to the memory of Dr. Salim Ali; Dr. Ali was an internationally renowned Ornithologist. This room contains his bust, photographs, write-ups and some items of personal use. In Sultanpur, 250 bird species have been recorded, 150 are resident while others come from distance regions like Siberia, Europe and Afghanistan. Some of the resident birds are : Common Hoopoe, Paddyfield Pipit, Purple Sunbird, Shikra, Little Cormorant, Eurasian Thick-knee, Gray Francolin, Black Francolin, Indian Roller, White-throated Kingfisher, Spot-billed Duck, Painted Stock, White Ibis, Black-headed Ibis, Little Egret, Great Egret, Cattle Egret, Indian Crested Lark, Red-vented Bulbul, Rose-ringed Parakeet, Red-wattled Lapwing, Eurasian-collared Dove, Red-collared Dove, Laughing Dove, Spotted Owlet, Rock Pigeon, Magpie Robin, Greater Coucal, Weaver Bird, Bank Mynah, Common Mynah and Green Bee Eater.

Every year, 90 migratory bird species arrive here in search of feeding grounds and to pass the winter time. In winter, the sanctuary provides a picturesque panorama of migratory birds such as Ruff, Greater Flamingo, Black-winged Stilt, Common Teal, Common Greenshank, Northern Pintail, Yellow Wagtail, White Wagtail, Northern Shoveler, Rosy Pelican, Gadwall, Wood Sandpiper, Spotted Sandpiper, Eurasian Wigeon, Black-tailed Godwit, Spotted Redshank, Starling, Blue Throat and Long-billed Pipit.

In summer, about 11 species of migratory birds such as Koel, Black-crowned Night Heron, Eurasian Golden Oriole, Comb duck, Blue-checked Bee Eater, Blue-tailed Bee Eater and Cuckoos arrive here.

A leisurely walk along the perimeter of the whole park can take up to two hours. In addition to the birds, antelopes like Neelgai (Blue Bull) and Black Buck are also seen here.

SOHNA

The Delhi-Alwar Highway boasts of a unique hilly attraction—Sohna, in Gurgaon district. Standing on the Aravalli Hills, Sohna looks out at a wide panoramic view of the plains below it. Sohna has been provided with landscaped gardens and an exclusive Barbet Hut, which is complete with its own sitting area and an attached kitchen. A motel wing has been built here where air-conditioned rooms are available for stay. In February, the statesman Vintage Car Rally vends it way to the Sohna hill and Haryana Tourism celebrates the day with great pomp and show.

It also has lawns full of flowers as well as greenary to reduce the visitor. Sohna is also famous for its hot water tank, which has amazing property to cure people of skin diseases (because of the presence of sulphur in its water).

DAMDAMA LAKE

It is located at a distance of 8 kilometres from Sohna. It is an ideal place for fishing. It has facilities like fishing, restaurant and air conditioned rooms. A motel is also operating here.

BADKHAL LAKE

It is located 3 kilometres off the Delhi-Mathura highway (NH1). It was constructed in 1947. It has a 13-set tourist bungalow, sprawling lawns, bar, Mayur restaurant and other facilities.

SURAJ KUND

It is located at a distance of 20 kilometres from Delhi. Its rocky terrain and the historic Surajkund are its main attractions. Hotel Rajhans caters to the needs of Indian and foreign tourists who visit this spot quite frequently. The diameter of the pond (at its bottom) is 130 metres. The remnants of the historic Sun temple can also be seen here. The lake close to Surajkund is known as Mayur Lake.

DABCHIK

It is located on Delhi-Agra National Highway (NH1). It has one restaurant, one bar, one tourist hut and places for sitting and moving around.

KURUKSHETRA

Kurukshetra is a great pilgrimage place for Hindus and tourists from all over the country who visit the venue of the Mahabharata war and the birth place of *The Bhagwad Gita*. Building on its historical and cultural traditions, Kurukshetra has developed to become a modern city. The Brahmasarovar, Sri Krishna Museum and the Science Museum (Panorama) are its chief attractions. Kurukshetra district is a tourist's delight; there are about 360 *tirthas* of religious and historic importance for him. Out of these, about 134 *tirthas* are being maintained by Kurukshetra Development Board, Kurukshetra.

KALA TEETAR

It is located at a distance of 325 kilometres from Delhi on Delhi-Ganganagar road on an area of 8.5 acres. It is situated on the intersection of Rajasthan Canal and Bhakra Canal near Punjab, Haryana and Rajasthan border. Facilities provided at this resort include the motel, restaurant, fast food counter, boating children's park, mini zoo, arrangements for gatherings, green lawn and parking facilities.

BHINDAWAS BIRD SANCTUARY

This is in district Jhajjar at a distance of around 15 kilometres from Jhajjar town and is about three-and-a half hour drive from Delhi. The lake and birds in it are the main attraction of this complex. The sanctuary is spread over an area of 1,074 acres, which makes it considerably larger than Sultanpur Bird Sanctuary. The peripheral embankment is man-made and constructed to store water escaping from Jawaharlal Nehru Canal through an escape channel at the time of power failure of the lift canal system. The Bhindawas lake is being used by the migratory and resident birds about 250 species. The best time to visit is December-January when one can watch the maximum number of birds. The winter timings are from 6:30 am to 5 pm and in summer, from 6 am to 6 pm.

The road to the lake is breath-taking with brilliant yellow mustard fields on all sides during the spring season. There are many species of water birds to be seen near the canal even before on reaches the sanctuary. A vehicle track goes all around the lake. The government officials at the sanctuary are quite knowledgeable and keep a track of various birds that visit the lake. There are two watchtowers on the edge of the lake and the whole lake, full of birds, is visible from there. Even the areas surrounding the sanctuary have a large variety of birds. Since it is difficult to get close to these birds, photographing them is difficult unless one owns an expensive camera with powerful lenses.

The sanctuary is facing a big problem in the form of the weed, which is water hyacinth. It has choked large sections of the lake. With the removal of water hyacinth, this sanctuary would attract many more birds. The State Government has made some efforts to clear this weed from the lake. Another problem is the drying up of this lake during the periods of lean rainfall and/or shortage of water in the nearby canal. Haryana Tourism also plans to build a resort here to provide food and lodging facilities to bird lovers who may like to spend the night here.

Blue Peafowl, Gray Francolin, Black Francolin, Graylag Goose, Ruddy Shelduck, Bar-headed Goose, Comb Duck, Gadwall, Eurasian Wigeon, Great Cormorant, Common Teal, Northern Paintail, Northern Shoveler, Red-vented Bulbul, Common Pochard, Black-rumped Flameback, Common Hoopoe, White-throated Kingfisher, Green Bee-eater, Black Drongo, Pied Cuckoo, Common Hawk Cuckoo, Rose-ringed Parakeet, Spotted Owlet, Blue Rock Pigeon, Great Egret, Purple Swamphen, Eurasian Collared Dove, Mallard, Crested Lark, Jungle Babbler, Ashy Prinia etc. are some of the more common birds found in this sanctuary. The antelope Neelgai (Blue Bull) and the Jungle Cat can also be seen in this sanctuary.

MORNI HILLS RESORT

Morni Hills are offshoots of the Shivalik range, which run as two parallel ranges. The village of Morni (Bhoj Jabial) lies on the mountainside, at height of 1220 metres or 3600 feet above sea level. Traditions assign the name of Morni to a Queen who is believed to have ruled this area. Situated in the lower reaches of the Shivalik range, Morni is ideal for a holiday with its cool climate, beautiful natural vistas and myriad opportunities for trekking, rock climbing and other adventure sports. The best time for visiting Morni Hills is from September to March.

Just five hours away from Delhi and 45 kilometres away from Chandigarh, Morni (in Panchkula district) combines the best of an idyllic retreat with action, adventure and fun. The road to Morni has breathtaking scenery as it goes past sleepy hamlets and cultivated terraces, chugging up a hill climb with wilderness all around.

Myth, mystery and history also have their places in Morni's landscape. The Mountain Quail Tourist Complex of Haryana Tourism is close to the ruins of an old fort. The climate is salubrious and the area is suitable for trekking. The Haryana Government has developed this only hill resort of Haryana and provides facilities to tourists; a motorable road was constructed to connect the Morni Hills with Haryana state Highway near Panchkula. A forest tourist hut—Lal Munia—and a PWD rest house were also constructed to accommodate tourists and trekkers.

Morni Hills have a fascinating range of flora and fauna. Pines crown the hilltops and trees like Sal, Neem, Mango, Ritha, Pipal, Jamun, Shisham, Amaltas and Jacaranda cover the slopes. When the flowering trees blossom, the hillsides are awash with colour. Morni is a paradise for wildlife enthusiasts and birdwatchers with its teeming population of birds like blue peafowls, quails, partridges, sand grouse and common doves as well as animals like jackals, langurs, hares, hyaenas, neelgais, sambars, kakads and even leopards.

There are two lakes or *tals*, which seem to be interconnected mysteriously even though they are separated by a hillock. The water level in both the *tals* always remains the same, as there is a hidden channel under the hill connecting them. The larger lake is about 550 metres long and 460 metres broad and the smaller one about 365 metres either way. Locals consider the lake to be auspicious and gather here on ceremonial occasions. A small temple on the banks contains a Trimurti (the Hindu Trinity), which dates back to twelfth century AD when a Shiva temple was also supposed to have existed at the site.

Morni offers many interesting trekking options. One can trek to the two *tals* and the fort. But for more adventurous people, there are treks leading of the bank of the river Ghaggar, which flows past Morni. Goat tracks lead out of the tourist complex for those keen on walks. Tourism authorities are examining the viability of hang-gliding in Morni.

SURKHAB

A restaurant with bar facilities of Haryana Tourism Corporation was inaugurated on November, 1980. It is located at a distance of 259 kilometres from Delhi on an area of two acres on the Delhi-Rohtak-

Sirsa-Fazilka National Highway. It has the motel, restaurant, bar, lawn, green landscape, fresh juice corner, gift and parking facilities.

SHIKRA

It is located at a distance of 326 kilometres from Delhi on Delhi-Ganganagar road on an area of three acres. It has the guesthouse, restaurant, musical, dancing fountains, joy riders in the children's park, merry-go-round, mini train, laughing joker, photography, green lawn and parking facilities.

HATHNI KUND

After a short drive from the town of Yamunanagar, the Sal forest reserve of Kalesar can be visited. At Paonta Sahib, the river Yamuna crosses over the last lap of the Himalayan foothills. It flows into the plains of Haryana. The waters of the western Yamuna Canal are caught in the barrage at Tajewala. The tourism centre of Haryana Tourism at Hathni Kund forms a link between these attractions. Hathni Kund is a delightful location. Built on a raises plinth, the complex overlooks the flowing waters of the Yamuna. At a distance, the foothills of the Himalayas slowly blend into the skyline.

The summers bring groups of adventurous river rafters. Launching off on an expedition from Paonta Sahib, the rafts bob on till Hathni Kund. The rapids in this stretch are of medium intensity. Perfect for amateurs, large numbers of expeditions have already been organised. Adding a special appeal to rafting is the facility to camp at the lawns of this complex. Rafting expedition, camping at night and trekking in the Kalesar forest reserve are the major attractions. Not only is the Kalesar forest a delight, but also is bird life. The Tree Pie, Drongo, Hornbills, Blue Peafowl and Partridges will delight the ornithologist in the visitors. Neelgai (Blue Bull), Kakad or Barking Deer, Monkeys, Jackals and an occasional Chital can also be spotted here. Kalesar covers about 5100 hectares and is the only Sal forest tract in Haryana. There are many flowering trees in the Kalesar forest, including Dhak, Kachnar and Amaltas.

The next halt can be made at an absolutely different location—the water-front of Tajewala. The barrage at this location has fascinated many an angler. The waters have the Mahaseer for all those who care for this very restful experience. A permit is necessary. Obtain it from the Officer-in-charge. Special adventure club camps can be tailored according to the preferences of tourists.

SKYLARK

The department of tourism of the state has set up a tourist complex on GT Road, near Panipat. Here, twenty rooms, two bar rooms, one petrol pump, one gift shop, lawns and one conference hall have been provided.

BLUE JAY

It has been developed at Samalkha, which is at a distance of 18 kilometres from Panipat (towards Delhi). Eight rooms, one bar room, one hotel and one motel are the chief attractions of this resort.

KALA AMB

It is situated at a distance of 5 kilometres from Panipat on Panipat-Sanauli road. The Third Battle of Panipat was fought here. Some rooms, one lawn, a war memorial and catering services are available at this resort.

OASIS

It has been built at village Uchhana, the site of the famous Karna Lake. It is located at a distance of 8 kilometres from Ambala (towards Delhi) on National Highway No. 1. The Oasis tourist resort is on the lakeside. It has two family huts, 22 rooms, one petrol pump, two restaurants, one bar, one dispensary, one bank and a motel. Boating facilities are available. Nearby 4.5 lakh tourists visit the resort every year. The tourism department of the state earns Rs. 2 crore on an annual basis through this resort. Haryana Tourism has recently commissioned a new Golf Course on the banks of Western Yamuna canal just near the Lake Oasis twin complex. The golf course has been designed and it lies on both sides of the National Highway No. 1; and one has to pass under the highway to continue playing. The combination of Karna Lake, Oasis Complex and the Golf Course is going to make this place in Karnal as one of the most visited tourist spots in the whole of Haryana.

JYOTISAR

It is located at a distance of 8 kilometres from Kurukshetra railway station, on the Pehowa road. It has a large tank (*sarover*). Lord Krishna had given the Gita sermon to Arjuna at this site. Some rooms, one lawn and one restaurant are available at the resort.

PARAKIT

It is located at Pipli on the Amritsar-Delhi Highway (NH 1). It has a motel, restaurant, gift shop as well as lawns.

SHAMA

It has been developed at Gurugram. It has one restaurant, one bar, twelve air conditioned rooms and other facilities.

ARAVALLI GOLF GROUND

It is located in Faridabad district. It has a nine-hole golf course, club, restaurant and bar. Tourist huts are available here. It is close to National Highway No. 2.

KINGFISHER

It is located in Ambala City on Ambala-Delhi Highway (NH1). It has one health club, one swimming pool, one gymnasium and other facilities. Motel, bar, restaurant and meeting hall are available.

RED ROBIN

It has been developed in Bhiwani district. There is a hotel as well as a restaurant in this complex. There are four rooms and lawns in the hotel.

DARENGO

It is located in Charkhi Dadri district. It has a hotel and restaurant.

JAL TARANG

It is located in Loharu sub-division. It has a hotel and a restaurant. It is being managed by the Loharu municipality.

GORAYA

It is located in Bahadurgarh on NH10. It has eleven air conditioned rooms, one restaurant and one bar.

YAMUNANAGAR TOURIST COMPLEX

The old canal rest house of the city of Yamunanagar was connected into a tourist complex in 1985. It has one restaurant, one bar, one/motel and other facilities.

TILIER TOURIST RESORT

It is located in Rohtak district. Its area is 123 acres. It has a lake, called Tilier Lake. It has mini zoo, one petrol pump, one fast food corner, one bar and some air conditioned room.

MAINA RESTAURANT

It is located at Rohtak. It has one conference hall and one bar.

CHAPTER 16

SPORTS

INTRODUCTION

Haryana has made notable contributions to the world of sports. The Government provides sports facilities, scholarships, sports gear and training to those prospective sports persons of the state who are likely to show their abilities in state, national and global sports arenas. Wrestling centres, yoga centres, sports stadia, rural games centre, schemes for talent hunting, sports hostel, sports equipment and state sports awards are a part of the policy of the Haryana Government. Further, it also gives training to budding sports persons, awards to trainers and coaches and motivation to the sports fraternity of the state.

There is a plan to construct at least one sports stadium in each district of the state. A sports hostel has been constructed in Gurugram. Players living in this hostel are provided free boarding and lodging facilities by the state. Under the sports wing scheme, all the players are kept at one place and imparted rigorous training.

POPULAR SPORTS PERSONALITIES

Kapil Dev, the Haryana Hurricane, has been given the award of "the best Indian sportsman of the century" by Wisden Magazine. The glorious saga of this legendary cricket player can be read in the chapter Famous Personalities.

Other sports stars of the state are as follows :

(A) Nawab M.A.K. Pataudi—Cricket

(B) Master Chandagi Ram—Wrestling

(C) Sunita Sharma—Wrestling

(D) Nirmala Gulia—Gymnastics
(E) Satpal—Wrestling
(F) Chand Ram—Athletics
(G) Bahadur Singh—Hammer Throw
(H) Girivar Singh—Boxing
(I) K Malleswari*—Weightlifting
(J) Vijender Kumar**—Boxing
(K) Sushil Kumar***—Wrestling
(L) Yogeshwar Dutt***—Wrestling
(M) Gagan Narang***—Shooting
(N) Saina Nehwal***—Badminton
(O) Sakshi Malik****—Wrestling
(P) Neeraj Chopra• — Javelin Throw
(Q) Ravi Kumar Dahiya#—Wrestling
(R) Bajrang Punia#—Wrestling
(S) Manu Bhaker•—Shooting
(T) Sarabjot Singh•—Shooting
(U) Aman Sehrawat•—Wrestling

Haryana is a traditional powerhouse in games like kabbadi, kho-kho, judo, boxing and wrestling. Sports in the state are managed by the Department of Sports & Youth Affairs, Haryana. Nahar Singh Stadium for international cricket was built in Faridabad in the year 1981. This ground has the capacity to hold around 25,000 people as spectators.

PARIS OLYMPICS–2024

In the Paris Olympics–2024 India won 6 medals and secured 71st position on the medal table. India won one silver and 5 bronze medals. Sports persons from Haryana exhibited high level of competitiveness in this event. Four sportsperson of Haryana won medals. Neeraj Chopra clinched a silver medal with a stunning throw of 87.5 m in the men's Javelin throw final. Chopra had won gold medal in Tokyo Olympics 2020. Manu Bhaker and Sarabjot Singh won bronze medals in shooting and Aman Sehrawat won bronze medal in wrestling.

---

* Malleswari had won the lone bronze medal at Sydney Olympics (2000) in 69 kg weightlifting category.

** Vijender Kumar had won the bronze at Beizing Olympics (2008) in 75 kg boxing category.

*** Won medal in London Olympics–2012.

****Sakshi Malik had won the bronze at Rio Olympics (2016) in 58 kg freestyle wrestling category.

Won medal in Tokyo Olympics–2020.

• Neeraj Chopra won gold medal at Tokyo Olympics (2020) and silver medal at Paris Olympics (2024) in Javelin Throw.

• Manu Bhaker won bronze medal at Paris Olympics (2024) in shooting.

• Sarabjot Singh won bronze medal at Paris olympics (2024) in Shooting.

• Aman Sehrawat won bronze medal at Paris Olympics (2024) in 57 kg Freestyle wrestling category.

SPORTS INSTITUTIONS

Motilal Nehru Sports School at Rai is famous all over India. It is situated in the district of Sonepat on National Highway No. 1. It is run like a boarding school. Sports persons are admitted to the school on the basis of merit. Poor and economically backward students are also granted scholarships by the school. This institution develops the multi-faceted personality of the student who gets admission here.

Within the premises of the Motilal Nehru Sports School, Kamla Nehru School is also working to train junior sports stars. So, this school is deemed the junior wing of Motilal Nehru sports school. Children between the age group 8 to 11 years get admission to this school.

Further, the Department of Sports (Haryana Government) also takes care of the needs (related to sports and games) of the populace of the state. All the three universities of the State have their sports departments. Students get training from coaches and play intra-university or inter-university matches to assert their supremacy in various games. Colleges also have sports facilities.

Popular games being played in Haryana are table tennis, wrestling, cricket, hockey, soccer, swimming, badminton, athletics, boxing and chess.

OTHER COMPETITIONS

In the times to come, several sports stars of Haryana are likely to steal the limelight in regional, national and global sports competitions. The Government is paying full attention to such talented men and women as are likely to win awards and victories on behalf of the State as well as the country.

During the 19th Asian games held in Hangzhou, China in 2023, India got 28 Gold, 38 Silver and 41 Bronze medals. 89 sports persons from Haryana participated in it and won 08 Gold, 04 Silver and 16 Bronze medals.

Commonwealth Games 2022 organized from 28 July 2022 to 8 August 2022 at Birmingham. India wins 61 Medals (22 Gold, 16 Silver, 23 Bronze) in Commonwealth Games 2022 out of which Contribution of Haryana is in 20 Medals. 9 Gold Individual, 2 Silver Individual, 2 Silver in Team events, 6 Bronze Individual and 1 in Team event Medals.

CHAPTER 17

AGRICULTURE

INTRODUCTION

The State of Haryana is one of the leading agricultural State of the country. This State, along with Punjab, is fondly known as the "bread basket of India." Wheat and paddy are its major crops. Its contribution towards the national foodgrains pool is one of the highest in the country. There was a time when the farmers of the State were on the brink of starvation and economic disaster. They witnessed troubled times in the fifties and sixties of the century goneby. But today, Haryana is a State of plenty. Most modern equipment for agricultural activities, contribution of two agricultural universities, toil of the people and the Green Revolution are the four causative factors that led to prosperity of the State.

THE KHARIF BASKET

Although Haryana is a major producer of Rabi Crops (like wheat), yet its supremacy in the field of Kharif Crops had been established a long time ago. The major Kharif Crops of the State are paddy, sugarcane, cotton, maize and barley. Paddy is the chief Kharif Crop of the State. A remarkable increase in foodgrains production is visible in Haryana since inception of the State. Production of total foodgrains in the State was 184.32 lakh tonnes in 2022-23. The Wheat and Paddy crops have played a major role in pushing up the agricultural production. The production of Rice was 59.21 lakh tonnes in 2022-23. Similarly, the production of Wheat was 110.64 lakh tonnes during 2022-23. Haryana is next only to Punjab in terms of average paddy output (in the country).

The paddy belt of the state is located in the districts of Karnal, Kaithal, Kurukshetra, Ambala, Panipat and Yamunanagar. The area under cultivation and production (of paddy) is nearly 80 per cent. The region on both the sides of GT Road, starting from Ambala and ending near Kundli (Sonepat) is the world famous rice belt. Basmati rice, the most widely demanded type of rice in the world, is a speciality crop of this belt.

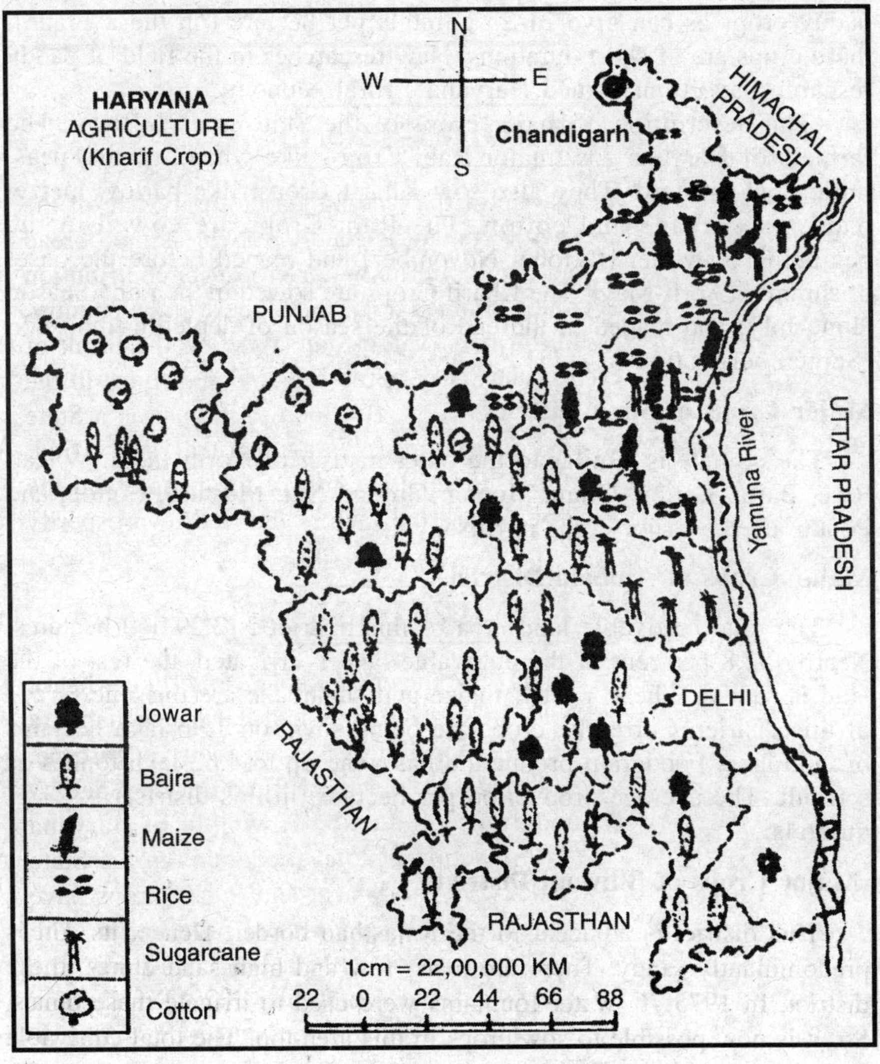

In 1970, the research work on paddy was initiated in HAV, Hissar. In 1992, Paddy Research Centre (Kaul), which is known as NARF, started the development of new paddy varieties. It also initiated steps for research in other crops, like wheat, pulses, vegetable oil crops etc. Today, the highly developed varieties of Haryana are PR-106, HKR-120 and HKR-126, which are medium-duration paddy breeds. The Central Government is persuading the state's farmers to plant such paddy crops as can give 21-23 quintals per hectare (on the average); these crops are of short durations. New researches in the field of paddy research have transformed Haryana's rural economy.

The description of major crops of the State is as follows. The farmers of Haryana sow major Rabi Crops, like wheat, grams, peas, millet and mustard. They also sow Kharif Crops, like barley, maize, paddy, sugarcane and cotton. The Rabi Crops are sowed in the beginning of winter (October-November) and reaped before the onset of summer (April-May). The Kharif Crops are sowed in the rainy Season (June-July) and reaped in the end of the season of depleting monsoon (September-October).

Major Crops of Sirsa District

The climate is similar to the other district of North India. Wheat, Rice, Bajra, Barley, Gram, Moong, Ground Nut, Mustard, Cotton, and Potato are the major crops in Sirsa.

Major Crops of Ambala District

The total cultivable land area of this district is 2,29,000 hectares. Nearby 52.8 per cent of the cultivable land is irrigated, the rest of the land is sandy. Wheat, paddy, maize and sugarcane are the chief crops of this district. Currently, crops are being sown on 1.96 lakh hectares of land area. Foodgrain production has gone up to 4.62 lakh tonnes as a result. The average production per hectare (in this district) is 23.57 quintals.

Major Crops of Bhiwani District

This district is adjacent to the Rajasthan border. Hence, its soil is predominantly sandy. There are many low and high sand dunes in the district. In 1975-76, water fountains were used to irrigate these dunes. So, it is now possible to sow crops in this area-too. The total cultivable land in the district is 4-12 lakh hectares; crops are sown on 3.47 lakh hectares of this land.

Dry land farming is done on 60 per cent of the land area of the district. Nearly 40 per cent of the land area is fed by canals and tubewells.

Major Crops of Sonepat District

The soil of this district is *domut*, sandy but fertile. Wheat and paddy are the major crops. Besides, sugarcane, millet, barley, pulses, oil-producing crops, sunflower and mushrooms are also grown here. Mango, malta, lemon, sweet lemon and guava are also grown.

In the Khadar area (near the river Yamuna) is used for growing watermelons and musk melons. Some farmers have also grown grapes here. This district is leading the nation in terms of mushroom production.

Major Crops of Yamunanager District

The total land area of this district is 1,72,626 hectares. Out of this, 1,26,946 hectares are used for cultivation purposes. Wheat, sugarcane, gram, maize and paddy are the major crops. Sunflower is also grown by many farmers. The production of fruits and vegetables is in large quantities. Popular fruits grown here are watermelon, muskmelon, mango, apricot etc.

Major Crops of Rohtak District

Three-fourth of the area of this district is used for crop cultivation. Major crops include barley, millet, sugarcane, oat, wheat, cotton and gram.

Major Crops of Gurugram District

The major crops of this district are barley, millet, oat and gram. Oat is the chief Kharif Crop of this area. It is used as green fodder for animals. Vegetables are also grown here. The farmers of this district also sow mustard, toria and taramira, which are cash crops.

Major Crops of Kurukshetra District

Wheat and paddy are the two major crops of the district. Sugarcane is a cash crop. A sugar mill in Shahabad Markanda accepts the sugarcane outputs of the areas in its vicinity.

Major Crops of Faridabad District

More than 60 per cent of the population of this district is associated, overtly or covertly, with agriculture. Major crops are wheat, millet and mustard. The cultivable land of the district is 1,63,000 hectares.

Major Crops of Karnal District

More than 70 per cent of the population of this district is associated overtly, or covertly, with agriculture. The economy of the district has its roots in agriculture. The Basmati rice produced here is exported to many countries. That is why, it is also known as the "rice bowl". Sugarcane production has touched new marks in this district. New techniques and good-quality seeds have also contributed to a growth in the production of sunflower.

Major Crops of Hissar District

Cotton, millet, maize, paddy, wheat, gram and mustard are the major crops of this district. Farmers are also taking interest in the production of sunflower and soyabean. Pulses and oil-producing crops are also being grown with the help of advanced agricultural techniques and latest seeds.

Major Crops of Kaithal District

The total cultivable land of this district is 20,095 hectares. Wheat and Basmati rice are cultivated in abundance. The rice mills of the district export rice to the Gulf countries.

Major Crops of Jind District

The total cultivable land of this district is 2,72,00 hectares. Paddy, millet, barley, pulses, cotton, sugarcane, oil-producing crops and wheat are the major crops of this district. Sunflower is also grown in this district.

Major Crops of Panipat District

The area of the district is 1,75,000 hectares. The cultivable land is 1,63,000 hectares and the total sowed land is 1,55,000 hectares. The chief Rabi Crop is wheat whereas the chief Kharif Crop is paddy. Sunflower is also being grown here.

Major Crops of Mahendragarh District

This district is rain-dependent in terms of agricultural work. Only 50 percent of its land area is irrigated. However the Department of Agriculture of the State as well as the farmers of this district has worked very hard to enhance the agricultural output in the district. That is why, this district has already become a leader in the field of mustard production. It is also trying to emulate Karnal and Kurukshetra districts in terms of wheat production. The major Kharif Crop is barley. The major Rabi Crops are wheat, gram, and mustard. Cash crops, like cotton and sunflower, are also being grown here.

Major Crops of Rewari District

Agriculture is major occupation of the people of this district. Due its proximity to Rajasthan, the soil of this area is sandy. The effects of poor rainfall, dust storms and high temperature affect the agriculture of this district in an adverse manner. However, irrigation facilities have increased in number in this district after the formation of the Haryana state. Wheat, paddy and sugarcane are its major crops.

Major Crops of Jhajjar, Fatehabad and Panchkula

Gram, wheat and paddy are grown in most of the land areas of these districts.

HORTICULTURE IN HARYANA

Haryana is also developing as a horticultural State of the Country. Mangoes of Ambala and Panipat are famous. Other fruits grown in the state are watermelons, guava, muskmelons, apricots and grapes. But the farmers would have to work harder to generate higher outputs of fruits in the state. The two agricultural universities of the state as well as the Department of Agriculture/Horticulture are providing advanced varieties/seeds to farmers. These institutions are also giving latest techniques of fruit production of these farmers.

In 2022-23, the total production of horticultural crops in the State was 64.18 lakh MT. Horticultural Crops cover 4.20 lakh hectare area which is 6.28 per cent of the grass cropped area of the state.

Irrigation Schemes of the State

Rainfall as well as water of canals and rivers is utilised to irrigate the fields of the state. Rainfall is not adequate in Haryana. So, farmers adopt, other measures to irrigate their fields. The following modes of irrigation are popular in the State.

Irrigation in North-eastern Parts

The north-eastern parts include the plains of Ambala and the Shivalik hills. Rainfall occurs in good quantities in this area. The plains of this region are fertile. Rainfalls are used to irrigate the fields in most of the areas of this region. After the construction of Nangal Lift Irrigation Scheme, canal irrigation was made possible in Ambala district. With this scheme, nearly 45,500 areas of land (of 75 villages) have started receiving canal waters for the purpose of irrigation.

Irrigation in the Central Region

The central region of the state comprises, Kurukshetra, Karnal, Jind, Rohtak, Panipat and Sonepat districts. Rainfall occurs in adequate quantities in these districts. Maize and paddy are grown here because these crops need large volumes of water. Rabi crops are grown with the help of tube-wells, wells and canals.

Irrigation in the South-eastern Region

This area comprises the districts of Gurgaon and Faridabad. Rainfall is less than normal in this area. The major crops of this region are maize, barley, millet, oat, wheat and gram. These crops are supplied water by canals and tube-wells.

Irrigation in the Sandy Region

This region comprises the districts of Hissar, Sirsa, Mahendragarh and Bhiwani. Rainfall is almost nil in this area. People use camels in agricultural tasks. Main crops of the region are barley, millet, gram, maize and wheat. Tube-wells are used to irrigate the fields; the latter get water through the water sprinklers.

Canal Irrigation

Canal irrigation is the major fulcrum that balances the lever of irrigation in the State vis-a-vis the rainfall. The canals of the State have

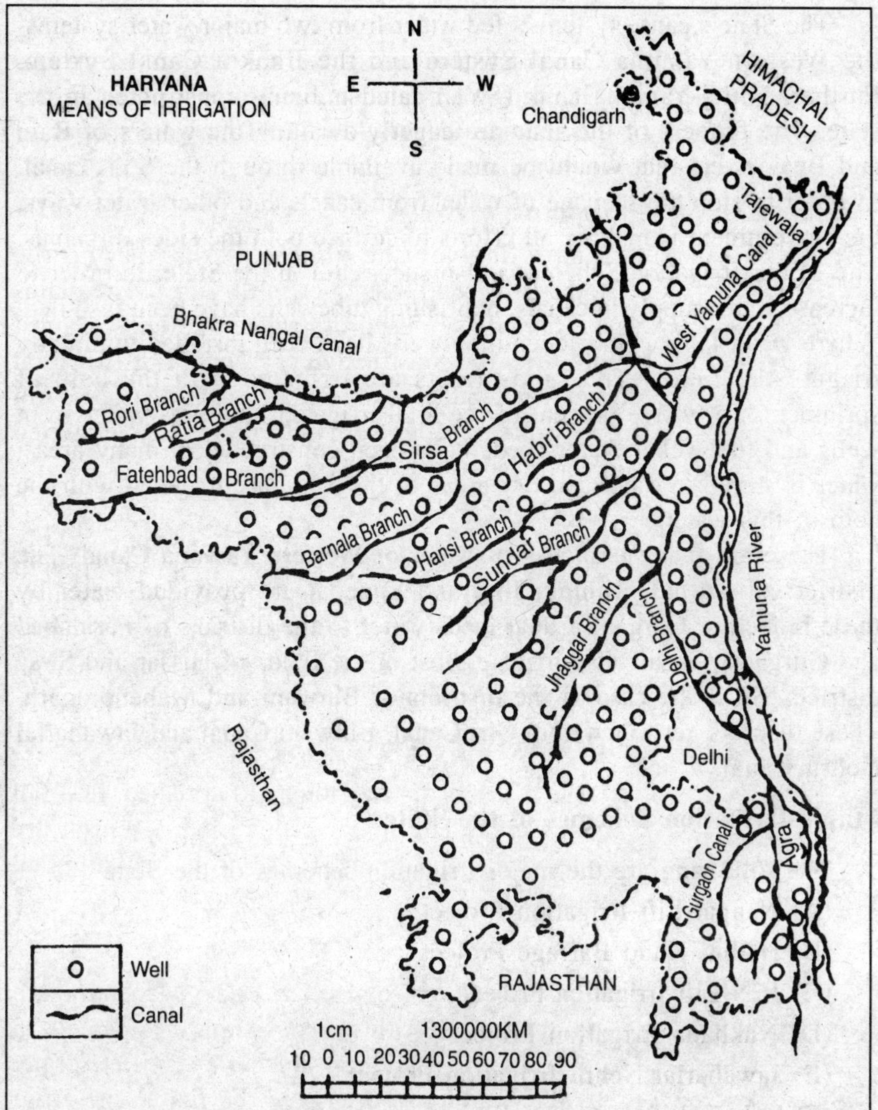

been described in the Chapter Geography. These are the main sources of irrigation in Haryana, rainfall playing only a minor role in this Herculean task. Fig. shows network of canals and also, that of wells in the State.

The State's canal system is fed water from two major water systems- the Western Yamuna Canal System and the Bhakra Canal System. Further, Sutlej-Yamuna Link (SYL) canal is being constructed in the state. The farmers of the state are eagerly awaiting the waters of Ravi and Beas rivers that would be made available through the SYL canal. In order to stop the seepage of water from canals and other water ways, the Government is making all efforts to surface both the sides of canals. The Minor Irrigation Scheme is also successful in the State. In order to increase water supply in canals, nourishing tubewells have been installed. Where water table is low, deep tube-wells have been installed to directly irrigate the fields. The sandy tracts are irrigated with the help of sprinklers. Forty-five percent of the total irrigated land gets water from wells and tubewells. Water sheds have been constructed in many areas; water is stored in them and dry areas of the State are irrigated with the help of this water.

There are many branches of water of Western Yamuna Canal. The districts of Karnal, Rohtak, Jind and Sonepat are provided water by these branches. Gurgaon Canal feeds water to the districts of Faridabad and Gurgaon. Canals also irrigate most of the fields of Hissar and Sirsa districts. So is the case of the districts of Bhiwani and Mahendragarh. These districts get water from Giri Canal, Bhiwani Canal and Jawaharlal Nehru Canal.

Major Irrigation Schemes of the State

The following are the major irrigation schemes of the State :

(A) Nangal Lift Irrigation Project

(B) Hathni Kund Barrage Project

(C) JLN Lift Irrigation Project

(D) Nakhana Irrigation Project

(E) Jawaharlal Nehru Irrigation Project

(F) Loharu Lift Irrigation Project

(G) Singa Lift Irrigation Project

(H) Western Yamuna Canal Project

(I) Giri Lift Irrigation Project

(J) Sewani Lift Irrigation Project

In 2022-23, the total land area of the State (which was used for agricultural purposes) was 65.80 lakh hectare. Foreign financial institutions (like World Bank) and Indian financial institutions (like NABARD) are giving aid to the Haryana Government so that irrigation facilities could improve in the State.

PRODUCTION OF PRINCIPAL CROPS

(000 Tonne)

Year	Wheat	Rice	Total Food-grains	Sugar Cane	Cotton (000 bales)	Oilseeds
1	2	3	4	5	6	7
1966-67	1059	223	2592	5100	288	92
1970-71	2342	460	4771	7070	373	98
1980-81	3490	1259	6036	4600	643	188
1990-91	6436	1834	9559	7800	1155	638
2000-01	9669	2695	13294	8170	1383	571
2010-11	11578	3465	16568	6042	1747	965
2011-12	13119	3757	18370	6953	2616	758
2012-13	11117	3941	16146	7500	2378	972
2013-14	11800	4041	16970	7427	2027	899
2014-15	10457	3989	15340	7035	1943	729
2015-16	11350	4142	16330	6992	995	841
2016-17	12310	4451	17877	8167	2046	956
2017-18	12263	4880	18032	9633	1626	1121
2018-19	12573	4516	18144	8505	2013	1278
2019-20	11877	5195	18322	7730	2463	1175
2020-21	12393	5634	19588	8588	1825	1261
2021-22	10447	5514	17226	8823	1316	1720
2022-23	11064	5921	18432	8914	1000	1473

The production of Oilseeds and Sugarcane during the year 2022-23 was 14.73 and 89.14 lakh tonnes against 17.20 and 88.23 lakh tonnes respectively during the year 2021-22. The production of Cotton in the State was 10.00 lakh bales in 2022-23.

CHAPTER 18

EDUCATION

INTRODUCTION

When the State of Haryana was created, the literacy rate of the entire State was 20 per cent. But now as per Census (2011), the literacy rate of the State is 75.60 per cent; the literacy rate of males is 84.10 per cent whereas the same figure for females is 65.90 per cent. The residents of the State, therefore, achieved a lot (in terms of education) during the period 1966-2011. Let us study the present scenario of educational activities in the State.

SCHOOL EDUCATION

There are 9,882 primary/pre-primary schools, 5,916 middle schools and 9,078 high/secondary schools till 2022-23.

Further, there are 21 Navodaya Vidyalayas in the State.

Primary education is free and compulsory. All the children can avail the facility of free primary education; their ages should fall in the age group of 6-11 years. There is one primary school in one square kilometre area, one middle school in 1.45 square kilometre area and one high school in 1.77 square kilometre area and one senior secondary school in 3.19 square kilometre area. From 1985-86 onwards the 10+2+3 System of education was put in force in Haryana. School children are also being taught computer operations in many schools of the State.

There are scholarship of various types available for meritorious students. Scheduled Castes (SC) girls get scholarships for attendance; under this Scheme, every SC girl gets some cash money per month; if she is regular to school. SC also get uniform free of cost. Further, students of primary schools also get free notebooks and writing material.

In March, 1980, the library class scheme was initiated in primary and middle school of the State. Students can read books in the library under this Scheme and also, can take some books to their homes to prepare themselves in academic terms.

COLLEGE AND UNIVERSITY EDUCATION

There are 373 Art and Science Colleges, 93 Engineering Colleges and 489 Teachers Training Colleges in the State till 2022-23. Further, 57 universities are operating in the State. Some main universities of the state are—

(A) Chaudhary Charan Singh Agricultural University, Hissar
(B) Kurukshetra University, Kurukshetra
(C) Guru Jambeshwar University, Hissar
(D) Maharshi Dayanand University, Rohtak
(E) Ch. Devi Lal University, Sirsa
(F) Central University of Haryana, Mahendergarh
(G) Deenbandhu Chootu Ram University of Sci. & Tech., Murthal
(H) Maharishi Markandeswar University, Mullana

The Haryana Private Universities Act, 2006 has been enacted and the following main Private Universities have been established under this Act:

1. O.P. Jindal Global University, Village Jagdishpur, Distt. Sonepat.
2. ITM University, Gurugram.
3. Appejay Stya University, Distt. Gurugram.
4. Amity University, Distt. Gurugram.
5. MM University, Sadopur, Ambala.
6. NIILM University, Kaithal.

Because of these educational institutions, the literacy rate of the State jumped to 75.60 per cent in 2011. But the people of Haryana have still a long way to go on the educational front. The rural areas of the State remain underdeveloped because of poor literacy rates among the rural masses.

At the time of inception of Haryana as a separate State in 1966, there were only 6 Polytechnics and only one Engineering College at Kurukshetra. In the Academic Session 2022-23 the number of Polytechnics was 191 and the number of Engineering Colleges was 93.

Degree and diploma providing institutes are imparting education in different technical field. Regional Engineering College (REC) at Kurukshetra is an accredited deemed university. Now, its name has become—National Institute of Technology. Chaudhary Devi Lal Smriti

Engineering College has been opened at village Pannawala Mota in Sirsa district. Seats are available in the following four main subjects namely—Computer Science and Engineering, Electronic and Communication Engineering, Electrical Engineering and Food Technology.

The main concern of the Government is to tackle the problem of illiteracy among its female population. The importance of education among girl and its overall impact of the welfare of children and community as a whole cannot be ignored. Concessions and incentives for girls, especially those belonging to backward classes and scheduled castes have gone a long way in promoting female education. Scheduled Caste/EWS girls in primary, middle and high classes are being given free uniforms. Scheduled Caste/EWS students are given grants for books and stationery articles and are awarded scholarships and reimbursement of tuition fees. The Government is providing free education to the women up to graduation level and also in technical institutes.

Chaudhary Charan Singh Agricultural University, popularly known as HAU, is located in Hissar district (Haryana). It was initially a campus of Punjab Agricultural University, Ludhiana, Punjab. In 1966, with the division of Punjab and Haryana, HAU became an independent institution. Since then, HAU has become internationally known not only for its advances in high yielding grain and cotton varieties but also for its scenic campus.

The first Vice-Chancellor of HAU, Mr. A.L. Fletcher dedicated many years of his life in making HAU one of the best known institutions in Asia. His vision and efforts led to an infusion of resources for creation of world class infrastructure, laboratories and other facilities on the main campus.

At present, the university has seven colleges: College of Agriculture, College of Agricultural Engineering, College of Animal Sciences, College of Basic Sciences, College of Home Sciences, College of Sports and College of Veterinary Sciences.

In fact, HAU was the first institution of higher learning to create a separate college for sports in India. The university also has a research and training farm of over, 3,000 acres (about 1,200 hectares) for faculty and students. The university recently annexed another, 2,000 acres for its seed operations. The university has a faculty of over 1,200 scientists most of whom have either been educated or trained abroad in their respective fields of specialization.

HAU is also one of the three Indian universities to be a recipient of the recent World Bank project on Agricultural Human Resource Development. The overall project cost was approximately US $ 240 million. Under the project, about 65 faculty members and deans/directors visited the United states, the United Kingdom and other countries. These visitors took four-and-a-half-month training at selected universities in these countries.

Vocational Education

Vocationalization of education refers to the inclusion of practical subjects or courses, which shall generate among the students some basic knowledge, skills, and disposition that prepare them to think of becoming skilled workers or entrepreneurs. The in-school vocational education in Haryana has been implemented based on the National Skills Qualification Framework (NSQF). The important highlights are as under: • Total 1,248 Govt. Schools stand covered under Vocational Education till 2023-24 with an enrolment of 1,89,349 students (classes 9th to 12th). • 15 Skills/Sectors are running in 1,248 Govt. Schools (1, 2 or 3 skills/sectors in each school). • 2,476 skill labs have been approved for 1,248 Govt. schools of the state. 2,238 skill labs in 1,074 schools are fully equipped with tools and equipment and the remaining 238 labs will be equipped in 174 schools.

NDRI

National Dairy Research Institute (NDRI), Karnal is the premier organization that provides R&D support for dairy development programmes. Over the years, it has gained prominence as the front ranking dairy research organization of the world. The institute works in close liaison with various national and international development agencies to assist the country in her dairy development programmes.

The NDRI evolved from the erstwhile Imperial Institute for Animal Husbandry and Dairying, which was established at Bangalore in 1923. In 1936, it was expanded and renamed as Imperial Dairy Institute. It was in 1955 that its headquarters were shifted to Karnal at a location, which was formerly called Central Cattle Breeding Farm. In order to consolidate the impressive infrastructure already developed at Bangalore, the unit was reorganized to serve as the Southern Regional Station of the Institute. In 1962 and 1964, two regional stations of the institute were established at Kalyani and Bombay, respectively; the former was the Eastern Regional Station whereas the latter was the Western Regional Station. However, the Western Regional Station (WRS) at Bombay was closed in 1984. The Southern and the Eastern Regional Stations continue to provide region—specific R&D support for dairy development in relation to the agro-climatic conditions that exist in those areas.

In 1970, the Institute's management was weaned away from the Ministry of Agriculture and brought under the wings of the Indian Council of Agricultural Research (ICAR) with a view to providing greater operational autonomy in research management functions. In 1989, the status of Deemed University was conferred on the Institute for further strengthening the academic programmes for human resource development. The institute provides high-quality education in the field of dairying, which has no parallel in Asia. It is noteworthy that the NDRI is an important contributor of dairying manpower and plays an important role in enhancing the teaching capabilities of the dairying staffs. This is evidenced by recognition, by the ICAR, of the institute as a Center of Advanced Studies at NDRI in Dairy Breeding and Dairy Technology disciplines to further strengthen the research and training components. During the Ninth Five Year Plan period, a National Research Centre on Biotechnology was commissioned at this Institute.

The Institute offers various teaching programmes at diploma, graduate, post-graduate and doctorate levels in order to develop trained manpower in dairying to meet challenges at national and international levels. All research laboratories are equipped with ultra modern equipment and State-of-the-art technological facilities.

National Dairy Diploma: The objective of this course is to develop trained manpower to meet the requirements at operational levels in dairy plants. The duration of the course is 2 years (full time). This course is offered at this Institute's southern regional station at Bangalore. The eligibility for admission is a pass in 10+2 or its equivalent examination with Physics, Chemistry, Mathematics and English as electives from a board/university recognized by the Institute. Only those candidates, who have obtained at least 50% marks or equivalent (45% in case of SCs/STs) in the aggregate of Physics, Chemistry and Mathematics, are eligible to apply for admission.

B.Tech. (Dairy Technology): This degree programme offers intensive training in processing of milk and its products, quality control and engineering aspects of dairy processing equipment. The duration of B.Tech. (Dairy Technology) is 4 years. The course is administered according to the semester system. One academic year consists of two semesters, each one of these being of a duration of 18 weeks. Students are sent for plant training for one year to the Model Dairy Plant located at the Institute's premises. The eligibility for admission to this degree course is 10+2 or its equivalent examination with Physics, Chemistry, Mathematics and English from a board/university recognized by the institute. Only those candidates, who have obtained at least 60% marks or their equivalent G.P.A in the aggregate of Physics, Chemistry and Mathematics, are eligible for admission to B.Tech (Dairy Technology).

Masters Degrees in Dairying: The Institute offers M.Sc and M. Tech degree programmes in the following disciplines: Dairy Microbiology, Dairy Chemistry, Dairy Technology, Dairy Engineering, Animal Biochemistry, Animal Genetics and Breeding, Livestock Production and Management, Animal Nutrition, Animal Physiology, Dairy Economics and Dairy Extension Education and finally Animal Biotechnology.

The duration of the Master Degree in Dairying is three years for graduates in pure sciences, B.A.S.C. (Food Technology) and B.Sc. (PCM) with IDD (DT) and two years for graduates with four-year professional degrees. However, it will be three years for those admitted to Master in Dairy Engineering with a degree of B.Sc/ B.Tech (DT). Candidates having bachelor's degree in the concerned field must have obtained at least 60% marks or an Overall Grade Point Average (OGPA) of 6.50 out of 10.00 or 3.25 out of 5.00 or 2.60 out of 4.00 (for SC/ST candidates 55% marks or an OGPA of 6.00 out of 10.00, 3.00 out of 5.00 or 2.40 our of 4.00) or a certificate of having an OGPA equivalent to 60% marks from the Registrar.

Doctorate Level Courses: Dairy Microbiology, Dairy Chemistry, Dairy Technology, Dairy Engineering, Animal Biochemistry, Animal

Genetics and Breeding, Livestock Production and Management, Animal Nutrition, Animal Physiology, Dairy Economics, Dairy Extension Education. *Eligibility:* Candidates having Master's Degree in the relevant field must have obtained at least 60 per cent marks or an Overall Grade Point Average (OGPA) of 6.50 out of 10.00 or 3.25 out of 5.00 or 2.60 out of 4.00 (for SC/ST candidates, 55 per cent marks of an OGPA of 6.00 out of 10.00, 3.00 out of 5.00 or 2.40 out of 4.00) or a certificate of having an OGPA equivalent to 60 per cent marks from the Registrar.

The Institute provides technical advice and guidance to Central and State Government Organizations, cooperative institutions and private entrepreneurs in the development of cattle and dairy industry in India. The Dairy Extension Division and Krishi Vigyan Kendra/ Teacher's Training Centres (KVKs/TTCs) are engaged in imparting training to farmers and entrepreneurs. The KVKs impart training to different clientele comprising farmers, farm-women, school drop-outs, rural youths and village-level extension functionaries of Karnal district. In addition, special requests from other areas of the country are also entertained.

Most of the training schedules of KVKs are organized on basis of the philosophy of "learning by doing" in important areas like dairy farming, crops including pulses and oil seeds, horticulture, bee-keeping, fisheries and manufacture of dairy products are followed. While imparting training through KVKs, three fundamental principles. These are: (*i*) agricultural production, the prime goal; (*ii*) work experience, the main method of imparting training; and (*iii*) weaker sections of the society, the main target. Every KVK concentrates its activities within district in which, it is located. Every TTC concentrates on giving training on different aspects of dairy farming as well as dairy processing to the trainers of KVKs, teachers of state agriculture universities and senior extension functionaries of the country.

NIT KURUKSHETRA

National Institute of Technology Kurukshetra (NIT Kurukshetra) is a public technical and research university located in Kurukshetra. In December 2008, it was accredited with the status of Institute of National Importance (INI). It is one of the 31 National Institutes of Technology established and administered by Government of India. It runs undergraduate and postgraduate in programme Engineering and Doctor of Philosophy programme in Engineering, Sciences and Humanities.

The first Prime Minister of independent India, Jawaharlal Nehru, sought to develop India as a leader in science and technology. Between 1959 and 1965, with this vision, the Government founded 14 educational institutions in different regions of India. The system of competitive entry (based on merit) gave access to higher education in these institutions. Such an institution was established in 1963 in Kurukshetra as a joint enterprise of the Government of India and the Government of Punjab, as the Regional Engineering College, Kurukshetra (REC Kurukshetra). In 2002, all the Regional Engineering Colleges were unified by a common entrance exam. Therefore, REC Kurukshetra was renamed to National Institute of Technology under the NIT Act and was given a Deemed University status.

Hostels: Being a residential institution, hostel accommodation is available for all the B.Tech. students. Hostel accommodation is also provided for M.Tech and B.E. students. There are 15 hostels, 11 for boys and 4 for girls.

Instructional Blocks : The instructional building includes, 6 blocks and 1 workshop. Each block has offices for the staff, lecture halls, tutorial rooms and various laboratories A mini-auditorium has been added to this set-up.

Residential Sector : The college provides almost hundred per cent facilities for its faculty and fifty per cent housing facility for its teaching staff. The campus extends over an area of about 300 acres and presents an impressive blend of modern architecture and rural landscape.

Departments of the College : Department of Electronics & Communication & Computer Engineering, Department of Civil Engineering, Department of Electrical Engineering, Department of Mechanical Engineering, Department of Physics, Department of Chemistry, Department of Humanities, Department of Mathematics, Institute-Industry Interaction and E.D. Cell and finally, Training and Placement Department.

Number of Recognised Universities/Colleges/Schools in Haryana

Type of Institution	2018-19	2019-20	2020-21	2021-22	2022-23
Universities (including State/Private/Deemed/ Cetral/Technical/ Others Universities)	55	56	56	57	57
Arts and Science Colleges	342	359	357	364	373
Engineering Colleges	109	101	90	91	93
Polytechnics	185	192	189	191	191
MBA Colleges	99	89	83	99	115
MCA Colleges	34	33	32	31	32
B.Pharmacy Colleges	43	52	66	67	72
B.Arch Colleges	–	–	–	7	7
Teachers Trainng Colleges	491	475	491	491	489
High/Senior Secondary	8,308	8,575	8,782	9,023	9,078
Middle Schools	5,673	5,704	5,833	5,888	5,916
Primary/Pre-Primary Schools	9,972	9,928	9,895	9,896	9,882

HARYANA INSTITUTE OF CIVIL AVIATION

Haryana Institute of Civil Aviation was conceived on April 1, 1999 by merging the erstwhile Karnal Aviation Club, Hissar Aviation Club and Pinjore Aviation Club into one organisation. The institute is situated 4 km away from Karnal on Karnal-Kunjpura Road, near Budha Khera village.

The institute aims to impart training to young boys and girls from all over the country for making them pilots and engineers. In order to achieve these objectives, it has a total fleet of 3 aircraft at Karnal, 4 aircraft at Hissar and 4 aircraft at Pinjore. Besides imparting flying training, gliding training is also given at its branches. The aircraft are of different categories *vis,* Pushpaks, Sheshnag, Swatis and Piper Cherokees. Flying training is provided in four phases as under:

Students Pilot License or SPL; Private License or PPL; Commercial Pilot License; CPL. Flying for Instructor Rating: PPL is obtained by a trainee after experiencing 40 and 60 hours of flying and for getting a CPL, one has to complete minimum 250 hours of flying, which includes cross-country flights, instrument flying, simulator training, flying skill tests etc. The institute also imparts training to the students for qualifying Aircraft Maintenance Engineer's License.

Intake of Students: Haryana state government sponsorship—for which, advertisements are published every year. Direct recruitment—admission for direct recruitment are open round the year. Duration of Course: Between 2 to 3 years, depending upon the aptitude of an individual.

Other Facilities: Chartered flights, joy rides and simulator training facilities are available at the club.

DR. B.R. AMBEDKAR NATIONAL LAW UNIVERSITY

Dr. B.R. Ambedkar National Law University, Sonepat (DBRANLU) was established by the State Government of Haryana in the year 2012 under the Haryana Act No. 15 of 2012 under the name of National Law University Haryana enacted by the legislature of the State of Haryana. As a tribute to Dr. B.R. Ambedkar, a great social reformer and architect of our present legal system and the Constitution, the State Legislature of Haryana through an amendment in 2014 changed the name of this university to Dr. B.R. Ambedkar National Law University, Sonepat. The University has its own space wherein the campus is coming up with high speed currently is under construction is situated in the education hub of India – Rajiv Gandhi Educational City, Rai, Sonepat – where more than thirteen renowned educational institutions and universities are located and are functional. The location provides a positive and congenial environment for legal education and professional training besides overall development of students. The University has firmly resolved to impart advanced legal education, to hone practical legal skills and inter disciplinary understanding, keeping in view the requirements of a just and equitable society.

The Chief Justice of India or his nominee, who shall be sitting Judge of the Supreme Court, shall be the visitor of the University. Hon'ble Governor of the State of Haryana is the Chancellor of the University.

CHAPTER 19

INDUSTRY AND ECONOMY

Haryana has emerged as one of the most progressive States of India with an impressive trail of achievements on the fields of agriculture, business, tourism and industrial development. Though small in terms of geographical spread, Haryana has 6,841 villages and 154 towns spread over 22 districts. Its compact size has been a contributing factor in its development. Demographically, Haryana shares a common border with Delhi on three sides, with easy access to its raw materials and commercial activities. The international airport, diplomatic enclaves and business centres in the immediate vicinity of the state are with just 1.37% of the total geographical area and less than 2% of the country's population, Haryana today is one of the leading states in the country in terms of per capita income. Today, it enjoys a unique distinction in India of having provided electricity, metallic roads and potable drinking water to all of its villages.

Haryana's economy has a significant agrarian component. Its annual foodgrain production is about 18 million tones and it is one of the largest contributors to the foodgrains pool of the Central Government. Cotton, sugarcane and oilseeds are the main commercial crops, which have triggered the growth of several agro-based industries.

Haryana has taken a lead for social and economic development. The state stands out for its progressive policies, which have led to the improvement of the quality of life for its residents through focused development of agriculture, industries, commerce and trade as well as through the creation of social infrastructure. It is recognized as a state that is trying to orchestrate improvement in every parameter involved in guiding investment decisions.

Haryana's achievements in the industrial sector have also been quite phenomenal during the last 55 years. Haryana has a large industrial base having more than 1,347 large and medium and 80,000 small scale units in the state.

Haryana accounts for more than 75 per cent of the total number of passenger cars, 50 per cent of tractors and 60 per cent of motor cycles manufactured in the country. It also produces more than 30 per cent of refrigerators and 25 per cent of bicycles and sanitary ware manufactured in the country on an annual basis.

The State has more than 500 large industrial units with foreign technical/financial collaborations. Some examples are—Maruti Udyog, Hero Honda, Escorts, Sony India, Whirpool India, Bharti Telecom, Perfetti India, DCM Benetton, TDT Copper, Modi Alcatel, Carrier Aircon etc. Some major units in the public sector are—HMT Ltd. National Fertilizers Ltd., Indian Drugs and Pharmaceuticals Ltd., Bharat Electronics Ltd. etc. The latest addition to this group is the Rs. 60-billion oil refinery set up by the Indian Oil Corporation Ltd. in Panipat district.

About 80,000 SSI units are functioning in the State. Twenty per cent of the country's total exports of scientific instruments, 60 per cent of the country's demand for ammunition boxes of defence forces and 60 per cent of total number of woollen blankets of Indian army are met by the SSI units of Haryana. These units also manufacture the largest number of electric mixies in the country.

The State Government promulgated "Haryana Enterprises & Employment Policy-2020 (HEEP-2020)" w.e.f. 01.01.2021 to propel the State's growth story. This policy seeks to establish Haryana as a competitive and favoured investment destination, achieve regional development, export diversification and augment livelihood opportunities for its people through resilient economic development. The policy objective is to attract investments of ₹ 1 lakh crore and generate 5 lakh jobs in the State. The Government is continuously working on implementing reforms to reduce the regulatory burden and attract private sector participation in the State's economy.

Apart from easing regulations, Haryana is adopting a three-pronged approach for Ease of Doing Business (EoDB). The State's EoDB strategy is being implemented in three phases i.e. 'Design & Develop', 'Implement & Use' and 'Improve'. The ultimate objective of Haryana's 3 phase strategy is to create a conducive environment for businesses. State Government has been working in close coordination with the Department for Promotion of Industry and Internal Trade, Ministry of Commerce, Government of India. The State secured "Top Achiever" status in the State Business Reform Action Plan 2020 assessment among 37 participating States/UTs rank in the Ease of Doing Business

Rankings released in 2022. Haryana was also accorded "Top Achiever" State in the Logistics Ease across Different States (LEADS) ranking released by GoI on 13.10.2022.

Agriculture is the main occupation of the people of Haryana. About 75 per cent of the population is dependent upon agriculture for their livelihood. Haryana is self-sufficient in foodgrains production and one of the top contributors of foodgrains to the central foodgrains pool. It contributes 40 to 45 lakh tonnes of foodgrains to the central pool, which is the second largest, contribution in the country by a state. The world famous basmati rice produced in Haryana finds vast markets abroad. Production of oil seeds and cotton has also gone up considerably. At present, an area of about 65.80 lakh hectares is covered under cereal crops like wheat, rice, maize and bajra. It yields a total cereal output of 184.32 lakh tonnes.

The State of Haryana has a geographical area of 44,212 square kilometres. About 86 per cent of the geographical area is cultivable, of which, 96 per cent has already been brought under the plough. Therefore, there is hardly any scope for bringing additional area under cultivation, except reclamation of degraded land affected by water logging, salinity and alkalinity. About 75 per cent of cultivated area in the state is irrigated. The contribution of tube wells/ pumping sets in this percentage is 50 per cent. The cropping intensity in the state is nearly 170 per cent.

The State has Asia's largest agricultural university, known as Chaudhary Charan Singh Agricultural University, located at Hissar. It has helped the state being about Green Revolution in the country. Haryana, together with Punjab, is called the "Grain Bowl of India". Electricity is supplied on subsidized rates to the agriculture sector. There is a network of canals and an effective lift irrigation system for the arid areas of the state. As a result of various incentives being provided to farmers, floriculture and horticulture are improving in this state. An ultra-modern fruit and vegetables market and food processing complex of international standards are being developed at Rai near Delhi to provide marketing and food processing facilities to the farmers and entrepreneurs of the northern region.

The main crops of Haryana are wheat, rice, sugarcane, cotton, oilseeds, gram, barley, corn, millet etc. There are two main types of crops of Haryana—Rabi and Kharif. The major Kharif crops of Haryana are rice, jowar, bajra, maize, cotton, jute, sugarcane, sesame and groundnut. For these crops, soil is prepared in April and May and seeds are sown on the commencement of rains in June. The crops are ready for harvesting by the beginning of November. The major Rabi crops are wheat, tobacco, gram, linseed, rapeseed and mustard. Soil is prepared either by the end of October or the beginning of November and crops are harvested by April/May.

The production of some of the main crops and the area under cultivation is an under:

Wheat	-	110,64,000 tonnes	-	23,77,000 hectares
Paddy	-	59,21,000 tonnes	-	16,61,000 hectares
Cotton	-	10,00,000 bales	-	5,75,000 hectares
Oil Seeds	-	14,73,000 tonnes	-	8,61,000 hectares

Dairy farming forms an essential part of Haryana's rural economy. It has been known as the "milk pail" of India. Dairy products like milk, ghee, butter, curd and cheese are a major part of the diet of Haryanvi people. Animal husbandry has been taken up as an integral component of its diversified agriculture. As per Livestock Census—2019, Haryana has a livestock population of 71.26 lakh. In order to give farmers good prices for their products and help them in marketing activities, a vast network of milk producers' societies has been set up in the state. About 1,500 milk societies are operating in the state. Six milk plants, set up in the co-operative sector are now working in Jind, Bhiwani, Ambala, Rohtak, Hissar and Ballabhgarh. An additional milk plant is being set up at Sirsa. Asia's best dairy research institute, the National Dairy Research Institute (NDRI), has been set up at Karnal. It has been now upgraded to the status of deemed university. Embryo transfer technology is being introduced to improve the quality of the livestock; by adopting this technique, a superior female can produce 12 offsprings through the techniques of multiple ovulation and embryo transfer. The state is regularly supplying eggs, chicks and broilers to the neighbouring states of Delhi, Rajasthan and Uttar Pradesh. However, it also has its markets in the States of Assam and Bihar.

PRESENT STATUS

- Haryana has announced its new Industrial Policy on 1st January, 2011. The objective of this policy is to generate employment and create investment.
- As per the Advance Estimates for the year 2023-24, the GSDP of the State at current prices has been estimated as ₹ 10,95,535.06 crore, recording the growth of 11.3% in 2023-24 as compared to the growth of 13.3% recorded in 2022-23. The GSDP at constant (2011-12) prices is estimated to be ₹ 6,34,026.56 crore with a growth of 8.0% in 2023-24 as compared to the growth of 7.9% recorded in 2022-23.
- The growth of Gross State Value Added (GSVA) is the same in the years 2022-23 and 2023-24 of the State at constant (2011-12) prices has been estimated as 7.6 per cent. The growth of 7.2 per cent in Industry Sector and 9.0 per cent in Service Sector led to the overall growth of 7.6 per cent in 2023-24.
- Per capita income is the average income earned per person. At the time of formation of Haryana State in 1966, the per capita income of State at current prices was only ₹ 608. Since then, the per capita income has increased multi fold. The per capita income in 2023-24 was ₹ 3,25,759.

AGRICULTURE

- Haryana ranks among the top ten agrarian States of the country with agriculture contributing around 35 per cent of GSDP and employing 53.4 per cent of the population.
- The gross irrigated area in Haryana as a percentage of gross cropped area is 84 per cent which is more than double the all India average, reflecting efficient land utilisation.
- Horticulture crops cover 4.20 lakh hectare area, which is 6.28% of the gross cropped area of the state.
- Production of horticultural crops in the state was 64.18 lakh MT during the year 2022-23.

INDUSTRY

- With the industrial sector contributing 29.1 per cent of the income of the State, likely to rank among the ten most industrialised States in the country.

- The total Exports from the State have increased from ₹4.50 crore during 1967-68 to ₹2,45,453.19 crore during 2022-23. It is a matter of satisfaction that, barring very few appeal cases, nearly all the old outstanding liabilities under the various old subsidy schemes have been cleared.

INFRASTRUCTURE

- As per infrastructure index developed by (CMIE), Haryana is at the fourth place in terms of infrastructural facilities which are 33 per cent higher than the national average.
- It is the first State to achieve hundred per cent electrification of villages provide potable water throughout the State and link all villages with metalled roads.

PHYSICAL INFRASTRUCTURE

- Almost all iligible villages have been connected with metalled roads in the state.
- The proportion of unsurfaced roads in the States is the lowest in India after West Bengal.
- The total installed capacity of power available to the state is 14,026.68 MW as on September, 2023.

POWER GENERATION AND DISTRIBUTION

Electricity is a primary input for ensuring development of every state or region. It is used by farmers, households, offices and industrial units. It is very important to generate enough of electrical power, so that growing demand of a State could be met. Further, transmission and distribution of electrical power are two vital fields that ought to be managed with utmost care. Transmission and distribution losses increase the cost per unit generated of electrical power. Thus, these ought to be minimised.

On November 1, 1966, Haryana emerged as a separate State on the map of India. At that time, it did not have a stable and on efficient system, for transmitting and distributing electrical power. So, it was not able to utilise the quota of 16 lakh units per day of power that was allocated to it by the Bhakra Nangal Project. So much so, it was also not able to fully utilise the power allocated to it by the Indraprastha Thermal Power Station. Nearly two lakh units to be supplied by this power station to Haryana on a daily basis, were utilised by other states results in lack of adequate transmission and distribution equipment in the state.

In such a problematic situation, the Government, under the leadership of Bansi Lal, initiated a campaign to deliver electrical power to each and every village of Haryana. After the Haryana efforts of the engineers and officials of the State, electricity was finally made available in all the villages of the State by November 29, 1970.

This development gave a filip to the all-round development process of the State. Thus, the demand for electric power surged ahead in all the sectors of the State's economy. Agriculture, households and industries were the major consumers of electricity. When the local areas were electrified, these areas used electric power to run tubewells and light up their homes. But slowly and surely, the local people started using electrical appliances quite frequently. So much so, electricity was also used for skimming milk, running flour mills and preparing fodder for cattle.

The total number of electricity consumers in the State has increased from 35,44,380 in 2001-02 to 78,13,955 in 2023-24 (upto September, 2023). Every year nearly 1.5 lakhs new electric connections are released. The per capita consumption of electricity increased from 700 units in 2006-07 to 2,272 units in 2022-23. In order to promote power generation through solar Energy, HAREDA intered into MoU with six Independent Power Producers in September 2008 to set up six SPV Power Projects.

Considering the need for maximising power availability in the State, various short term and long term measures such as addition in capacity generation, improvement in operational efficiency, rehabilitation and extension of distribution network etc. have been taken. The total installed capacity available to the state till September, 2023 is 14,026.68 MW. With the increase in availability of power, it was possible to meet the demand of all categories of consumers in the State. A massive programme has been undertaken to add the generation capacity in the State, through State as well as through private sector participation.

Number of Electricity Consumers

Year	Domestic	Non-domestic	Industrial	Tubewells	Others	Total
2002-03	28,22,384	3,54,144	64,310	3,69,716	9,314	36,19,868
2005-06	31,19,788	3,87,520	70,181	4,11,769	11,402	40,00,660
2010-11	36,84,410	4,62,520	85,705	5,20,391	34,896	47,87,922
2015-16	44,19,364	5,73,848	99,195	6,13,973	45,790	57,52,170
2016-17	45,69,311	5,97,063	1,01,388	6,21,571	50,825	59,40,158
2017-18	48,41,143	6,23,455	1,04,124	6,30,487	25,328	62,24,537
2018-19	51,50,007	6,53,356	1,09,076	6,38,191	26,428	65,77,058
2019-20	53,91,944	6,83,042	1,11,569	6,43,588	27,466	68,57,609
2020-21	56,06,807	7,17,355	1,13,773	6,50,800	28,649	71,17,384
2021-22	58,10,407	7,59,112	1,18,751	6,64,882	29,684	73,82,836
2022-23	60,23,446	8,03,128	1,22,372	6,83,480	32,449	76,64,875
2023-24 (upto Sep. 2023)	61,38,865	8,26,789	1,25,923	6,87,492	34,886	78,13,955

Source: HVPN Ltd.

The per capita consumption of electricity increased from 57 units in 1967-68 to 2,272 units in 2022-23. The consumption of electricity in the State during 2022-23 was 8,36,757.30 lakh units (LUs). The consumption of electricity by the Industrial Sector was maximum *i.e.* 2,89,108.30 LUs followed by domestic sector *i.e.* 2,39,799.40 LUs. For agriculture sector, subsidy amounting to ₹ 5,769.94 crore was given by State Government in the year 2023-24.

Sector-wise Electricity Consumed in the State

(Lakh Units)

Sector	2022-23	2023-24 (upto Sept. 2023
Industrial	289108.30	153570.10
Domestic	239799.40	135539.70
Agriculture	162616.00	79971.74
Commercial	84556.78	50452.46
Public Services (Public Lighting & Public Water Works)	24048.54	9935.14
Railways	1660.50	517.62
Miscellaneous	34967.77	22556.50
Total	**836757.30**	**452543.20**

Source: HVPN Ltd.

ENERGY CONSERVATION PROGRAMMES

Haryana Government is also promoting energy efficiency as a measure for energy transition. The State has been awarded second prize at National level in the large States category for effective implementation of energy conservation policies by the Ministry of Power, Government of India. Transport, Industry, Building and Agriculture have been identified as the major sectors having potential for energy efficiency and energy transition. An action plan has been prepared for reducing carbon footprint of the State in these sectors.

Installation of Solar Power Plants on Government Buildings

Solar Power Plants of 1 kW to 500 kW (with/without battery) are installed in CAPEX mode and the Department concerned bears the cost. Solar Plants are procured through a Rate Contract arranged by the DS&D. So far, solar power plants of 196 MW have been installed. During 2023-24, solar power plants of total 10.4 MW capacity are proposed to be installed. Subsidy Pattern: • ***Govt. Buildings (1-500 kW):*** No Subsidy • ***Social sector institutions (1-50 kW):*** 50% subsidy (New Scheme) • ***SC-BC Dharamshalas (1-5 kW):*** 75% subsidy (New Scheme)

In RESCO mode, Solar Power Plants of capacity >50 kW and up to 500 kW are installed. The plant is installed by a RESCO firm at its cost and it supplies power at a tariff discovered through tendering done by the DS&D. During 2023-24, solar power plants of total 30 MW capacity are proposed to be installed.

Solar Water Pumping Programme

To meet the irrigation needs of farmers with clean energy and to replace diesel pumps with solar pumps, the Department of New and Renewable Energy, Haryana, is implementing a scheme to provide 3 HP to 10 HP off-grid solar water pumps with a 75% subsidy (Central + State) for irrigation purposes in the State under component B of the Pradhan Mantri Kisan Urja Surkha Evam Utthan Mahabhiyan (PM-KUSUM) scheme of the Ministry of New & Renewable Energy (MNRE), Govt. of India. From 2020–21 to 2022–23, 50,230 Solar Pumps were installed. These 50,230 Solar Pumps have resulted in a solar capacity addition of about 339 MW in the State, which resulted in a saving of about 335.66 million units (MUs) of electricity annually and will save an emission of about 2.68 lakh tonnes of CO_2 annually. Furthermore, there is an annual financial savings of ₹ 225 crore in electric (RE) subsidies for agriculture pumps.

Installation of Solar Power Plants in Gaushalas

Haryana Government has decided to install Solar Power Plants in all the Gaushalas in the State to meet their energy requirement with 80% State grant (for the power plant without battery bank) and 85% grant (for hybrid solar power plants with battery backup).The balance is to be borne by Gau Sewa Aayog. So far, 331 Solar Power Plants with aggregate capacity of 2.00 MW have been installed in 330 Gaushalas. During 2023-24, it is proposed to install solar power plants of about 900 KW in 150 Gaushalas.

Biomass Power Projects

The Haryana Govt. has notified the Haryana Bio-Energy Policy-2018 with a target of installation of biomass based power projects. To tackle the issue of straw burning and to promote paddy straw based biomass power projects in the State, the Govt. had allotted 4 paddy straw based biomass power projects of 49.8 MW capacity in Kurukshetra (15 MW), Kaithal (15 MW), Jind (9.90 MW) and Fatehabad (9.90 MW). These projects will consume about 5.70 lakh ton of paddy straw as fuel annually. The projects at Kurukshetra and Kaithal have been commissioned whereas the project at Jind is likely to be commissioned by September 2024.

SPV Street Lighting for Rural Area

Energy Department is implementing 'SPV Street Lighting for Rural Area' Scheme with the objective of enhancing social security in rural areas and to reduce the dependence on conventional power for street lighting. Proposals for this scheme are invited through respective Additional Deputy Commissioner-cum-Chief Project Officer of the district from the interested Gram Panchayats, Block Samitis, eligible non-commercial institutions/organizations etc. Under this scheme, standalone Solar Street Lighting Systems, each system consisting of 75 watt solar panel, Lithium Ferro Phosphate battery of 12.8V30 Ah and 12 watt LED Luminaire at pole of 5 meter height with dusk to dawn operation and Solar High Mast lighting systems, each system consisting of SPV module of aggregate capacity 440 watt, 12.8V200Ah LiFePO4 Battery and 4 × 22 watt LED Luminaires, Pole of 7 meter height with dusk to down operation are installed through the approved suppliers.

The total installed capacity available to the State is 14,026.68 MW as on September 2023. It includes 2,582.4 MW from State's own stations, 846.14 MW from jointly owned projects and the balance as share in Central Projects and independent Private Power Projects. The **power availability** from these sources during the year 2022-23 was 5,96,678.02 lakh KWH.

The progressive increase in power availability has been as follows:

Installed Generation Capacity & Power Availability in Haryana State

Year	Installed generation capacity (MW)	Total installed capacity (MW)	Power available (lakh KWH)
1967-68	29	343	6010
1970-71	29	486	12460
1980-81	1074	1174	41480
1990-91	1757	2229.5	90250
2000-01	1780	3124.5	166017
2010-11	4106	5997.83	296623
2015-16	3611.37	11053.3	445111
2016-17	3621.00	11065.00	454659
2017-18	3621.37	11262.30	506044
2018-19	3638.54	11750.72	515733
2019-20	3428.54	11950.70	521775
2020-21	3428.54	12241.41	495874
2021-22	3428.54	12201.52	529358
2022-23	3428.54	13442.77	596678
2023-24 (upto Sept., 2023)	3428.54	14026.68	326416

Under the new electricity policy, proposals from 18 firms have been received to generate 44 MW of power through non-conventional sources. These firms would produce electric power by using biomass waste products of cities and waterfalls available near canals. The private firms would invest ₹ 220 crore in the power generation sector.

The Ministry of Non-Conventional Energy sources of Government of India has praised the Integrated Rural Energy Programme of Haryana. It has asked other States of the country to adopt this model.

CHAPTER 20

Religious Places and Pilgrimage Sites

INTRODUCTION

Haryana is a land of temples, mosques and gurudwaras. The Sacred place of the Hindu pantheon, Kurukshetra, is located in the State. Lord Krishna had given the divine message and guidance to Arjuna, his cousin and disciple at Jyotisar. Besides, there are many religious places associated with the Muslims and the Sikhs. Let us discuss these in a nutshell.

RELIGIOUS PLACES OF THE HINDUS

Kurukshetra

Kurukshetra is a great pilgrimage place for Hindus and tourists from all over the country who visit the venue of the Mahabharta War and the birth place of *The Bhagwad Gita,* Building on its historical and cultural traditions, Kurukshetra has developed to become a modern city. The Brahmsarovar, Sri Krishna Museum and the Science Museum (Panorama) are its chief attractions. Kurukshetra district is a tourist's delight, there are about 360 *tirthas* of religious and historic importance for him. Out of these, about 134 *tirthas* are being maintained by Kurukshetra Development Board, Kurukshetra.

Nava Graha

It is located in Kaithal city. There are 9 *kundas* at this place. Lord Krishna had got them constructed. In old times, there were *pucka ghats* at this place where people used to take bath. Today, most of the *kundas* have become extinct, the remaining ones are in a pathetic stage.

Baba Ladana's Shrine

It is located at a distance of 10 km from Kaithal, at a place called Rajpuri. Baba Ladana was a Saint. On the day of the Dussehra, a fair it organised at this shrine, which comprises a *Samadhi* and a pond.

Brahma Sarovar

It is located in Kurukshetra, quite near the Thanesar railway station. Its size is 1219.2 m × 608.6 m. There are some small islands and Pauranic temples at this site. The Shravan Nath Math has been connected to other islands by bridges. King Kuru has got this Sarovar dug. Stairs are visible only on the western side of the Sarowar. On its northern part, there are temples and dharamshalas. In its centre, there is a Shiva temple. There is a platform of 6.10 metre width around the Sarovar. On the periphery of the Sarovar there are *sadris,* which were got constructed by the Kurukshetra Development Board.

Sannihit

It is located at a distance of 1.5 km from Kurukshetra Railway Station on the Kurukshetra-Pehova road. It is nearly 472.44 metre long and 137.16 metre wide. People come here to offer homage and respect to their ancestors. It is deemed as the permanent abode of Lord Vishnu.

Jyotisar

It is located at a distance of 8 km from Kurukshetra Railways Station. It is located on the Pehova road on the bank of river Saraswati. Its literal meaning is "pond of knowledge." At this, place, Lord Krishna had given divine guidance to Arjuna. His teaching are better known as *Shrimad Bhagwad Geeta.* The remains of a pond, Akshay Vata and Shiva Temple are still here. Its length is 1000 ft (393.7 m) and its width is 500 ft (196.85 m). It was also known as *Pawan Hriday* and *Marut* (according to *the Mahabharata).* Water for the pond is provided from the Narwana Canal. If someone takes bath at this shrine and pays homage to Lord Shiva, he is eligible for the supreme status *(Shaiva Pada).*

Kamli Wale Baba Ka Dera

It is located near Sannihit in Kurukshetra. It was set up by Swami Vishuddhanand. Here, statues of Lord Shankar, Lord Krishna and Arjuna can be seen. *Dharamshalas* and eating places are available.

Chandrakoop

It is situated near Kurukshetra's shrine. It has well and a temple, which was got built by Yudhishthira after the War.

Gandiya Muth

It is located on the northern side of Kurukshetra's shrine. It is inhabited by the Shri Bengali disciples who are followers of Lord Krishna. Here beautiful statues of Radha and Krishna can be seen. It related to the *Bhakti* era of starting of the sect of Chaitanya.

Geeta Bhawan

It is located at the northern bank of Kurukshetra shrine (the Soraovar). It was set up by the king of Rewa in 1921. It has a palace like structure in which statues of Lord Krishna, Durga and Lord Shankar are placed. There are adequate arrangements of boarding and lodging at this shrine.

Valmiki Ashram

It is located opposite Thanesar Railway Station in Kurukshetra. Baba Lakshman Giri had taken *samadhi* as well as the Balmiki temple is the famous site to be visited.

Baan Ganga

It is located on the Thanesar-Jyotisar road near village Narkatali. Arjuna had made the Ganges erupt at this point. So that it could quench the thirst of Bhishma, who was lying on a bed of arrows during the War.

Kamal Nabha Teerth

It is located in Kurukshetra district. It is believed that Lord Brahma had made his appearance here, There is a pond at this place, where males and females take bath (at separate places).

Kaleshwar Teerth

It is located in Kurukshetra district. Ravana had established the idol of Lord Rudra here, There is also a Shiva temple and a *ghat* at this places.

Prachi

It is located in Kurukshetra district, It is located towards north of Bhadrakali temple, near the Kuber shrine. People pay homage to their ancestors here, *i.e.,* carry out the rituals of *pitra tarpan.*

Kuber Teerth

It is located on the banks of Saraswati river in Kurukshetra district (near Kali Mata's temple). Kuber had organised *Yajnas* here. Here, the residential place *(Kutia)* of Chaitanya Mahaprabhu is also located.

Markandeya

This shrine is located on the bank of Saraswati river. On the road to Pipli (in Kurukshetra district). Markandeya had achieved a divine status by carrying out *tapa* (meditation) at this spot. A temple is located here.

Narkatari

It is located in Kurukshetra district. Its relationship has been established with Brahma, Vishnu, Mahesh and wife of Rudra. It is located at a distance of 1 km from the Kurukshetra University. A deep pond is located here, it is called Baan Ganga.

Kamodha

It is a forest area located at a distance of 14 km from Thanesar in Kurukshetra district. The Pandavas had stayed here. Here, a temple and *math* of Kameshwar Mahadev, both are made of bricks. There is another small room made of bricks in this area, called Draupadi's store. Draupadi had cooked food for the Pandavas here.

Aapga

It is located in Kurukshetra district, it was located on the bank of full Aapya (Aapga) in the ancient times. *Rigveda* has mentioned Drishadvati, Saraswati and Aapga rivers. Vedic civilisation had originated on the banks of these three rivers. It is located at a distance of 0.5 km from Kurukshetra University near Karna Ka Tida. The old pond has been filled with soil with passage of time.

Pehowa

Its old name was Prithudak. King Prithu had prayed for his father *(i.e.,* done the *tarpan)* at this site, Hence, it is a popular place for the people of Punjab, Haryana, J & K and Rajasthan, to carry out *pitr shraadh.* It is located at a distance of 25 km. towards west of Thanesar. There are many temples at this place, which has become a town with passage of time.

Panchavati

It is located at Palwal and has a temple as well as a pond. The Pandavas had taken rest during the year of solitary stay *(agyaat vaas)* at this place. The pond is called Draupadi Ghat.

Pandu Pindara

It is located near Jind on the Jind-Gohana road. The Pandavas had carried out the ritual of *pind daan* at this place after the War. Every year, a fair is organised on the day of Somvati Amavasya at this place. *Pind daan* rituals are also done here.

Ram Rai

It is located on the Jind Hissar road. A fair is organised here on every *Puranmasi* day. But fairs of Kartik and Baisakh are more important. Lord Rama, Sita and Lakshman had visited this place. Lord Parashuram has conducted *Yajna* here. A place called Dhundwa is located nearby here, Duryodhana had hid himself after he was defeated in the war. Bheema had killed him after locating him at this spot.

Hansdehar

It is located on the Patiala Narwana road, at a distance of 10 km from the Narwana Subdivision headquarters, Kardam Rishi had meditated here, his son Kapil Muni, was also born here.

Jamni

It is located at Jind-Safidon road. Rishi. Jagdamni had meditated here.

Pushkar

It is located in Jind district at a distance of 2-3 km. A Sarovar is located here.

Dhosi

It is located at a distance of 9 km from Narnaul. Rishi Chwan had prayed for 7000 years at this place. The Shiva temple. Shiva *Kunda*, Chandra *Kunda* and other *Kundas* are worth seeing. The peak of the hillock can be approached after climbing 459 steps. People flock to this place on the day of Somvati Amavas and take bath in these kundas. The large statue of Chwan Rishi is also worth a visit.

Pundarik Sarover

It is located in the township of Pundri. Vrindavan ghat, Triveni wala ghat, Ganga ghat, Gau ghat and main ghat are the main attractions of this area.

It is located at a distance of 5 km from Bhiwani. Here, fairs are organised in the Chaitra and Ashwin months every year. The temple located here was got built by a businessman *(Mahajan).*

Shri Kaleshwar Mahadev Math

It is located on the Yamunanagar Paonta Sahib road near Kaleshwar, on the bank of Yamuna. It is one of the 12 oldest *mathas* of the world. It is the place of confluence of Saraswati, Yamuna and Sukhna. On the hillock's top, there are caves of Shiva and Parvati. The statues of Brahma, Vishnu, Mahesh, Sheshnag and Parvati can be seen in these caves.

Asthal Bohr

It is located in Rohtak and is famous for its darshani Sadhus (whose ears are split). These Sadhus consider Gorakhnath to be their first teacher. This shrine was established by Shri Chaurangi Nath Ji. Nearly 250 years, ago, it was got separated by Baba Mastnath Ji. The main temple has been built with marble. There is an Ayurveda College and an eye hospital in the complex. The temple is called Siddh Smriti Mandir. A fair is organised every year from Phalgun Shukla Navami (in the memory of Baba Mastnath Ji).

Kapaal Mochan

It is located at a distance of 20 km from Jagadhari at a place called Bilaspur (formerly Vyaspur). Som Sarovar is located here.

If one takes bath in this Sarovar one can get rid of all the evils. They must take bath between the *ekadashi* and *panchmi* of the Kartik purnima to do so. Besides, it people take bath in the Shukla paksha and visit the Shiva Lingum (phallus of Shiva) then all of their desires are fulfilled.

Sthaneshwar Mahadev Temple

It is located near Thanesar (Sthaneshwar). It was got built by the ancestor of king Harshvardhana, Raja Pushya Bhuti. It is dedicated to Mahadev. Here, the Pandavas has prayed to Lord Shiva and got his blessing to win the War. The temple has regional architectural style. Mahmood Ghaznavi took the original statue of the temple to Ghazni. Lately, Sadashiv Rao, the Maratha Chieftain, got the temple rebuilt.

Devi Koop

It is also called Bhadra Kali temple. It is located near Kurukshetra Railway Station, on Sansa road, near Sthanu (Shiva) temple. It is dedicated to Goddess Bhadra Kali (Sati). At this place the right knee of the goddess (Sati) had fallen. People come to pray at this temple. Their desires are fulfilled here.

Dukh Bhanjaneshwar Temple

It is located near the Sannahit Sarovar. People come to pray before Lord Dukh Bhanjaneshwar Mahadev Ji in this temple.

Narayan Mandir

It is also located on the bank of Sannihit Shrine (in Kurukshetra). The Statues of Chaturbhuj Narayan, Dhruva Bhakta, Hanuman and Durga Devi are seated in this temple.

Lakshmi Narayan Mandir

In Kurukshetra a grand temple of Lord Lakshmi Narayan is located near the Sannihit Sarovar. Its style is based on Southern architecture. It has been constructed according to the Chola style of architecture. Baba Shiv Giri Maharaj, a saint of the Giri community, had got it built. The top of its upper most storey is too thin to be stepped at.

Salveshwar Mahadev Temple

It is located in the middle of the Brahma Sarovar (Kurukshetra). A small bridge is the only passage for approaching this temple. It was got constructed by Baba Shravan Nath. The statues of Lord Garuda, Narayan Shiva and Ganesha are located here. Besides, the statues a goddess Parvati, Nandis and a Shiva Lingum (Shiva's Phallus) are also located here. The statues of Lord Krishna as well as those of Balrama and Hanuman are also the main attractions. At this place, Kunti had played before Lord Shiva during the Mahabharta era.

Birla Mandir

It is located near Thanesar Railway Station on the Kurukshetra-Pehova road. In 1955, Jugal Kishore Birla had got it constructed and named to Bhagwadgeeta Mandir. It is located on the bank of Kurukshetra Shrine (Brahma Sarovar). The marble chariot of Lord Krishna seems to be giving the elixir of *the Geeta* to Arjuna. On the marble walls of this temples the teachings/statements of great sages and religious preachers have been engraved. The sacred hymns *(shlokas)* of *the Geeta* have also been engraved on marble in this temple. The statues of Hanuman, Lord Krishna and Arjuna can be seen in the temple premises.

Madhowala Mandir

It is also called Lord Shiva Temple. It is located in Narnaul (near the bus stand) on the Narnaul-Rewari road. On the occasion of Raksha Bandhan a large fair is organised here.

Gyarah Rudri Shiva Mandir

It is located at Kaithal. In this temple, Arjuna has appeased Lord Shiva and obtained the Pashupatastra from him. The construction of the present temple was got done by the wife of Uday Singh nearly 250 years ago. There are 11 Shiva Lingas in this temple. On the dome of the temple, paintings of gods, goddesses, peacocks and *garudas* (eagles) can be seen. Statues of Lord Shiva and Hanuman have been installed in the precincts of the temple.

Ambakeshwar Mahadev Mandir

It is located at Kaithal and dates back to pre Mahabharata time. The lingum located here is also called Swayam Linga or Pataleshwar.

Hanuman Mandir

It is located in the centre of Kaithal city. It is located at a height of one storey from the ground level. It also, has one well, one *Satsang* hall, *Chowk* and *verandahs.* Janam Ashtami and Hanuman Jayanti are celebrated as festivals in this temple.

Shiv Mandir (Devi Talab)

It is located at Panipat. It was got built by the Maratha Chieftain Mangal Raghunath, during the Third Battle of Panipat (1761).

Shiva Mandir

It is located in Chaura Bazaar at Karnal. A large fair is held on the day of Shiva Ratri in the temple.

Aditi's Temple

It is located at village Amin in Kurukshetra district, Aditi had played here before giving birth to Surya, the Sun god.

Panchvati Mandir

It is located at Palwal. The Pandavas had stayed here during the period of secret exile at this temple.

Dau Ji's Temple

It is located at Vanohari village which is located at a distance of 55 km from Faridabad on G.T. Road. It is dedicated to Balrama, the brother of Lord Krishna.

Shiva Mandir (Badhot)

It is located at a distance of 40 km from Mahendragarh in the Kanina-Dadri road at village Badhot. It is associated with King Dilip of the Ikshawaku dynasty. It is presumed that king Dilip had got it constructed and named it. Bagheshwar. Later, this name was corrupted to become Badhot. Large fairs are held on the Shiva Ratri (of Shravana) and Maha Shiva Ratri (of Phalguna).

Chamunda Devi's Temple

It is located in the centre of Narnaul city. People get their wishes fulfilled in this temple. There were 84 pillars in this temple. But only a few of these are left today, According to the legend King Noonkaran (of Circa twelfth Century AD) had got it built because his queen had given birth to two sons, The signs of Ashokan age are visible in the remains of the temple. Noonkaran was a disciple of Chamunda Devi.

Ghanteshwar Temple

It is located at Rewari. The statues of all the gods and goddesses of the Sanatan Pantheon have been installed here.

Hanuman Mandir

It is located at Rewari. It has a huge pond. A fair is organised every Tuesday at this temple.

Shitla Devi Temple

It is located at Gurugram. Dronacharya gave training to Kauravas and Pandavas at this place. The 1.5 kg gold statue of mother Kirpi, the wife of Dronacharya is the main attraction. The temple area is 500 square yards. In the months of March and October, fairs are organised in this temple. Kirpi had become Sati after the death of her husband, Dronacharya.

Shivalaya of Deeghal

It is located at Deeghal village in Jhajjar district. Lala Dhaniram had got its construction initiated. It was constructed with Lakhauri bricks and lime. Inside the deepest chamber of the Shivalaya, the paintings, referring to the stories/fables of *Mahabharta Ramayana* and Puranas, can be seen every today.

Radheshyam Temple

It is located at Pundarik township. It has statues of Radha and Lord Krishna. A small temple of Lord Shiva as well as another temple of

Gauri Shankar is also located here. A fair is organised here on the occasion of Janam Ashtami.

Geeta Mandir

This temple is located near Mardane Ghat on the way to Pundarik. It has holy hymns *(Shlokas)* of *the Geeta, Ramayana* and other religious scriptures written on its walls.

Shiva Temple

It is located in the premises of the Pundarik Shrine. In Circa 1520 AD, a temple *(matha)* was seen on this site, it was then known as the matha of Baba Thandi Puri. He was a disciple of Lord Shiva.

Old Shiva-Parvati Temple

It is also located at Pundarik. People use water and sweets *(batashas)* to pay their respects to Shiva and Parvati during the days *(Jagaran Kaal)* of Maha Shiva Ratri.

Rudhmal Temple

It is located at Beri in Jhajjar district. It has a 105-year old Shivalaya whose height is 116 feet. The statues on figurines of 24 *avataras* (incarnations) of the lord have been created in the temple (from bottom to top). The Shivalaya was built in 1892. In 1953, it was renovated. Again, in 1990, it was refurbished. One Hanuman temple, one Durga temple and one Radha-Krishna temple are also located in the premises of this temple. The Radha-Krishna temple is also called Shri Nand Nandan Thakur.

Thakurdwara of Kutani

It is located at village Kutani at a distance of 23 km from Jhajjar. It was got constructed by Shauji Singh in 1901. The height of this temple is 50 ft. An 8-metal alloy *(Ashta dhatu)* has been used to make the statues of Radha and Lord Krishna. For these statues, jewellery (weighing 50 *Tolas)* was got made. This jewellery is intact and decorating the idols. In the deepest chamber *(Sanctum Sanctorum)*, the tales from the life of Lord Krishna have been depicted as paintings. But their colours are fading now-a-days.

Chitta Temple of Yamunanagar

It is located at Yamunanagar. It was got built nearly 60 years ago. The praying site of Mahant Shri Ganga Nand Giri Ji is located here when the Pandavas were heading towards Kurukshetra for waging the War against the Kauravas, they had taken rest here. Hanuman was residing, albeit in a secret manner, on the top of the chariot of Arjuna, When the Pandavas stopped here, Hanuman showed Himself as a white person at the site. Later a white statue of Hanuman was installed here and that is why, it was called Chitta Mandir (white temple). A fair is organised every Tuesday at this temple and desires of the masses are fulfilled here.

Sarvadharma Temple

The Sarvadharma temple of Lord Parashuram is located at Jagadhari. It has an architectural style of the medieval age. The statues of the prophets and saints of all the religions have been installed in this temple.

Its depth is 42 ft. and the number of its storeys is 11. Its height is 55 ft. 3 inches. A hospital and a training centre (sewing) is also located in the premises of this temple. Pancham Kaal Jain Temple.

It is located at Budia in Yamunanagar district. Several years ago, a statue of Lord Parshva Nath was found here. It was installed in the temple. It is also called Digamber Nath Jain Temple. The statues of Lord Mahavir Swamy), Vimal Nath, Devi Padmavati and Lord Parshva Nath can be seen here.

Adi Badri Narayan Temple

It is located at a distance of 35 km, from Jagadhari on the Bilaspur Ranjitpur road near Kathgarh villlage. It is located in the Shivalic hill range. The river Saraswati had originated here. During the Mahabharata era, Lord Badrinarayan had visited this temple. Ved Vyasa had sat on the western bank of Saraswati and written *Shrimad Bhagwat Mahapurana.*

Later, Adi Shankaracharya located this place and got a temple constructed. In 1823, Purushottam Ashram got this temple renovated. Towards its eastern side, there is a temple of Lord Kedarnath. Towards its northern side, goddess Mantra has her presence. Towards its west, there is a temple of Adi Badri Narayan. Towards its south, the Saraswati river is located (which does not flow in the present era). On the occasion of the seventh Teej of Baisakh, an annual fair is organised here.

Panchmukhi Hanuman Temple

Located at a distance of 5 km from Chhachhrauli, this temple is only 23 km away from Jagadhari (on the Chhachharauli Bilaspur road). The statue of this temple is believed to be nearly 350 year old. Devouts throng the temple every Tuesday and Saturday.

Shiva Temple (Kiloi)

This 300 year old Shiva temple is located at village Kiloi in Rohtak district. On the phalluns (Shiva lingum), there is a statue of Lord Shiva, this is a rare event. Newly married couples seek blessings of the Lord at this temple. People offer milk (every Monday) to the Lord. Fairs are organised in the months of February and August.

Mansa Devi Temple (Mani Majra)

It is located at a distance of 9 km from Chandigarh near Mani Majra. Fairs are organised during the *Navratra* days of Chaitra and Ashwin months (Every year) in this temple.

RELIGIOUS PLACES OF THE SIKHS

Dhamtan Sahib Gurudwara

It is located in the Narwana sub-division on the Narwana-Tohana road. Guru Tegh Bahadur had stopped here on his way to Delhi (to offer himself for martyrdom). The area of the land under the gurudwara is 621 acre, it is fully cultivable. Fairs are organised on the days of Dussehera, Holi and Amavasya (dark moon nights). People also take bath in is pond.

Gurudwara Ninth Patshahi

It is located close to the Sthaneshwar Mahadev temple in Kurukshetra district. During the time of solar eclipse, Guru Tegh Bahadur had held discussions (on religion) with sages and *Sanyasis* at this place. He had also organised the community kitchen *(langar)* at this place.

Rajghat Gurudwara

Guru Gobind Singh Ji had visited this place on the occasion of solar eclipse. This shrine is located at Kurukshetra.

Gurudwara Neem Sahib

It is located near Pratap gate at Kaithal. Guru Tegh Bahadur had visited this place, along with his family members, in 1723. He had given the margosa leaves of the tree (under which, he was sitting) to a sick person. The sick person had recovered from the disease.

Gurudwara Manji Sahib

It is located at Kaithal Guru Tegh Bahadur had visited the home of a carpenter at this place and sat under a margosa tree. The carpenter had given the place for the construction of the gurudwara.

Gurudwara Sixth Patshahi

It is located near the Sannihit Shrine in Kurukshetra. Its building is new, though it is an old gurudwara. People from far and wide visit the shrine.

Gurudwara Kapal Mochan

It is located at Bilaspur in Yamunanagar district towards the east of the Kapal Mochan Sarover. It is dedicated to Guru Gobind Singh Ji. In 1687, Guru Ji had stayed here for 52 days after fighting the forces of the kings of the hilly areas. He had also washed his weapons at the Rina Mochan pond. That is why, this place is also called the Shastra Ghat of Guru Gobind Singh Ji.

Gurudwara Lakhan Majra

It is located at a distance of 20 km from Rohtak on the Rohtak-Jind road. This famous Manji Sahib Gurudwara is dedicated to Guru Tegh Bahadur. While going towards Delhi (to offer himself for martyrdom), Guru Ji had stayed here for 13 days. On the one side of the pond, there is the Gurudwara. On the other side, there is a two-storey *dharamshala*. On the day of Phalgun Shudi Pooranmasi, thousands of devouts had bid adieu to Guru Ji at this place.

RELIGIOUS PLACES OF THE MUSLIMS

Dargah Bu Ali Shah Kalander

It is located at Panipat. It is believed that the bricks or body of Bu Ali Shah Kalander were brought here from Buddha Khera. It is a sacred shrine of the Chishti Sect. It is believed that when Bu Ali Shah Kalander had died, his body was buried at Buddha Khera. Later, the residents of Panipat had taken either the body or the bricks of this shrine to Panipat. Historians have not been able to confirm the real facts regarding this transfer.

Mazaar of Sheikh Anam Allah

It is located at Panipat.

Mazaar of Altaf Hussain Hali

Hali was a sensitive Urdu poet. His mazaar is located at Panipat.

Mazaar of Ghaus Ali Shah

It is also located at Panipat. It is frequently visited by the devouts.

Dargah of Hamza Pir

It is located at a distance of 10 km from Narnaul at village Dharsun. The full name of Hamza Pir was Hazrat Shah Kalamuddin Hamza Pir Hussain. Ladies were not allowed to visit this shrine.

Dargah of Pir Mubrak Shah

It is located at Kaliyana village in Charkhi Dadri district. A fair is organised every Thursday at this dargah. On the occasion of Bakr Eid an *Urs* is organised on the twenty-sixth day of the month.

Mazaar of Seikh Junaid

It is located at Hissar towards South of the Nagaur Gate.

Mazaar of Sant Mir Shah

He was also known as Baba Shah Khan. His Mazaar is located at Fatehabad. A rock edict of Humayun can also be seen in the precincts of this mazaar.

Tomb of Sheikh Chehli

Sufi Saint Sheikh Chehli (also called Sheikh Chilli) had come to visit Hazrat Qutab Jalaluddin at Thanesar. He had come from Iran During the reign of emperor Shah Jahan.

Unfortunately, Sheikh Chehli died at Thanesar. He was buried at Thanesar and a beautiful marble tomb was built at the place of his burial. Its total area is 4 hectares. Its construction is so beautiful that it is also called the Taj Mahal of Haryana. The ASI has declared it as a monument of natural importance.

Dargah Chaar Qutab

It is located at Hansi. It has the mazaars of four Sufi Saints—Qutab Sheik Jamaluddin Ahmed, Qutab Maulana, Basohuddin, Sufi, Qutab-ud-din Manavvar and Qutab Nur-ud-din. An *Urs* is organised every year at this shrine and *chadars* are brought from Ajmer Sharif and put over the four mazaars.

Pucka Pul Mazaar

The Pucka Pul's Mazaars belong to five saints. It is located at Madhuban near Karnal. The five mazaars belong to Hazrat Ali Ilahi Baksh, Bahadur Khan Durrani, Mohammad Ali, Sabar Singh Bori and Kesar Mal Bori.

Sheeshe Wali Masjid

It is a large mosque, which is located at Rohtak. Its entrance gate is made of marble. The outer facade of the mosque has beautiful ceramic tiles. The walls of the major shrine have a length of six feet each . The domes and inner roofs have beautiful paintings on them. Glass pieces have been fixed on the walls of the mosque. But these glass pieces are being destroyed by the vagaries of time and also, due to negligence of authorities. Three large domes and minarets are in a very poor condition. The lower parts of the two minarets at the front of the mosque have been made from marble. In one part of the mosque, there is a long verandah having 14 pillars. In another part of the mosques two religious priests (*maulvis*) live along with their families. This mosque has been built on a platform whose height is 8 ft.

Deeni Masjid

It is located at Rohtak. The ancient Mahavira temple is located within its precincts. The legend says that there was a temple at the site of the mosque. During the reign of Aurangzeb, the temple was converted into a mosque. After 1947, the mosque was converted into a temple. The old statues and figurines of the Hindu gods and goddesses were also found here; these have been displayed in the mosque. The lower part of this building has a beautiful architectural design. Many destroyed or broken statues were also found at this site. Probably, they were destroyed under the orders of emperor Aurangzeb.

Lal Masjid

It is a famous and beautiful mosque of Rohtak. It is located close to Bhiwani bus stand. A businessman, Haji Ashiq Ali, had got it constructed in 1939. The entrance gate of this mosque has been made from carved red stone. The stones installed on the entrance gate have been carved and cut with an artistic precision. These depict the architectural grandeur of the yore. There are three storeys in this mosque. There are also two verandahs in its main building. Ceramic tiles bearing pleasant designs have been fixed on the pillars of the mosque. At some places inside the mosque, glass pieces have also been fixed. Both minarets of the mosque have 50-step stairs each. Besides, 19 windows have also been made in each one of the minarets. Three domes of the mosque are in ruins now. However, rest of the mosque is in a good condition. The entire mosque has been constructed on a 10-foot high platform. The Muslims pray here every Friday and take part in the Jummah namaaz with religious fervour.

Mosque of Village Sarai Alawardi

It is located at village Sarai Alawardi in Gurugram district. It is a very old mosque. It dates back to the reign of Allauddin Khilji (also Khalji). The religious priests (*maulavis*) of this mosque claim that it has ancient historical linkages.

Qazi Ki Masjid

It is located at village Dujana in Jhajjar district. A priest named Qazi Ji had got it constructed nearly 200 years ago. There is also an underground chamber (*tahkhana*) in this mosque. Qazi Ji was quite popular among the local masses. When one goes towards the underground chamber, one finds the mazaar of Qazi Ji on his right hand side. People put cloth sheets on this mazaar and pray that their desires be fulfilled. The minarets of this mosque have an approximate height of 50 ft. Circular step stairs have been made in these minarets, just like the stairs of the Qutab Minar (Mehrauli). The entire mosque has been made from white stone. However, it is being neglected by authorities.

Red Mosque of Rewari

This famous historical mosque is located at Rewari (near the old Courts). It was constructed during the reign of Akbar in Circa 1570 AD. Two tombs are also located near this mosque.

Durgah Pir Jamal

It is located at Gohana in Sonipat district. The Hindus as well as the Muslims visit this dargah with equal devotion. There is a berry garden in the immediate vicinity of the dargah. The Hindus and Muslims come to this place every Thursday to get their wishes fulfilled.

Mazaar Baba Meeran Nau Bahar

The shrine (mazaar) of Guhla Cheeka Baba Meeran Nau Bahar is nearly 960 year old. A fair is organised here every years. This saint had buried himself live. Devouts must also pay respects to Pir Chetan Shah at his mazaar (which is nearby) before visiting the mazaar of Baba Meeran Nau. The mazaar of Baba Meeran Nau Bahar is located at Kaithal and that of Pir Chetan Shah is located near the bus stand of Kaithal.

CHAPTER 21

Research Projects

INTRODUCTION

Haryana is a symbol of historic and cultural unity of India. It was once the cradle of the Vedic civilisation. *The Bhagwadgeeta* was written here. Several sages and philosophers stayed here and created such holy scriptures as are unequalled in the world. In this chapter, we shall study various research projects that were undertaken to unearth the ancient glory of this State. Such projects were undertaken by the agencies of the government, especially the ASI and private researchers in the fields of archaeology, literature, arts and crafts. In the hills of the Shivalik range, some implements dating back to the stone age have been recovered. These were recovered from the region of Pinjore and Kalka. Thus, we can conclude that the earliest man was an inhabitant of this area. It is believed that Manu, who was the creator of the human society in India, was the king of this region that is now known as Haryana. In *Avanti Sundari Katha*, he has been introduced as the resident of Sthaneeshwar (now Thanesar). According to archaeologists, concrete evidences and artefacts have been obtained from Banawali, Siswal, Kunal, Mirzapur, Daulatpur and Bhagwanpura. Excavations at these sites have yielded enough objects and evidences that relate to pre-Harappan, Harappan and post-Harappan eras. These objects included painted figurines, utensils, items of daily use, ornaments, etc. One gets an idea of the cultural and material prosperity of people of those times from the remains, earthen utensils, copper items, jewellery and items of everyday use that have been found at the aforementioned sites. These evidences confirm that the post-Harappan people used to live in houses made of raw bricks. Their jewellery was made of precious stones, baked earth and other items. They used to make their weapons and defence gear from copper. The sharp blades of javelin. (made of copper), chisels, needles, bangles, hooks for catching fish, stones for rubbing and grinding and finally, tools for digging have been found from these excavation sites. The painted earthen vessels found from Bhagwanpura (in Kurukshetra district) throw light on the cultural ethos of the people of that era. Excavations have revealed that the people of that civilisation used to make their huts in the shape of a crescent (half) moon. Roofs of such huts used to be made of cane. Later, they started making homes from earth and still later, they started making these with baked bricks.

Several written scriptures, coins, currency coins, imprints of currency coins, remains of art objects (sculptures) and other articles have been found from various exacavation sites. These give ample evidences of the social, political, cultural, economic and artistic activities and aptitude of the people of Haryana over various (historical) periods/eras.

In 1862, Alexander Cunnigham started the process of archaeological research for the first time in the State. Till 1990, several artefacts and remains of historical importance have been unearthed and/or found in the State. The history of human civilisation in Haryana begins from the Stone Age. Several implements and tools of this age have been found from Pinjore. The research and excavation tasks carried out in Sirsa, Jhajjar and the upper valleys of Kaushalya river inform us that the Stone Age man used to inhabit these areas. In the area towards the west of Kalka station, implements belonging to the Stone Age have been found. Similar implements have also been found in Ambala district. Although it is difficult to assign the age of these objects, yet experts and scholars believe that these could be dating back to 1,00,000 years.

Dr. Surajbhan has come across very important artefacts and objects by excavating sites at Mithathal (in Bhiwani district). In the first phase of his excavations, he found post-Harappan utensils that are quite similar to those found at Kalibangan. In the second stage (A and B) of his research he has found the remains that belong to the Harappan civilisation.

Exacavations were carried out under the direction of Dr. Udayvir Singh at Balu. These have led to the discovery of post-Harappan are pre-Harappan remains from that place. The remnants of a post-Harappan and Harappan fort have also been found/unearthed. This fort was made from raw (unbaked) bricks. From Daulatpur, the remains of the Harappan era and later, the painted earthen vessels were found.

During the first (B) age (as described by Dr. Udayvir Singh), people belonging to the post-Harappan culture lived here. But later, people of painted slate vessel civilisation came to live in this region. The proof of the co-existence of both these types of civilisations has been found from Bhagwanpura. Evidences about the painted slate vessel civlisation have also been found at other places. However, many facts were learned about their living styles and life patterns from Bhagwanpura. During the first stage, these people used to live in circular or crescent-shaped huts. During the second stage, they started living in homes made of earth. Archaeologists have found a house, which contains 13 rooms, all made from the walls of earth. The size of each room of this house was 1.60 m × 1.60 m or 3.35 m × 4.25 m. Nearly 2.5 per cent vessels, belonging to post-Harappan civilisation, have also been found. In the rooms of the aforementioned house, slate vessels, pens made from bones, toys and beads in large numbers. These findings give an idea of the social exchanges prevalent among those people. During the third stage, these people started living in houses made of baked bricks. Five different types of bricks have been found here.

Archaeologists have also found some oval-shaped creations at some sites. Perhaps, they may have been used for some religious ceremonies. Archaeologists have discovered two burial places. In one of these, a child's skeleton has been found and in the other, the skeleton of a man has been discovered. Both the skeletons have been found to be lying in the north-south direction. The earthen toys, figurines of humans, pens of bones, needles and children's toys of the painted slate vessel civlisation are worth mentioning here.

The excavation tasks done at Bhagwanpura brought the time period of the painted slate vessel civilisation to the middle of second century AD; it also connected this civilisation to the time period of the post-Harappan age. During the post-Harappan age, the painted slate vessel civilisation had come to its end.

Besides the aforementioned places, dozens of mounds are located in Haryana, whose lists are available. Many mounds of post-Harappan, Harappan and painted slate vessel civilisation are included in them. A large mound belong to the Harappan civilisation is located at Rakhi Garhi (in Jind district). It seems to be a large city of Harappan civilisation. Some *Samdhava* coins have also been found; these are believed to be belonging to Swami Omanand Ji. Several mounds of Haryana that are similar to the one at Rakhi Garhi pose a challenge of connecting several hidden links of ancient civilisations.

Among the remains of the Mauryan dynasty, the famous pillar (272-232 BC) of emperor Ashoka is worth mentioning. This pillar was located at Topra (Ambala). In 1356 AD, Feroze Shah Tughlak got it removed from Topra and installed it at Kotla. Shams Shiraz has recorded the details of this transfer. There is also a scripture of king Visal Dev. Besides, two parts of a pillar have been found, one each at Hissar and Fatehabad. It is just possible that these two parts (of the same pillar) may have been located at Hansi and Agroha and later located at Hissar and Fatehabad. Further, remains of a *stupa* have been found at Chaneti (at a distance of 3 km from Jagadhari) have been discovered. The height of this mound is 3 m and its circumference is 20 m. Archaeologists opine that this could be a *stupa* of the Mauryan age.

A sculpture has been found from Palwal. It is made of red stone. It shows a *yaksha* who is wearing a scarf and a necklace. He has large ears and an object in the shape of a mollusk. This sculpture belongs to the early Shung age and is said to date back to second century BC.

In Amin (in Kurukshetra district), two pillars have been discovered. These are excellent examples of the art of the Shung age. On the first pillar, *yaksha*, has been shown. On the second one, again, a *yaksha* can be seen; he has been made from baked earth. The second figure, obtained from Pehowa, insinuates the Gandhar art style. It could not be known how this figure had arrived at this site (Pehowa).

During first or second century AD, supremacy of the Yodheyas, Agreyas (Agrohas) and Kuninda was established over Haryana. Several coins are found (even today) from many places/sites of Haryana that confirm their dominance of this area during those times. Further, coins of Indo-Greek, Indo-patheon, Indo-cynthion, Indo-Lasasanian kings have also been found in this State.

Several coins and sculptures of the *Kushana* age have been found from various places of the State. These are vital from the viewpoints of history and art. A scripture written in the *Kharoshti* Script has also been found from Karnal, it is lying in the Lahore museum.

A sculpture made from baked earth has been found at Ashtipur (Thanesar).

It is a plaque in which, two men—one having curly hair and the other having long hair—have been shown fighting against each other. It has the insinuation of the Gandhara style of art.

From Khokhra kot, two pairs of lions have been found. These lions are sitting back to back. On the backside of this figure, a *yaksha* and a *Yakshini* are seated. The lions of these figures do not have feathers. This art object dates back to second century AD and has been kept in the National Museum.

During third century AD, the *youdheyas* reigned supreme in the area of Rohtak. Several coins have been found from this area that belong to the *Youdheyas*. Their prime deity was Lord Kartikeya, His images have been found on these coins.

Some earthen sculptures and a mould of Shridevi have been found from the fort of king Karna. A golden coin (of the shape of a *Parashu*) has been found at Mitathal (Bhiwani). Besides this coin, several other gold coins have also been found. A gold coin belonging to the age of Samudragupta has been found at Jagadhari. A scripture belonging to the Gupta era has been found at Tosham. There are three scriptures in it. These throw light on the contemporary religious activities of the State. From Kapal Mochan (in Ambala district), a scripture, on the Vaishnava religion, has been found, it dates back to 484 AD. Several coins of the Gupta era have been found from various places of the State.

The copper coin of Harshvardhan has been found from Sonepat. This coin describes the details of the Pushyabhuti clan.

Hiuen Tsang has described the city of Thaneshwar (now Thanesar) in detail. There were 3 Buddha *viharas* (during the time period of his visit) at Thaneshwar where 700 Buddhist monks used to live and pray. Hiuen Tsang has mentioned that there was a *stupa* of Ashoka's period at a place towards north-west of Thaneshwar. Rogers had found the desecrated figurine of Lord Buddha from a place near the pond of Kurukshetra.

Archeological excavations were carried out for many years by the ASI under the guidance of Bri Mohan Pandey at Thaneshwar (Thanesar). These excavations give us an idea of rich cultural history of the region. In the first phase of these excavations remains of painted vessel civilisation have been found; in the second stage, those of Kushana age; in the third, those of the Gupta age; in the fourth, those of the Harsha's age, in the fifth, those of the Sultanate period; and finally, in the sixth, those of the Mughal era. These excavations have revealed that there was an earthen structure at Thaneshwar during the Kushana age. The Mughals had got a structure built with baked bricks at the same place.

Sug, a place near Jagadhari (in Yamunanagar district) is an ancient place. Hiuen Tsang had also given a reference to this place in his works. He has written that during ninth century AD, these ancient remains were in a good conditon. He has also stated there was a Buddha *Vihara* at a place towards south-west of this city and also, an Ashoka *Stupa* at a place towards west of Yamuna. There was another *stupa* beside this (first) *stupa* where the hair and nails of Lord Buddha had been kept. There were many other *stupas* in the vicinity of these two *stupas*. Lord Buddha had given sermons at Sug during his previous incarnation. Under the aegis of Punjab University, Dr. B.C. Chhabra and Dr. Surajbhan Chaudhary arranged and supervised excavations at this site and found painted slate vessels as well as vessels made of bright black soil (dating back to the first age). It is believed that the city of Sug was built during the first age. Many coins were also found of which, the *pancha martha* silver coins and the coin of Menender are deemed very important. The first age dates back to 500-100 BC.

During the second age, houses were constructed in a planned manner with raw and baked bricks. At Sug, sculptures of the Kushana era have been found in large numbers. Several beads and coins have also been found from this place. On a coin of third century AD, found from Sug, Uyaghra Raj has been written. On another coin, *Sugha* has been written. At some distance towards south-west of Sug, remnants of a rectangular structure have been found, it is just possible that it may have been the same Buddha *Vihara* that was described by Hiuen Tsang in his works.

At a distance of 20 km towards north-west of Agroha, the remains of an ancient *Agrodaka* are present in the form of a gigantic mound. H.L. Shrivastava of the ASI had got the excavations done at this place.

It has been presumed that the foundation of this city could have been laid in fifth century BC. In Agach district, 51 coins as well as several figurines and sculptures made of baked earth have been found. Coins belonging to the Kushana and *Youdheya* ages have also been found here. The figurines of Mahishasur Mardini and Varaha are quite charming. A handwritten book (*grantha*), which has been written on *bhojpatras*, has also been found from this site.

The writing of Pehowa (formerly Prithudak) informs us that the Tomars used to rule the area of Karnal. Two beautiful sculptures of the Pratihara era have been found from this place, one of the Lord Shiva and the other one of Lord Buddha. Several sculptures of the times of Pratiharas and Tomars (which date back to ninth century AD) have been found throughout the State.

On the Kaithal-Narvana road, at a place known as Kalayat, remains of three temples still exist. These temples were made from bricks. Two of these are in good condition while the third one has only a door to represent its lost glory. These temples date back to seventh or eight century AD. If we carefully study their architectural style, we are reminded of the Gupta temple of village Matir. The temple of Kapil Muni is quite similar to the Gupta temple in this context. Further, in the Bhagwat, temple, which is one of these three temples, statues of Ganesha and Mahishasur Mardini are very elegant. These statues have been carved out of black stone. It is said that Surajtal Tome had got the Surajkund constructed during the tenth century, it is located in Gurgaon district. There are stairs in the main structure of Surajkund that are in the shape of a crescent moon. It is believed that there was a Sun temple on its western side. Feroze Shah Tughlak had got it repaired in 1351-58. At a distance of 2 km from Surakund towards south-west, a dam has been found. It was got constructed by Anang Pal. The remains of Bhima Devi temple have been found near Pinjore. This temple dates back to tenth century AD. Several figurines have been found at the site of this temple; those of Mithuna, Yaksha, Varuna and Apsara are very beautiful.

During eleventh century AD, Haryana as well as its neighbouring areas was invaded by Mahmud Ghaznavi's army. After his attack, several mosques, mausoleums, *baolis*, places of rest and minarets were constructed in Haryana. These are the symbols of architectural supremacy of the medieval age. Among these, the fort, palace and minaret of Ferozeshah in Fatehabad (Hissar) is a prominent historical landmark of the medieval age. The Humayun Masjid is also located in the State. It is said that Humayun had offered namaz prayers at this mosque while he was heading for Amarkot. Hansi was a renowned centre of Sufis, Sheikh Baba Farid had lived here for 12 years. The fort, Baras Gate, Baradari, Khangah, the four mazaars of Chehar Qutab, the mausoleum of Mir Taza, the mosque of Feroze Tughlaq (which has an old mazaar) are the excellent examples of architectural finesse during the medieval age.

Narnaul, also known as Nandi Gram in ancient times, is also referred to as Chwavan Rishi. It has many remains of the architectural marvels of the medieval age. In 1137 AD, Shah Vilayat had come to Narnaul. He was a brave warrior. A tomb, a mosque and a school were built to honour him. All these are loacated near the tomb of Ibrahim Khan Sur. During fifteenth century AD, Ibrahim Khan was ruling the region of Narnaul. During the reign of Akbar, a mint was set up at Narnaul. Several gardens and buildings were also constructed during those times.

Further, Sher Shah Suri got the mausoleum of his grandfather (Ibrahim Kuwan) built at Narnaul. It was built in 1538-46. It is a square-shaped mausoleum built in *Pathani* style. It has red, grey and white stone slates. The roof of the mausoleum has beautiful paintings.

Shah Kuli Khan (1578-89) got a garden made; its name was *Aram-e-kauser*. He also got the Tripolia Gate constructed during his reign. Jal Mahal and Jami Masjid are the other magnificent buildings of this area.

Mukund Das, who was Deewan of Narnaul during the reign of Akbar, got a building constructed. It is known as Chhatta Rai Mukund Das. There is another building at Narnaul, called Sarai Mukund Das. It dates back to the period of Shahjahan. There is a scripture in it. Nowadays, this building is bring used as a government office.

Sardar Fidai Khan was the governor of Sirhind during the reign of Aurangzeb. He was impressed by the environs of Pinjore. He got a garden made according to the Mughal architectural style (at Pinjore). At the entry of the garden (near the road), there is an entrance gate. After this gate, there is a huge garden, which has been made in seven distinct steps. Each level connects to the lower one below it through a system of stairs. Fountains present a beautiful view in the garden. Sheesh mahal, Jalmahal and Rangmahal are also a part of this garden; they add to the beauty of the garden.

Finally, the fort and *baoli* of the post-Mughal era, located at Farrookhnagar, remind visitors of the old architectural traditons and styles.

CHAPTER 22

SOCIAL LIFE

Haryana is a State dominated by the Hindus. Nearly 87.5 per cent of its residents are Hindus. The rest 12.5 per cent comprise Muslims, Christians, Sikhs, Buddhists and Jains. The Socio-cultural ethos of this State has been defined by the Hindus, especially Jats. Besides, the Sikhs, Muslims and Jains have also contributed towards the creation of a unique multicultural society of the State.

Among the Hindus, we can find Brahmins, Jats, Rajputs, Gujars, Sainis, Kshatriyas, Ahirs, Khatris, Khatis, Rudis and Harijans. There are *36 gotras* of Gaur brahmins in this State. Jats are in abundance in this State. Jats are in abundance in rural and semi-urban areas. The societal status of Jats, Gujars, Rajputs, Ahirs, Sunars and Sainis is the same. These people are engaged in agriculture, military service and the police force. Harijans live in most of rural areas, they are craftsmen and craftswomen. Among the Muslims, Pathans, Meos, Rangrej and blacksmith (*lohar*) castes thrive in the State.

The common castes of Hindus in the State are—Sharma, Chaudhary, Mallik, Kadyan, Saini, Arora, Verma, Malhotra, Bhadana, Sood, Suri, Singh, Bathla, Jangda, Dahiya, Gaur, Saraswat, etc. This list is not exhaustive.

COSTUMES AND DRESSES

The males living in the State wear the following clothes, accessories and ornaments :

S.N.	Traditional Name	Use
1	*2*	*3*
1.	Dhoti	Cloth used to cover waist and legs
2.	Kurta	Cloth used to cover the torso, just like shirt, mostly white, rounded arms
3.	Kameej	Collared shirt
4.	Khandwa	Turban
5.	Safa	Turban in military style
6.	Paagri	Marwari Turban
7.	Paag	Rajputi turban
8.	Kamri	Half-sleeve shirt up to waist, used by elders
9.	Angrakha	Embroidered long flowing kurta
10.	Dohar	A hand-woven sheet of thick double cotton yarn; worn in winter
11.	Khes	A thick sheet of thick cotton yarn, worn in winter
12.	Topi	A cap like the Gandhi cap
13.	Kamri (cotton)	A blanket made by filling cotton; used in winter, also called mirjai
14.	Loi	Loi, a blanket-type warm cloth

The females in the State wear the following clothes, accessories and ornaments :

1.	Ghaghri	Ghaghra, worn to cover waist and legs
2.	Daman	A ghaghra of red or black cotton cloth
3.	Laih	A ghaghra made by creating designs in yellow colour on the cloth of blue colour
4.	Laih of Guldan	A ghaghra made by dying a coarse cotton sheet by the *bandhai* technique
5.	Kairi	A ghaghra made with red patches on blue coarse cotton cloth
6.	Khara	Coarse cotton cloth (khaddar) made by using four red and four blue threads, made without *kalis*
7.	Chand Tara	A ghaghra made from khaddar cloth having imprints of the dooj moon and star

1	2	3
8.	Kamri	A kamri of vasket-like shape, having full or half sleeves; worn only by married women
9.	Angi	Angia, inner garment
10.	Samij	A cloth worn under the kamij (shirt of women)
11.	Kamij	Collared shirt for women
12.	Jumphar	A cloth used to cover waist and legs, also called jumper
13.	Silwar	Punjabi-style dress to cover waiste and legs, also called shalwar or salwar
14.	Odhna	A head-dress (*odhni*) with *gotas*
15.	Dukania	An odhna made of deep red khaddar and embroidered with yellow thread
16.	Chhyama	An embroidered odhana of yellow strip
17.	Sopli	A deep-red-coloured odhni having print on its side/edge
18.	Dimas or Dimach	A silken odhna; put over the bride in marriage
19.	Gumti	An odhni made from coloured cotton cloth and embroidered with silken *boondis*.
20.	Lahria	An odhna prepared by dying it through the bandhai technique
21.	Bol	An odhna made from cotton cloth and and embroidered with silken embroidery on a stripe
22.	Pilia	An odhna made from thin yellow cloth and having red edges (*kinaries*), given to mother (of a newborn child) by her parents.
23.	Chundri	A thin odhni with red sides (*pallas*) and blue-dyed cloth in the centre.
24.	Maudia	A fine/thin *odhna* with yellow or blue dyed *pallas*.
25.	Kangh	An *odhna* of fast red colour, embroidered in many ways

1	*2*	*3*
26.	Phulkari	An odhna made by putting phulkaris (of square shape) made of yellow stripe or wool.
27.	Fargal	A cap for children
28.	Jhugla	A dress for children
29.	Saud	A quilt of course cotton (*khaddar*)
30.	Saudia	A mattress of course cotton (*khaddar*)
31.	Rijai	A quilt, rajai

JEWELLERY

The traditional jewellery of Haryana is as follows :

1. Paatti
2. Phool Paatti
3. Taatti
4. Chhail Kada
5. Gitian Ke Kade
6. Gajrian
7. Kadi
8. Jhanan Chudi
9. Ramjhol
10. Chhoti Neori
11. Neori of big trinkets
12. Bichhua
13. Bankdi

Note : The jewellery to be worn in feet (ankles) is made of silver.

The following jewellery is used for decorating hands :

1. Aarsi (of thumb)
2. Ring
3. Hathphool
4. Pauhachi
5. Kadulla
6. Gajra
7. Chhann

8. Pachheli
9. Kangni
10. Chhann Kangan
11. Tad (of arm)
12. Taddia (golden tad of arm)
13. Bajubandh

The following items of jewellery are used to decorate the throat :

1. Hansla (of gold/silver)
2. Hansuli (of gold/silver)
3. Mohanmala (of gold)
4. Galshree (of gold)
5. Kanthi (of gold)
6. Zanjira (of gold/silver)
7. Gulubandh (of gold)
8. Jhalra (of guineas or silver coins)
9. Button (of gold or silver)
10. Necklace (of silver)
11. Garland (of gold)

The following items of jewellary are worn on the head or mouth :

1. Phool : It is worn over head. It is made of gold or silver.
2. Singaar Patti : It is worn over head. It is made of gold or silver.
3. Bessar : It is held on the forehead. It is made of gold.
4. Tagga : It is held on the forehead. It can be either of gold or of silver.
5. Borla : It is worn in the centre of forehead. It is made either of gold or silver. It has precious stones studded in it.
6. Tikka : It hangs from the forehead. It is made of gold.
7. Klaf : It is put in the hair. It is made of gold or silver.
8. Boojni : It is worn in the ears. It can be of gold or silver.
9. Dhedhas : These are meant to be worn in the ears. These are made of silver.
10. Karnaphool : These are worn in the ears. These can be of gold or silver.
11. Balis : These are worn in the ears. These can be made of silver or gold.
12. Danda : These are hung near the ears. These are made of silver.

13. Nanth : It is worn in the nose. It is made of gold.
14. Purli : It is worn in the nose. It is made of gold.
15. Kokka : It is made of gold and worn in the nose.
16. Chhaj : It hangs on the forehead. It is made of silver.
17. Long : It is worn in the nose. It is made of gold.

Other items of jewellary are as follows :

1. Gof : It is the neck jewellery of males.
2. Kathla : It is the neck ornament of males and is made of gold.
3. Murki : It is the ear ornament of males.
4. Zanjeera : It is the ear ornament of males.
5. Patri : It is the neck ornament of both males and females.
6. Tagadi : It is the waist ornament of ladies.
7. Nada : It is the ornament (made of silver) that is worn along with the string (*nada*) of the ghaghra.
8. Pallu : It is an ornament made of silver. It is tied to the side of the odhna of the lady.

Signs of Good Omen

The following signs are of good omen whenever someone is about to start a piece of work or set out for a journey :

1. A pitcher full of water : If a water carrier is spotted and she has a pitcher full of water, then it is deemed a good omen.
2. A sweeper with a broom : If a black-coloured sweeper (with across the person on his way, it is deemed a good sign or omen for that person.
3. Gau Darshan : If a cow is spotted in the morning, then it is deemed a good omen.
4. Curd or Silver Coin : If any one of these is spotted, then this is a sign of good omen.
5. Deer spotting : If a deer comes from left to right of the person while he is going on a foreign tour, then this is good for that person.
6. Scratching on the Palm : If there is irritation/scratching on the left palm of the woman or the right palm of the man, then it is a sign of possibility of receiving money.
7. Pulsation of an Eye : If the right eye of the male or the left eye the female is pulsating, then it is deemed a good omen.

8. Call of the Crow : If a crow calls on the wall or entrance door of the home, then it is assumed that a guest is about to arrive.
9. Bending of the Chapati : It is also a premonition of the arrival of a guest.
10. Bathing of a Sparrow in the Sand : This indicates that rains are about to arrive in the area.
11. A sleeper/shoe on Another : This indicates that the owner of those sleepers/shoes may have to undertake a long journey.
12. Scratching of Foot : It also indicates that the concerned person may have to travel.
13. Sight of a Married Women : This is a good omen.
14. Sight of Neelkanth : It is deemed very auspicious. If a neelkanth is spotted on the day of the Dussehra, then the person is deemed absolved from all the sins.
15. View of the Green Grass : If a person sees a green grass upon getting up from the bed in the morning, he can hope to spend the entire day in great comfort.
16. SIght of one's Own Hand : If a person views his own hand (anjali) when he gets up in the morning (without looking at any other person's face), then it is deemed a good sign/omen.
17. Sight of a Brahmin Girl : If a brahmin's girl is spotted by a person early in the morning, then it is a good omen for the person.
18. Coming Across a water Bearer (*Bhishti*) : If a *bhishti,* carrying a sack full of water is spotted, then it is deemed very much auspicious.

Signs of Bad Omen

If a person sets out to travel or starts some pious task, then the following signs are deemed by him as those of bad omen :

1. Empty Pitcher : If a water bearer meets the person with an empty pitcher, it is deemed an ill omen for the person who comes across her.
2. A Casket Full of Fuel : If someone having a casket (full of fuel comes across the person, then it is deemed the sign of bad omen for that person.
3. Black Cat : If a black cat crosses a person from his right to his left, then it is deemed a bad omen for that persons.

4. Sneezing : If a pious task is about to be done or being undertaken, then sneezing by anyone is not deemed a good sign.
5. Coming Across a Pig : This is also the sign of a bad omen in Haryana.
6. Wailing of Jackals in the Cremation Ground : This is a premonition for death of someone in the colony. Even otherwise, a wailing jackal is deemed a bad omen.
7. Wailing of Dog : This is deemed the premonition of a tragedy that may strike the area in the time of come.

CHAPTER 23

WELFARE SCHEMES

The Haryana Government has started many welfare schemes to improve the living standards of Haryana's society and social welfare of the masses of the State. It has also taken adequate case of weak and backward sections of Haryana's populace by definin and implementing schemes for them. The Government has started several other schemes to eliminate evils from the society.

Some of the various welfare schemes being run by the State are follows :

SOCIAL WELFARE

Haryana the first State of the country in which, old persons, widow, orphans and disabled people are given pension (on a regular basis) on the seventh day of every month. A total of 18,52,859 old citizens are being given Old Age Samman Allowance in the State till Oct. 2023.

"Widows and Destitute Pension Scheme" is also being implemented to provide security and financial assistance to widows and destitute women. Under this scheme, widows and destitute women aged 18 years and above, who have no other financial support and her own income from all sources is below ₹ 2 lakh per annum are provided pension @ ₹ 3000 per month. A total of 8,33,809 such women had been benefitted upto October, 2023. In addition, the State is running 3 women homes at Karnal, Rohtak and Faridabad for young widows and destitute women and their dependent children to rehabilitate and provide them the facilities of boarding, lodging, education and vocational training in various trades.

In the area of social security, a scheme known as **Rajiv Gandhi Parivar Bima Yojana** launched from 1st April, 2006 is providing social security to the citizens of the State. Under this scheme, all the persons of Haryana in the age group of 18 to 60 years will be provided compensation of ₹ 1 lakh in case of unnatural death or permanent total disability due to accidents like rail or road or air accidents, tractor or farming equipment, riot, earthquake, strike, terrorist activity, storm, cyclone, snake bite, drowning, poisoning, electrocution, falling from height, collapse of house or building, fire, explosion, implosion, murder, attack of animals, stampede and suffocation, lightening, frost bite, sun burn (loo), burn injuries, death or permanent total disability due to any other unnatural event, within 72 hours of the submission of claim form.

Under the Mukhya Mantri Vivah Shagun Yojana, financial assistance ranging from grant to ₹ 31,000 to ₹ 71,000 is being provided to various categories of the resident of the State, whose annual income is upto ₹ 1.80 lakh, such as (i) ₹ 51,000 for the widow/divorced/ destitute/orphan of all sections of the society on their re-marriage (ii) Grant of ₹ 71,000 for the marriage of the daughter of SC/Vimukt Caste/Taprivas Caste. (iii) Grant of ₹ 31,000 for the marriage of sports women (any caste). (iv) Grant of ₹ 31,000 for the general category and backward class people for the marriage of their daughters. (v) Grant of ₹ 51,000 for Divyangjan if both of spouse are disabled and ₹ 31,000 for marriage of Divyangjan if one of spouse is disabled.

The Haryana Scheduled Castes Finance and Development Corporation provides loan/benefit to only those identified Scheduled Castes families whose annual family income is upto ₹ 1.80 lakh in rural areas and in urban areas as well as his/her name should be figured in BPL Survey list for various bank assisted income generating schemes such as dairy farming, sheep rearing, animal driven carts, leather and leather goods making, kiryana shop, atta chakki, carpentary, cyber cafe, photography and auto rickshaw etc.

Haryana Backward Classes & Economically Weaker Sections Kalyan Nigam is working for the economic upliftment of Backward Classes, Minority Communities and Persons with Disabilities for self employment in various income generating schemes, with the collaboration of National Corporations on low rate of interest. During the financial year 2023-24 the Nigam proposed the target to disburse loan of ₹ 25 crore for providing financial assistance to 5,000 persons of Backward Classes, ₹ 15 crore to 3,000 persons of Minority Communities and ₹ 10 crore to 2,000 persons with Disabilities during 2023-24. The Nigam has disbursed loans amounting ₹ 4.30 crore to 507 persons of Backward Classes, ₹ 4.39 crore to 396 persons of Minority Communities and ₹ 8.69 crore to 792 persons with disabilities upto 31.10.2023.

Hostels have been started in Karnal, Ambala, Faridabad, Rohtak and Rewari for such children as belong to Scheduled Castes but are engaged in clean occupations. Hostels have been opened at Jind for the children of nomad tribes. The reservation policy (in Government Services) has been implemented in the right manner (in the context of reservation for SCs, OBCs, ex-servicemen and physically disabled persons). It has been ensured that only those candidates are appointed on reserved posts, which have been reserved for their respective categories.

Post Matric Scholarship Scneme for Scheduled Caste Students: Scheduled Caste students studying in the Post Matric Classes are awarded with Scholarship under the Govt. of India's Post Matric Scholarship to Scheduled Castes students Scheme Academic allowance ranging from ₹ 2500 to ₹ 13,500 p.m. is paid. Besides this, compulsory non-refundable fees are also reimbursed to the students, provided their annual family income should be less than ₹ 2.50 lakh. An amount of ₹ 12,138.74 lakh has been spent on 79,116 candidates during the year 2022-23. A provision of ₹ 14,360.70 lakh has been made for the year 2023-24, out of which ₹ 7,548.16 lakh has been spent on 43,729 students upto 31.12.2023.

Mahatma Gandhi National Rural Employment Guarantee Act (MGNREGA) was launched in the district of Mahendergarh and Sirsa by Govt. of India during February, 2006 and was extended to districts Ambala and Nuh during 2007-08. All the remaining districts have also been covered under the programme w.e.f. 1st April, 2008. The basic objective of the scheme is to enhance livelihood security in rural areas by providing at least 100 days of guaranteed wage employment in a financial year to every household whose adult members volunteer to do unskilled manual work. 1/3rd of the jobs are reserved for women. Minimum wages applicable in the State are being paid to the persons being engaged under the scheme.

Swarna Jayanti Gram Swarozagar Yojna is an important programme among the Poverty Abolition Programmes. Accoding to this programme, it is expected to raise the living standard of those people who are living below poverty line within 3 years. The objective of the scheme is to bring every assisted family above the poverty line.

PROHIBITION

Mr. Bansilal, the former Chief Minister of Haryana, had declared complete prohibition in the State w.e.f. July 1, 1996. According to the law passed by the State Government in this context, there was a ban on manufacturing, selling, keeping, consuming and transporting liquor of any type in the State. This law was passed according to the spirit of directive principles of State policy. Article 47 of the Indian Constitution clearly mentions that the State shall try to ban the use of deleterious intoxicating liquids/drinks and medicines for better health of people. The Punjab Aabkari Act (1914) was amended to make the law of prohibition much more strict. The prohibition law did bring cheers in the lives of housewives, especially those belonging to rural areas of the State. But smuggling of liquor from Delhi, UP, and Rajasthan forced the Government to think about its decision. Further, the Government also started losing ₹ 600 crore per annum due to the lack of sales of liquor. Hence, Mr. Bansilal, the then CM of Haryana, decided to lift the prohibition order on April 1, 1998.

CHILD WELFARE SCHEME

Under the scheme of welfare of destitute children in need of care and protection, the department of Social Justice and Empowerment, Haryana is providing grant-in-aid to the voluntary organizations for the maintenance of orphan/destitute children. This scheme of Govt. of India has been taken over by the State Govt. w.e.f 1.4.1992. Before that the Central Govt./State Govt. was running it on 50:50 sharing basis.

The following categories of destitute/orphan children are admitted in the Children Home who fulfill prescribed conditions mentioned in the scheme:

(*a*) Children who do not have either parents or near relation.

(*b*) Children who were found without any home or settled place of above or any other ostensible means of subsistence.

(*c*) Children of single parent families deprived of adequate family care due to death, desertion, prolonged, illness, imprisonment of one of the parent.

(*d*) As a result of enforcing these conditions, no child who has already been admitted in the homes, should be sent out. The voluntary organizations, are, however, required to review the case of all children from time to time to ascertain their continued eligibility for the benefits of the scheme taking into account the frequency of absence from homes to got the relatives places etc. As such absence are indications of the persons who can take care of the children. Also any new facts that had come to light should also be taken into accounts, of the time of such reviews.

Further the Juvenile Justice (Care and Protection of Children) Act, 2000 has been passed and implemented w.e.f. April 1, 2001. It was previously known as Juvenile Justice Act (1986). Under this Act, care, protection and rehabilitation service are given to neglected and delinquent children. Homes have been created for such children. In these homes, free boarding, lodging, clothing, education and training are provided to these children.

The following homes (for these children) are being run by the government :

(A) State After Care Home, Sonepat

(B) Observation Home, Sonepat

(C) Special Home, Sonepat

The following homes are run by NGOs (District Council for Child Welfare)

(A) Juvenile Home, Rewari

(B) Observation Home, Rewari

(C) Observation Home, Chhachhrauli (Yamuna Nagar)

Financial Assistance to Destitute Children Scheme

This is a State Scheme under which parents/guardians of the children upto the age of 21 years who are deprived due to various reasons as per scheme is being provided financial assistance. Initially financial assistance @ ₹ 200 per month per child w.e.f. 01.03.2009 subject to maximum for two children of one family as per eligibility criteria laid down in the scheme. The rate of pension under this scheme has been increased to ₹ 500 per month per child from January, 2014, ₹ 700 w.e.f. 01.11.2016, ₹ 900 w.e.f. 01.11.2017, ₹ 1,100 w.e.f. 01.11.2018, ₹ 1,350 w.e.f. 01.01.2020 and ₹ 1,600 w.e.f. 01.04.2021, ₹ 1,850 w.e.f.)1.04.2023 and ₹ 2,100 w.e.f. 01.01.2024.

WOMEN'S WELFARE

At Rohtak, Karnal and Faridabad, Home-cum-Training centres for widows and destitute women and their dependent children have been opened. There is one such centre at each one of the aforementioned cities. Further, there is State After Care Home (for girls) at Karnal. Finally, a Protective Home has been built at Faridabad.

WELFARE OF THE HANDICAPPED

The Persons with Disabilities (Equal Opportunities, Protection of Rights and Full Participation) Act (1995) has been implemented in the State with full force. The following steps have been taken to ensure welfare of the handicapped persons living in Haryana :

(A) A Training Centre for Adult Blind has been opened at Sonepat.

(B) Scholarships are being given to physically handicapped students.

(C) Unemployment allowance is given to educated physically handicapped.

(D) Prosthetic aids and equipment are provided to handicapped persons of the State.

(E) Blind persons are being given employment.

(F) Drug de-addiction and counselling centres have been set up throughout the State.

(G) The Government has instituted awards in the field of welfare of the handicapped. These awards are given to those persons who achieve outstanding landmarks in this field.

(H) The scheme, Assistance to Disabled and Infirm Persons (ADIPs) is in Vogue.

WELFARE OF SENIOR CITIZENS

The Home for the Aged and Infirm Persons is being run at Rewari. There are many other Old Age Homes and Day Care Centres in Haryana. These take care of the old citizens who want to avail their services.

New Old Age Homes are being constructed. Old ones are being repaired and/or maintained by the State Government.

Old Age Samman Allowance Scheme

Such schemes have been started for old persons who cannot sustain themselves (with their own resources) and fulfil some eligibility criteria to avoid these schemes. The person, who seeks pension under the scheme, should : *(a)* have Haryana as his/her domicile; and *(b)* be more than 60 years of age. Under this scheme, old persons in the age of 60 years or more, whose husband/wife's annual income from all sources is below ₹ 3 lakh is given benefit @ ₹ 3,000 per month per beneficiary to eligible senior citizens. 18,52,859 eligible senior citizens covered under this scheme upto October, 2023.

Pension Scheme for Women

Further, there is also a pension scheme for widows and destitute women. Its objective is to give social security to those widows and destitute women (or married ladies) who are unable to sustain themselves from their own resources and are in need of financial assistance. In order to avail this scheme, a woman should be : *(a)* of the age of 18 years or above : and *(b)* should have Haryana as her domicile.

Every beneficiary is given ₹ 3,000 on a monthly basis. A total of 8,33,809 such women had been benefited upto October, 2023. New pensions are being sanctioned every month and disbursed by the seventh day of every month, Just like Old Age Pension.

Pension for Divyang Persons

To provide social security to Disabled Persons, the scheme called Haryana Disabled Persons Pension Schemes was introduced in the year 1981-82. The aim of the scheme is to provide social security to disabled persons who are unable to sustain themselves from their own resources and are in need of financial assistance from the State. The rate of pension, which was ₹ 50 per month at the beginning of the scheme is now ₹ 3,000 w.e.f. 1.1.2024. An amount of ₹ 356.59 crore has been spent for the year 2023-24 upto 31.10.2023 for 1,90,737 beneficiaries.

Ladli Social Security Allowance Scheme

To remove the sense of economic insecurity in the mind of parents who have only daughters, Ladli Social Security Allowance Scheme is being implemented w.e.f. 1st January, 2006. Under this scheme, the rate of allowance is ₹ 3,000 per month per beneficiary. The allowance is paid to the families from the 45th years of the father/mother, who ever is older of the two till their 60th birthday i.e. for 15 years. Thereafter, they are eligible for Old Age Samman Allowance.

Project for Children (0-6 years)

The Integrated Child Development Project has been implemented in Haryana. Its major objectives are—physical, mental and social development of children, increasing the dexterity of mothers in the field of infant rearing, reduction in Infant Mortality Rate (IMR) and improvement of the levels of health and nutrition of mothers. In order to attain these objectives, in all the *aanganwadis* of Haryana, nutritive food is arranged for children of age group 6 months to 6 years, pregnant women, lactating women and those women who are rearing their children. Further, immunisation services are provided free of cost to pregnant women and children in the age group of 0-6 years. Mothers are educated on matters related to health and cleanliness. Finally, little children are also given informal education.

For the development of the children and women of the State, the Government of Haryana has implemented many welfare schemes, such as *Devi Roopak Yojana, Kanyadaan Yojana, Balika Samriddhi Yojana, Kishori Shakti Yojana* and *Mahila Mandal Yojana* etc.

Financial Assistance to Women and Girls Acid Attack Victims

A Scheme namely financial assistance to Women and Girls Acid Attack Victims has been implemented by Social Justice and Empowerment Department, Haryana on 26th February, 2019 for empowering the women and girls whose faced disfigurement of any part of body due to acid attack. Male and Transgender acid victims have also been including in the scheme on 22nd January, 2020. Any victims residing in the Haryana State is eligible for financial benefits in this scheme.

'Saksham Yuva' Scheme

The Government of Haryana has launched the "Educated Youth Allowance and Honorarium Scheme- 2016" popularly known as "Saksham Yuva" Scheme on 1st November, 2016 on the occasion of Haryana Swarn Jyanti Varsh to provide unemployment allowance and honorarium to the eligible post-graduate youth of Haryana in lieu of 100 Hours of honorary work. Later, the Scheme has been extended to include registered Science, Engineering, Science equivalent and Commerce Graduates of the State. Arts Graduates 10+2 pass applicants have also been included in the scheme from August, 2019.

Under the scheme ₹ 3,000, ₹ 1,500 and ₹ 900 are given as Unemployment Allowance to Post-Graduate, Graduates and 10+2 pass applicants respectively and in lieu of 100 hours ₹ 6,000 per month for honorary assignment to eligible registered Post-Graduate (PG), Graduates (G) and 10+2 pass applicants. During the period April, 2023 to December, 2023, total 22,444 Saksham Yuvas applications have been approved under the scheme. During the same period, ₹ 199.99 crore and ₹ 31.03 crore have been disbursed as unemployment allowance and honorarium respectively. From April, 2023 to December, 2023, a total 1,281 Saksham Yuva has been placed in different sectors. During the same period 79 youths of 'Antodaya' families have been approved for the benefit of the Saksham Yuva Scheme under Mukhyamantri Antodaya Parivar Uthan Yojna.

Welfare Schemes for Freedom Fighters

The State Samman Pension of Freedom Fighters/their Widows belongs to Haryana State have been increased from ₹ 20,000 to ₹25,000 per month (including fixed medical allowance at the rate of ₹ 750 per month) with effect from 1.4.2014. In addition to Samman Pension some other schemes/facilities are also extended to the Freedom Fighters/ Widows and their dependents which are as under:

(*i*) The State Samman Pension after death of Freedom Fighters and their spouse is to be transferred further to their unmarried unemployed daughters and disabled unmarried unemployed sons with 75% disability. If there are more than one eligible children, they will get proportionate share in the pension.

(*ii*) Financial assistance for meeting the funeral expenses on the death of Freedom Fighters of the State has been enhanced from ₹ 1500 to ₹ 5000 w.e.f. 13.7.2009.

(*iii*) Financial assistance to the Haryana State Freedom Fighters/INA personnel and their widows for the marriage of their daughters, grand daughters and dependent sisters is given at the rate of ₹ 51000 in each case w.e.f. 20.8.2009.

Welfare Schemes for Defence Personnel

It is matter of pride that every 10th soldier in the country belongs to Haryana State. The State Govt. is committed for the welfare of Defence Personnel, Ex-Defence Personnel and their families in recognition to the services and supreme sacrifices made by them. The State Govt. is providing One Time Cash Award to Gallantry Award Winners. The amount of Cash Awards being paid to Gallantry Award Winners (War Time and Peace Time) is given in the following table:

One Time Cash Award to Gallantry Award Winners

Sr. No.	War Time Gallantry Award	One Time Cash Award (in ₹)
1	Paramvir Chakra	2,00,00,000
2	Mahavir Chakra	1,00,00,000
3	Vir Chakra	50,00,000
4	Sena /Nao/Vayu Sena Medal (Gallantry)	21,00,000
5	Mention-in-Despatches (Gallantry)	10,00,000
	Peace Time Gallantry Award	
1	Ashok Chakra	1,00,00,000
2	Kirti Chakra	51,00,000
3	Shaurya Chakra	31,00,000
4	Sena /Nao/Vayu Sena Medal (Gallantry)	10,00,000
5	Mention-in-Despatches (Gallantry)	7,50,000

Source: *Sainik and Ardh Sainik welfare Department, Haryana.*

The State Govt. is also providing the Annuity to Gallantry Award Winners prior to 05.10.2007. The amount of Annuity being paid to Gallantry Award Winners is given in the following table:

Annuity to Gallantry Award Winners

Sr. No.	Gallantry Award	Annuity (in ₹)
1	Paramvir Chakra	3,00,000
2	Ashok Chakra	2,50,000
3	Mahavir Chakra	2,25,000
4	Kirti Chakra	1,75,000
5	Vir Chakra	1,25,000
6	Shaurya Chakra	1,00,000
7	Sena /Nao/Vayu Sena Medal (Gallantry)	50,000
8	Mention-in-Despatches (Gallantry)	30,000

Source: *Sainik and Ardh Sainik welfare Department, Haryana.*

Disabled Ex-Servicemen have been given the facility to travel free in the Haryana Roadways buses. Also Defence Colonies are being developed at various places in Haryana. The Govt. has given the financial assistance at the rate of ₹ 15,000 per month to Victoria Cross winners and their Widows. The Govt. of Haryana has also granted financial assistance of ₹ 5,800 per month to the ESM of the age of 60 years and above and their Widows. The State of Haryana has also granted the financial assistance at the rate of ₹ 5,800 per month to all war Widows of defence forces personnel's in addition to their to family pension already granted by the Govt. of India. The State Govt. is providing Govt. service of Class-II, Class-III and IV category to any one dependent of the Martyrs of Defence Forces Personnel on ex-gratia basis. In addition, the State Govt. is also providing the Ex-gratia Grant to the martyrs.